Dynamics 365 Application Development

Master professional-level CRM application development for Microsoft Dynamics 365

Deepesh Somani
Nishant Rana

BIRMINGHAM - MUMBAI

Dynamics 365 Application Development

Commissioning Editor: Aaron Lazar
Acquisition Editor: Karan Sadawana
Content Development Editor: Akshada Iyer
Technical Editor: Supriya Thabe
Copy Editor: Safis Editing
Project Coordinator: Prajakta Naik
Proofreader: Safis Editing
Indexer: Rekha Nair
Graphics: Jisha Chirayil
Production Coordinator: Arvindkumar Gupta

First published: January 2018

Production reference: 1250118

Published by Packt Publishing Ltd.
Livery Place
35 Livery Street
Birmingham
B3 2PB, UK.

ISBN 978-1-78839-978-4

www.packtpub.com

I dedicate this book to my parents

-Deepesh Somani

I would like to dedicate this book to my family members who have always supported me; without their blessings nothing would have been possible.

-Nishant Rana

`mapt.io`

Mapt is an online digital library that gives you full access to over 5,000 books and videos, as well as industry leading tools to help you plan your personal development and advance your career. For more information, please visit our website.

Why subscribe?

- Spend less time learning and more time coding with practical eBooks and Videos from over 4,000 industry professionals

- Improve your learning with Skill Plans built especially for you

- Get a free eBook or video every month

- Mapt is fully searchable

- Copy and paste, print, and bookmark content

PacktPub.com

Did you know that Packt offers eBook versions of every book published, with PDF and ePub files available? You can upgrade to the eBook version at `www.PacktPub.com` and as a print book customer, you are entitled to a discount on the eBook copy. Get in touch with us at `service@packtpub.com` for more details.

At `www.PacktPub.com`, you can also read a collection of free technical articles, sign up for a range of free newsletters, and receive exclusive discounts and offers on Packt books and eBooks.

Contributors

About the authors

Deepesh Somani is a Microsoft Dynamics CRM solutions architect at Dynamisity and a corporate trainer. He is a Microsoft MVP awardee and has been an active contributor to the global technical community. He's authored *Mastering Dynamics CRM 2016* for Packt. His blog has had over 280,000 hits and has 500 followers. He's developed 14 free tools with 7,000 downloads and a Learning Dynamics CRM app with 1,500 downloads and 4.4 rating on the Play Store. He's experienced in working in different domains, such as banking, telecommunication, and retail, with teams from different countries and multinational companies.

I would like to thank my wife, Yamini; without her support this book wouldn't have been possible. I would like to thank the professional and extensive support offered by the Packt team: Venkatesh, Akshada, and Supriya. Thanks to Debajit Dutta, who reviewed this book and Nishant Rana, for giving me the opportunity to write with him. I would also like to thank my team members in Dynamisity for their extended support.

Nishant Rana is a Microsoft MVP – Business Solutions (Dynamics 365) with over 10 years of experience in Microsoft Dynamics CRM, Microsoft SharePoint, and other Microsoft .NET technologies. He has worked as a consultant at Microsoft for 7 years. He is a Microsoft Certified Professional in Microsoft Dynamics CRM, SharePoint, and Azure .NET. He is also a technical reviewer of popular books on Microsoft Dynamics CRM. He is an avid blogger and is also the author of *Nishant Rana's Weblog*, a technical blog on Microsoft.NET technologies, which has had more than 2.5 million hits and has 1,000 followers.

I would like to thank all my mentors and friends at Microsoft and KPIT Cummins for always encouraging me. The list could be endless, so just for brevity, I am not including their names here; they'll know who I am referring to. I would also like to thank all the MVP(s) and community leaders who have been my inspiration since I started my CRM journey. Last but not least, thanks to Packt for giving me this opportunity.

About the reviewer

Debajit Dutta is a Dynamics CRM MVP, with 11 years of IT experience and 8 years of dedicated experience in Dynamics CRM. He is currently working as a freelance architect in Dynamics and enabling CRM setups for clients. He is also an avid blogger and shares any new or interesting topics related to Dynamics 365 through his blog. His previous employers include SanDisk Corporation and Microsoft Corporation.

Currently, he is setting up his own initiative, Xrmforyou, which specializes in end-to-end CRM consulting/delivery and ISV offerings.

> *I would sincerely like to thank my wife, Mrittika Ray, for her constant support. Special thanks to my ex-colleagues Deepesh Somani and Nishant Rana, without whom this wouldn't have been accomplished. Lastly, my fellow colleagues in XrmForYou, Sakthi, and Chandana, who have been diligently working with me and have kept me updated about Dynamics 365. It helped me a lot while reviewing this book.*

Packt is searching for authors like you

If you're interested in becoming an author for Packt, please visit `authors.packtpub.com` and apply today. We have worked with thousands of developers and tech professionals, just like you, to help them share their insight with the global tech community. You can make a general application, apply for a specific hot topic that we are recruiting an author for, or submit your own idea.

Table of Contents

Preface

This book will introduce you to the components of new design tools such as SiteMap, App Module, and Visual Designer for business processes. Going deeper, you will get to know how to develop custom Software-as-a-Service (SaaS) applications, leveraging the features of PowerApps available in Dynamics 365. You will learn how to automate business processes using Microsoft Flow then we'll explore the Web API, the most important platform update in Dynamics 365 CRM. You'll also learn to implement the Web API in custom applications write an Azure-aware plugin to design and integrate cloud-aware solutions. The book concludes with configuring services using newly released features such as Editable Grids, Data Export Service, LinkedIn Integration, Relationship Insights, and Live Assist.

Who this book is for

This book targets skilled developers who are looking to build business-solution software and are new to application development in Microsoft Dynamics 365, especially for CRM.

What this book covers

Chapter 1, *Customize Application Navigation*, explores the Site Map Designer, which is a new web-based tool, introduced in Dynamics 365 CRM, which lets the customizer quickly define navigation within an app. Previously, one had to export the Sitemap XML and update it manually in the XML editor, or had to use some third-party tools. The built-in Site Map Designer makes editing the site map for an application much easier.

Chapter 2, *Design Apps Using App Module Designer*, covers App Module Designer, which makes it easy to add components to a specific app for users. Basically, an app is a collection of related entities, dashboards, and business process flows streamlined in such a way that end users can see only those components of Dynamics 365 CRM that matter to them.

Chapter 3, *Define Processes Using Visual Process Designer*, explains Visual Process Designer, which brings drag-and-drop design capabilities to Dynamics 365 CRM for business process flows. Business Process Flow in Microsoft Dynamics 365 CRM is a tool meant to help guide users through a business process in the system.

Chapter 4, *Define Business Rules Using Business Rule Designer*, walks you through Business Rules, which is a new interface that has been introduced in Dynamics 365 CRM. It has been enhanced with a complete UI overhaul, from being a step-by-step action addition to a drag-and-drop action addition.

Chapter 5, *Creating Custom Business Apps*, explains PowerApps, which provides templates to build custom Software-as-a-Service (SaaS) applications. Microsoft PowerApps allows users at any level in an enterprise to create usable mobile apps.

Chapter 6, *Automate Business Processes Using Microsoft Flow*, walks you through the creation of automated workflows between your favorite apps and services, in order to work less and do more. It is a cloud-based tool that can be easily used by Power Users without the need for a developer's help. The automated workflows are called flows. To create a flow, the user specifies the actions that should take place when a specific event occurs.

Chapter 7, *Develop Apps Using Web API*, covers Web API, which is one of the most important platform updates in Dynamics 365 CRM. It replaces OData and, eventually, SOAP-based services in Dynamics 365 CRM. It is based on the OAuth v2.0 and Open Data Protocol (OData) v4.0 standards. Both of these technologies are well established and are platform-agnostic. So, it can be consumed from different types of applications on different platforms.

Chapter 8, *Leverage Azure Extensions in Dynamics 365*, explains Azure extensions, which post message request data to any of the listener applications listening on the Microsoft Azure Service Bus. This opens up an infinite number of possibilities for integration between CRM and other LOB applications, be they in the cloud or on-premise.

Chapter 9, *Using Editable Grids in Apps*, explores Editable Grids, which is one of the most highly requested features now available in Microsoft Dynamics 365 CRM. It provides rich inline editing in main grids and sub-grids (web and mobile apps) so that users can perform operations with fewer clicks, without having to navigate to the main record.

Chapter 10, *Configure Microsoft Cognitive Services with Dynamics 365*, explains the configuration of cognitive services, which enables artificial intelligence to be incorporated into and integrated with Dynamics 365 CRM, specifically to make product recommendations and to suggest knowledge articles. Recommendation Service and Text Analytics Service connections can be configured easily inside Dynamics 365 CRM.

`Chapter 11`, *Train the Users through Learning Path*, takes a look at Learning Path, which allows user to author a custom, in-app help experience that could be specific to the CRM Solution. It facilitates learning and user adoption of Dynamics 365 CRM implementation.

`Chapter 12`, *Other New Features in Dynamics 365*, gives a brief description of some of the other new features in Dynamics 365 CRM that haven't been covered in the earlier chapters.

To get the most out of this book

This book assumes that the reader has some basic knowledge of Dynamics CRM and would like to learn the new features introduced in Dynamics 365. However, someone who hasn't worked with the previous versions and is starting afresh with Dynamics 365 will equally benefit from it. Developers, customizers, administrators, and power users will be able to enhance their skills by learning about the latest features and changes introduced in Dynamics 365.

You can try out all the features and topics mentioned in the book using a trial instance of Dynamics 365 (`https://trials.dynamics.com/`) along with the free community edition of Visual Studio 2017 (`https://www.visualstudio.com/vs/community/`). Some of the topics covered do not apply to the on-premise version of Dynamics 365.

Download the example code files

You can download the example code files for this book from your account at `www.packtpub.com`. If you purchased this book elsewhere, you can visit `www.packtpub.com/support` and register to have the files emailed directly to you.

You can download the code files by following these steps:

1. Log in or register at `www.packtpub.com`.
2. Select the **SUPPORT** tab.
3. Click on **Code Downloads & Errata**.
4. Enter the name of the book in the **Search** box and follow the onscreen instructions.

Once the file is downloaded, please make sure that you unzip or extract the folder using the latest version of:

- WinRAR/7-Zip for Windows
- Zipeg/iZip/UnRarX for Mac
- 7-Zip/PeaZip for Linux

The code bundle for the book is also hosted on GitHub at `https://github.com/PacktPublishing/Dynamics-365-Application-Development`. We also have other code bundles from our rich catalog of books and videos available at `https://github.com/PacktPublishing/`. Check them out!

Download the color images

We also provide a PDF file that has color images of the screenshots/diagrams used in this book. You can download it here: `https://www.packtpub.com/sites/default/files/downloads/Dynamics365ApplicationDevelopment_ColorImages.pdf`.

Conventions used

There are a number of text conventions used throughout this book.

`CodeInText`: Indicates code words in text, database table names, folder names, filenames, file extensions, pathnames, dummy URLs, user input, and Twitter handles. Here is an example: "The listener application needs to implement the `IServiceEndpointPlugin` interface's `Execute` method along with `WS2007HttpRelayBinding`, to which `RemoteExecutionContext` is passed from the Azure Service Bus."

A block of code is set as follows:

```
Request: GET [Organization URI] /api/data/v9.0/contacts?
 $select=firstname&$top=5
 Accept: application/json
 OData-MaxVersion: 4.0
 OData-Version: 4.0
```

Bold: Indicates a new term, an important word, or words that you see onscreen. For example, words in menus or dialog boxes appear in the text like this. Here is an example: "Do all the changes, and click on the **Save** Entity button:"

 Warnings or important notes appear like this.

 Tips and tricks appear like this.

Get in touch

Feedback from our readers is always welcome.

General feedback: Email `feedback@packtpub.com` and mention the book title in the subject of your message. If you have questions about any aspect of this book, please email us at `questions@packtpub.com`.

Errata: Although we have taken every care to ensure the accuracy of our content, mistakes do happen. If you have found a mistake in this book, we would be grateful if you would report this to us. Please visit `www.packtpub.com/submit-errata`, selecting your book, clicking on the Errata Submission Form link, and entering the details.

Piracy: If you come across any illegal copies of our works in any form on the Internet, we would be grateful if you would provide us with the location address or website name. Please contact us at `copyright@packtpub.com` with a link to the material.

If you are interested in becoming an author: If there is a topic that you have expertise in and you are interested in either writing or contributing to a book, please visit `authors.packtpub.com`.

Reviews

Please leave a review. Once you have read and used this book, why not leave a review on the site that you purchased it from? Potential readers can then see and use your unbiased opinion to make purchase decisions, we at Packt can understand what you think about our products, and our authors can see your feedback on their book. Thank you!

For more information about Packt, please visit `packtpub.com`.

1
Customize Application Navigation

A site map can be defined as a set of links through which a user can navigate and find their way around the website. In Dynamics 365 and in its earlier version, a site map is an XML file that is used for defining the navigation of the application or specific app module for the users. Until CRM 2016, there had been only one site map file for an organization. With the advent of apps in Dynamics 365, now we have one site map file for each of the app modules. As far as customizing the site map was concerned, until now we had to either update it using XML Editor, a text editor or some third-party tools. However, with Microsoft Dynamics 365 we have the built-in Site Map Designer in the product itself. This designer allows the administrator, customizers, or users with appropriate privileges to easily define navigation for an app by simply adding, dragging, and dropping the components within the Site Map Designer canvas. In this chapter, we will be covering the following points:

- Overview of the site map in Dynamics 365
- Understanding the designer interface and its components—areas, group, and sub areas
- Common operations that can be performed on the site map

Overview of the site map

For every app that is configured, we will have a separate site map defined for it. By default, we will have a Dynamics 365 custom app configured during the set up of the Dynamics 365. We can also have other apps configured while provisioning the Dynamics 365 instance such as **Sales**, **Field service**, **Project service automation**, or **Customer service**, if we have opted for them while provisioning Dynamics 365. For now, let's try to understand the basics of using the Site Map Designer using Dynamics 365 for a Sales app. Suppose we have selected **Sales** while provisioning Microsoft Dynamics 365, shown as follows:

 The link for the *Dynamics 365 Trial with Enterprise Plan 1* can be found here: `https://signup.microsoft.com/Signup?OfferId=bd569279-37f5-4f5c-99d0-425873bb9a4b&l=DYN365_ENTERPRISE_PLAN1`.

This will provision Dynamics 365 with a Sales app. This is how the navigation will look for the Sales app:

Now, as we have covered the basics of site map, let us look at the Site Map Designer interface and what components it has and how we can use it to update our site map for sales.

Overview of Site Map Designer

To access the Site Map Designer for our Sales app, perform the following steps:

1. Log in to the Dynamics 365 Sales app with a user having System Customizer, System Administrator, or any appropriate security role to customize the site map.
2. Go to **Settings | Solutions.**
3. Create a new solution with the appropriate details. For example, we have created a solution with the name of Site Map Solution, the publisher as default publisher, and the version as 1.0.0.0.

We can also log in to the default *Dynamics 365 - custom* app and create a new solution and add the Sales App Site Map in it.

4. Click on **Client Extensions** and add **Sales App Site Map** in it, shown as follows:

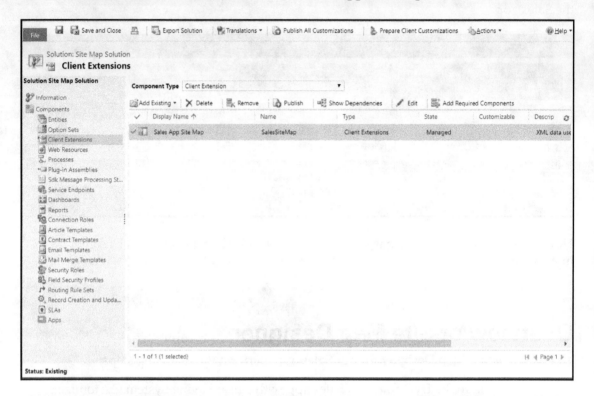

We can go to **Settings** | **Customizations** and update the site map in the default solution as well. However, as a best practice, we should create a separate solution and add the required components that need to be customized in it.

Double-clicking on it will open the **Sales App Site Map** on the Site Map Designer for us to edit. The Site Map Designer canvas allows us to work with **Area**, **Group**, and **Subarea** components:

Within the designer canvas, we can **Add, Cut, Copy, Paste, Clone**, and **Delete.**

Let us look at these components in detail.

Understanding components in the site map

Site map consists of three main components:

- **Area**: Area can be defined as the main node or area inside the navigation pane that consists of groups and their corresponding subarea. A new area can be added or the existing area can be updated or deleted. If an area doesn't consist of any visible subarea, the area will be hidden.
- **Group**: Groups can be defined as a collection or group of subareas. Just like an area, a new group can be added or an existing group can be updated or deleted.
- **Subarea**: A subarea can be defined as a navigation link within the area that defines what should load inside CRM's main pane when clicked. The subarea can point to a dashboard, an entity, a URL, or a web resource. Just like area and group, a new subarea can be added and an existing subarea can be updated or deleted.

Referring to our Sales app interface:

- **Sales**, **Marketing**, **Settings**, and **Training** are termed as areas
- **My Work**, **Customers**, **Sales**, **Collateral**, **Marketing**, **Goals**, and **Tools** are groups within the Sales area
- **Dashboards**, **What's New**, and **Activities** are subareas inside the **My Work group**.

The Sales area would have subareas specific to Sales, arranged inside what are termed as groups. Similarly, the Marketing, Settings and Training Area will have corresponding subareas inside the corresponding group. As shown in the following screenshot, the **Marketing** Area has **Dashboards**, **Activities**, **Accounts**, **Contacts**, **Leads**, **Marketing Lists**, **Campaigns**, **Quick Campaigns**, and so on. It also has subareas specific to the marketing module. These subareas are arranged inside the **My Work**, **Customers**, **Marketing**, **Collateral**, and **Tools** groups:

Now, as we have got the overview of the site map components, let us look at the different properties of each of these components in the next section.

Getting to know the area, group, and subarea properties

Let us look at the different properties of these components before we start customizing our Sales app navigation.

- The area component comprises of following properties:

AREA			
General			
	Title		For specifying the display name for the Area in the base language.
	Icon		For specifying the URL for the image used for the Icon. Size - 85 * 71 Pixel (width * height). An image can be selected from the list of web resources available in the solution.
	ID		For specifying the unique identifier for the Area. The designer only allows a-z, A-Z, 0-9 and underscore.
	Show Groups		Checkbox for specifying whether to Show/Hide all the Groups inside the Area including the Subarea within them.
Advanced	More Titles		
		Locale (LCID)	For Specifying the Locale ID for the title.
		Title	For specifying the text.
	More Descriptions		
		Locale (LCID)	For specifying the Locale ID for the description.
		Description	For specifying the text for the description
URL			For specifying the URL for Dynamics 365 for Outlook Folder.

- Group component shares most of the same properties as Area:

GROUP			
General			
	Title		For specifying the display name for the Area in the base language.
	ID		For specifying the unique identifier for the Area. Valid values include a-z, A-Z, 0-9 and underscore.
Advanced	More Titles		
		Locale (LCID)	For Specifying the Locale ID for the title.
		Title	For specifying the text.
	More Descriptions		
		Locale (LCID)	For specifying the Locale ID for the description.
		Description	For specifying the text for the description
URL			For specifying the URL for Dynamics 365 for Outlook Folder.
Set as Profile			This property is only applicable for Workplace Area. It is a Checkbox for specifying whether this group represents a user-selectable Profile for the Workplace.

Set as Profile property of Group might not be relevant for Dynamics 365, as the Workplace area has been discontinued starting CRM 2013.

Subarea has few more properties compared to Area and Group:

SUBAREA			
General			
	Type		For specifying the Subarea type • Dashboard • Entity • Web resource • URL
	Entity		For specifying the Entity for the subarea. (Available for Type - Entity)
	URL		For specifying the URL to be shown when the subarea is clicked. For Type - URL, we can specify URL of a web page and for Type - Web Resource, we need to specify URL of a Web Resource. The field is disabled for Type – Entity.
	Default Dashboard		For specifying default Dashboard when Type is selected as Dashboard. Inside the Site Map XML, the designer adds the GUID of the dashboard selected for Default Dashboard attribute of SubArea tag. We can also set an interactive dashboard as the default dashboard.
	Title		For specifying the display name for the Area in the base language.
	Icon		For specifying the URL for the image used for the Icon. Size - 32 * 32 Pixel. An image can be selected from the list of web resources available in the solution.
	ID		For specifying the unique identifier for the Subarea. Valid values a-z, A-Z, 0-9, and underscore (_).
	Parameter Passing		Checkbox for specifying whether to pass information about the organization and language context to the URL. Available only if Type is either Web resource or URL. The name of the corresponding tag in SiteMap XML is PassParams.

Advanced	Privileges	Defines whether to show or hide the Subarea based on privileges the user has through security roles assigned.	
		Entity	For specifying the name of the entity to check privileges for. We can specify more than one Entity.
		Miscellaneous	For specifying privileges not specific to an Entity. We can specify more than one Miscellaneous privileges. • Allow Quick Campaign • Create Entity • Import Customization • Learning Path • Use Internet Marketing
	More Titles		
		Locale (LCID)	For Specifying the Locale ID for the title.
		Title	For specifying the text.
	More Descriptions		
		Locale (LCID)	For specifying the Locale ID for the description.
		Description	For specifying the text for the description
	SKU's	For specifying which version of Dynamics 365 to display this subarea. • All • On-Premise • Live • SPLA	

	Client	For specifying the client for the SubArea. It has the following valid values → All, Outlook, OutlookWorkstationClient, OutlookLaptopClient and Web. We can select more than one values.	
		Outlook Shortcut	For specifying the icon to be displayed in Dynamics 365 for Outlook.
		Offline Availability	For specifying whether the subarea should be available offline in Dynamics 365 for Outlook.

- As we know that the site map is basically an XML file, any changes that we are doing through Site Map Designer are basically updating the site map's XML behind the scenes:

- To get the Sales App Site Map definition, export the solution containing the Sales App Site Map client extension and unzip it. Then, open the `customizations.xml` file and search for the `SiteMap` tag.

- The following is the sample XML for the My Work group of the Sales area inside the Sales App Site Map. We can see the `Area`, `Group`, and `SubArea` tags along with their corresponding attributes:

```xml
<SiteMapUniqueName>SalesSiteMap</SiteMapUniqueName>
<SiteMap IntroducedVersion="8.2.0.0">
  <Area Id="SFA4_324324" ResourceId="Area_Sales" DescriptionResourceId="Sales_Description" Icon="/_imgs/
sales_24x24.gif" ShowGroups="true" IntroducedVersion="7.0.0.0">
   <Group Id="MyWork" ResourceId="Group_MyWork" DescriptionResourceId="My_Work_Description"
   IntroducedVersion="7.0.0.0" IsProfile="false" ToolTipResourseId="My_Work_ToolTip">
     <SubArea Id="nav_dashboards" ResourceId="Homepage_Dashboards" DescriptionResourceId="Dashboards_Description"
      Icon="/_imgs/area/18_home.gif" Url="/workplace/home_dashboards.aspx"
            DefaultDashboard="2701de60-8f2a-48a4-8262-4a35ca7441fa" IntroducedVersion="7.0.0.0"
            GetStartedPanePath="Dashboards_Web_User_Visor.html"
            GetStartedPanePathAdmin="Dashboards_Web_Admin_Visor.html"
            GetStartedPanePathAdminOutlook="Dashboards_Outlook_Admin_Visor.html"
            GetStartedPanePathOutlook="Dashboards_Outlook_User_Visor.html"
            AvailableOffline="false" PassParams="false" />
     <SubArea Id="nav_personalwall" ResourceId="Whats_New_Label" DescriptionResourceId="Whats_New_Description"
      Icon="/WebResources/msdyn_/Images/Wall_16.png" Url="$webresource:msdyn_/PersonalWall.htm?
      data=HideUserProfile=0" IntroducedVersion="7.0.0.0" GetStartedPanePath="Dashboards_Web_User_Visor.html"
      GetStartedPanePathAdmin="Dashboards_Web_Admin_Visor.html"
      GetStartedPanePathAdminOutlook="Dashboards_Outlook_Admin_Visor.html"
      GetStartedPanePathOutlook="Dashboards_Outlook_User_Visor.html" OutlookShortcutIcon="$webresource:msdyn_/
      Images/Wall_16.png" AvailableOffline="false" PassParams="false" />
     <SubArea Id="nav_activities" DescriptionResourceId="Activities_SubArea_Description" Icon="/_imgs/
      imagestrips/transparent_spacer.gif" Url="/_root/homepage.aspx?etc=4200" IntroducedVersion="7.0.0.0"
      GetStartedPanePath="Activities_Web_User_Visor.html"
      GetStartedPanePathAdmin="Activities_Web_Admin_Visor.html"
      GetStartedPanePathAdminOutlook="Activities_Outlook_Admin_Visor.html"
      GetStartedPanePathOutlook="Activities_Outlook_User_Visor.html" Entity="activitypointer"
      AvailableOffline="false" PassParams="false" />
   </Group>
```

- As mentioned earlier, instead of using the Site Map Designer, we can manually update the site map's XML using any text editor, and can import back the solution (and publish it) to see the changes.

Site map XML reference : `https://msdn.microsoft.com/en-us/library/gg334430.aspx`.

In this section, we looked at the properties of the area, group, and subarea components of Site Map Designer. In the next section, we will learn how to perform some basic operations such as updating, adding, deleting, and so on, on these components through Site Map Designer.

Common operations using Site Map Designer

Now, as we have gone through all the properties of the components of site map in detail, let us see how we can perform some common operations using Site Map Designer.

Editing an existing component in the site map

To edit an existing area, group, and subarea in the site map, we need to select that component in the designer and go to the **properties** tab of that component. Let us take a simple example to understand this. Suppose we want to rename the existing **Training** area to Help, we need to select the **Training** area on the site map, go to its **Properties** tab, and update its **Title** property.

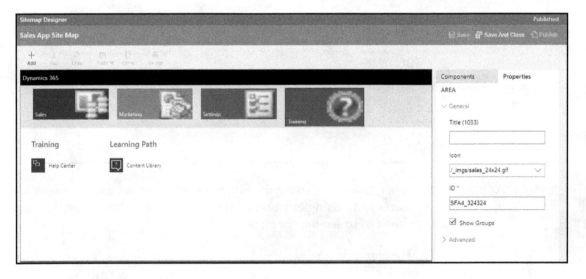

Let us specify **Help** as the value for the **Title** property. This updates the area's title from Training to Help, as shown as follows:

We can also update the title property of the site map components through inline editing. For this, hover over the component to reveal the pencil. We can click on the pencil icon to edit the **Title**. Similarly, we can edit or update the corresponding properties of the group and subarea components, and as we mentioned earlier, any changes made in the designer will reflect back in the XML for the site map.

Adding a component to the site map

To add an area, group, or subarea to the site map, we need to click on the **Add** button on the Action Bar in the **Sitemap Designer**. Let's add an area here to understand this. Click on the **Add** button and select **Area**:

Or, drag-and-drop the Area from the **Components** tab.

Once added, we need to select the component (Area here), and then edit its properties in the
Properties tab. For example, the **Properties** tab for the new Area component added is
shown in the following image:

This will add a new Area named **New Area** in the site map.

Similarly, we can add or drag and drop new groups and subarea components in the
Navigation and specify their properties.

Cutting, copying, and pasting a component to the site map

Through Site Map Designer, we can also cut, copy, and paste site map components. Let's select our **New Area** and click on the **Cut** button on the Action Bar to cut the component. The component will be grayed out.

Similarly, we can select the component and click on the **Copy** button to copy the component. The **Paste** button gives us the option of pasting the component to the right or left in case of Area and Group components, shown as follows:

Cloning a component to the site map

To clone or make a copy of an existing Area, Group, and Subarea to the site map, we can select the component and click the **Clone** button on the Action Bar in the **Sitemap Designer**. The clone will add the respective component to the next component being cloned with the -Copy suffix added to its Title. For example, cloning the **Sales** Area, as shown in the following image, will add a new area named **Sales-Copy** next to the **Sales** Area that is cloned:

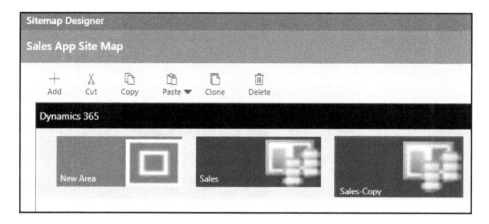

Deleting a component from the site map

To delete an Area, Group, or Subarea from the site map, select the component and either click **Delete** from the Action bar or press the **Delete** key:

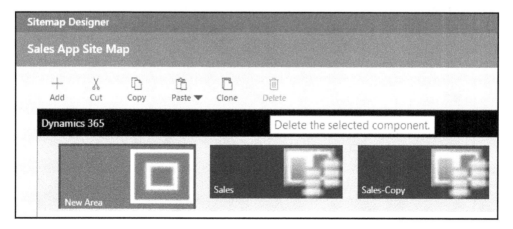

Deleting an Area will also delete the Group and Subarea in it. Similarly, deleting the Group will delete the Subarea in it.

Organizing a component within the site map

Using Drag and Drop, we can move the components around the site map before we rearrange it:

For example, we can move the **Sales** Area to be the last Area in the site map, **My Work** to be the second group within the **Sales** Area, **Dashboard** as the last Subarea inside the **MyWork** Group, and so on, shown as follows:

We can also move a Subarea to a different Group. For example, the **Dashboards** Subarea can be moved to any of the other Groups such as **Customer**, **Sales**, **Collateral**, and so on, and a Group to be part of a different Area. That is, we can move the **My Work** Group to be part of the **Settings**, **Training**, and **Sales** area.

Saving, validating, and publishing changes in the site map

To reflect any of the preceding changes for the users, such as add, clone, delete, and so on, we need to click **Save** and then **Publish** it in the Site Map Designer canvas. Here, ***Draft** indicates that there are unsaved changes:

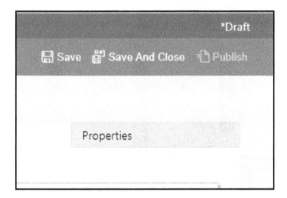

On saving the changes and clicking on **Publish**, it changes to **Published** to indicate that changes have been applied and are available for the users to see:

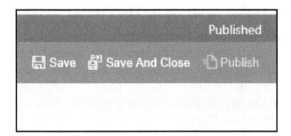

Clicking on the **Save** button will also validate and show up if there are any errors in the site map. For example, if we have not provided values for any of the required fields or specified unallowed characters for any of the properties. In the following screenshot, we have not provided a value for the entity property in the Subarea and clicked on **Save**, which is a mandatory field:

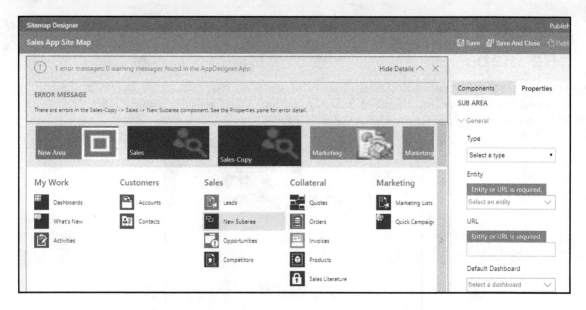

This shows the **ERROR MESSAGE** notification in the designer with all the details. We will only be able to save and then publish the changes after fixing the error.

Adding a Subarea component in the site map

Let's take a simple scenario here to understand how we can add a new Subarea component. We realize that our Sales app users would be frequently accessing the Open Leads View inside CRM, so it would be helpful for them if we could add a Subarea for Open Leads View in the My Work Group in the Sales Area for them. To implement it, we will need to add a new Subarea inside the My Work Group of type URL. To do so, we need to click on **Add** in the Action bar in **Sitemap Designer** and add a new Subarea and drag and place it below the Activities SubArea in the My Work Group:

Here, the URL pattern for the view needs to be the following:

```
=/_root/homepage.aspx?etc=<entity code >&viewid=%7b<GUID value of view
id>%7d"
```

For the `etc` and `viewid` query parameters, we need to go to the **Open Leads** view in CRM and click on the **EMAIL A LINK| Of Current View** ribbon button to get the link:

The link will have the value of `etc` and `viewid`. We will then copy the value of the `etc` and `viewid` query string parameters from the link. We can then set the properties for our new **SUB AREA**, shown as follows:

We will save and then publish it. After publishing, inside the Sales app the user will be able to see the new Subarea named **Open Leads**:

Clicking on the **Open Leads** Subarea will open the **Open Leads** view, shown as follows:

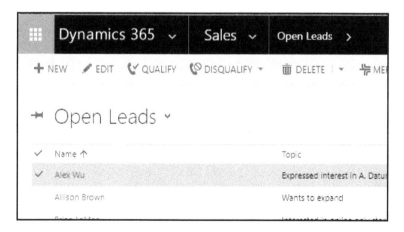

Hiding a Subarea component in the site map

As we saw earlier, the Subarea component has a privilege property. It defines whether to show or hide the Subarea based on privileges the user has through the security roles assigned. Let us try to understand this with an example as well. Suppose we want to show the Open Leads Subarea we just added to only those users who have a Create privilege on the Lead entity. To define this, let us go back to the **Properties** tab of the Open Leads Subarea in Site Map Designer. There, we need to go to **Privileges** inside the **Advanced** section. Inside the Entity drop-down, we can select the Lead entity and click on the + (plus) button to add the record. We will leave all the checkboxes unchecked, except **Create**:

Save and publish the changes. Now, let us log in with the user that has only the Salesperson security role assigned. Here, we have updated the security role and have set **None** for **Create** Privilege on **Lead** Entity; that is, the first option that we see in the following screenshot:

The users who do not have the Create privilege on the Lead record, will not be able to see the Open Leads Subarea in their site map.

Passing parameters to a URL from the site map

As we saw earlier, the Subarea component has a Parameter Passing checkbox property. It specifies whether to pass information about the organization and language context to the URL. The property is only available for Subareas of type web resource or URL. Suppose we have the following URL defined in our URL property of Subarea:

`http://mydomain/mypage.aspx`.

Checking the Parameter Passing checkbox will pass the following parameters to it:

`http://mydomain/mypage.aspx/?orglcid=1033&orgname=org29d341dd&userlcid=1033`.

- `orglcid`: language code identifier of the base language of the organization
- `orgname` : unique name of the organization
- `userlcid`: language code identifier used by the current user

This information could be used to create solutions that support multiple languages.

 Creating solutions that support multiple languages is detailed at `https://msdn.microsoft.com/en-us/library/hh670609.aspx#Anchor_0`.

Editing the site map and support for clients

Let us look briefly at separate ways of editing the site map apart from Site Map designer and the ways in which clients are supported for the different type of site map that we now have in Dynamics 365.

Site map editors

A site map, as we essentially know, is an XML file. Any XML text editor is good enough to edit site map XML files. For this, we can export the unmanaged solution that contains the site map XML, edit it either in NotePad, Visual Studio, or any other XML editor, and import it back. The important thing to remember here is, if we are importing the site map as a managed solution, it will create a new site map record with all the latest changes, and in the case of unmanaged, the existing site map XML is overwritten.

 Editing the site map XML with schema validation is detailed at `https://msdn.microsoft.com/en-us/library/gg334493(v=crm.8).aspx`.

Apart from Site Map Designer, we can use one of the third-party site map editors to edit the site map. One of the most popular tools is site map editor that is included as part of the XRM Tool Box. This is how our Sales App Site Map loads up inside site map editor:

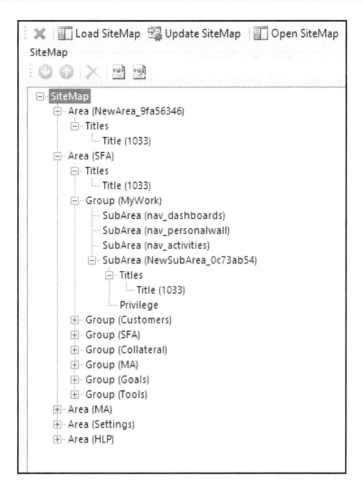

The tool makes it easy to edit the site map compared to editing the XML manually. The tool has been one of the most popular tools for editing site maps and has been available since CRM 2011. The tool has been recently updated to support multiple site maps available in Dynamics 365. The other option is programmatically updating the site map. For this, we can make use of the site map entity and update its `sitemapxml` property, shown as follows:

- Create an object of the site map entity:

```
Entity siteMap = new Entity["sitemap"];
```

- Update its `sitemapxml` property with valid XML:

```
siteMap["sitemapxml"] = "valid site map xml";
```

- Update the entity using Organization Service's instance:

```
service.Update(siteMap);
```

- Publish the changes using the `PublishXmlRequest` class:

```
PublishXmlRequest request = new PublishXmlRequest();
 request.ParameterXml =
"<importexportxml><sitemaps><sitemap></sitemap></sitemaps></imp
ortexportxml>";
 service.Execute(request);
```

We can also create and delete app-specific site map records programmatically. However, it is recommended you use Site Map Designer instead of doing it programmatically. Another point to note is that the default site map record cannot be created or deleted.

 It is strongly recommended that we export the existing site map XML file and save a copy of it before we start editing, which can help us to restore it back in case of any errors while editing.

Supported clients

The default site map, which is the site map for Dynamics 365 – custom app is supported for both Dynamics 365 web applications and Dynamics 365 for Outlook. The site maps for any new custom apps, or the business apps such as Sales, Customer Service, Field Service, and Project Service Automation, are only supported by Dynamics 365 web applications.

Summary

In this chapter, we saw how the site map has evolved in Dynamics 365. Now, we can have multiple site maps per app and the built-in Site Map Designer tool in the product itself. We also had a detailed look at the new Site Map Designer and some common operations that can be performed through it. In the next chapter, we will cover the new Visual Process Designer and how it can be used to create business process flows with intuitive drag and drop capabilities.

2
Design Apps Using App Module Designer

Apps are a new feature introduced in Dynamics 365 or Dynamics CRM version 9.x. Prior to the following versions of Dynamics CRM, it was not possible to create custom apps catering to any module in Dynamics CRM implementations. There used to exist one single layer of the site map which provided links to various entities, dashboards, and more, for the entire organization. However, with Microsoft Dynamics 365, Microsoft has introduced the concepts of apps which can cater to specific business areas or modules. Also, we have the built-in App Designer in the product itself. This designer allows the administrator, customizers, or users with appropriate privileges, to easily design an app by simply adding, dragging, and dropping the components, within the App Designer canvas.

In this chapter, we will be covering the following points:

- Overview of apps in Dynamics 365
- Prerequisite privileges required for configuring apps
- Configuring Dynamics 365 apps
- Understanding the app properties
- Understanding the App Designer interface
- Adding and removing components, validating, publishing, and securing an app
- Exporting and importing apps

Overview of apps in Dynamics 365

Apps are a new feature introduced in Dynamics 365 to provide quick navigation for the users to quickly access the most relevant entities, and so on. Apps are convenient and each app has its own site map. The details of designing a site map in Dynamics 365 will be discussed in `Chapter 1`, *Customize Application Navigation*. Briefly, a **site map** is a component which stores navigation links and is internally stored in XML format in Dynamics 365. Apps can contain components such as:

- Entities
- Dashboards
- Forms
- Views
- Charts
- Business process flows

Privileges required for configuring apps

Before we start discussing the steps required to configure apps in Dynamics 365, it is important to understand the prerequisite security privileges which are required for a particular user, before they are able to have access to configuring apps. This is particularly important if you wish to give a power user or end-user the ability to design and use their own apps. The following table summarizes the minimum privileges required to configure apps in Dynamics 365:

Sr. No.	Entity name	Read	Write	Create
1.	App	Yes	Yes	Yes
2.	Solution	Yes	-	-
3.	Customization	Yes	Yes	-

A detailed look at the security roles area via CRM screens is given here:

1. Under the **Customization** tab in Dynamics 365, **Security Role: Read**, **Write**, and **Create** privileges for **App** should be configured. Please refer to the following screenshot:

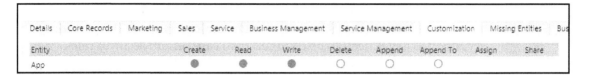

2. Under the **Customization** tab in Dynamics 365, **Security Role**: **Read** and **Write** privileges for **Customizations** should be configured. Please refer to the following screenshot:

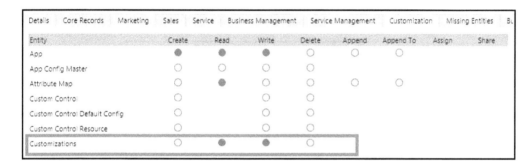

3. Under the **Customization** tab in Dynamics 365, **Security Role**: **Read** and **Write** privileges for **Customizations** should be configured. Please refer to the following screenshot:

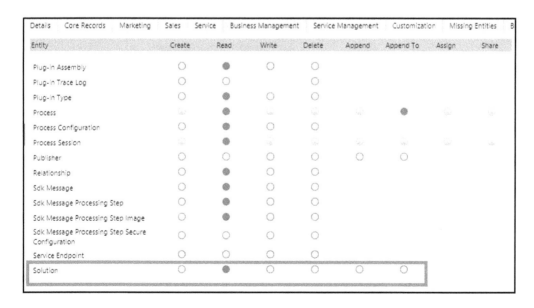

Note: The system administrator and system customizer roles already have the prerequisite privileges to configure Dynamics 365 apps. The preceding security privileges need to be configured, in case certain security roles, other than those mentioned, need access to configure Dynamics 365 apps.

Configuring Dynamics 365 apps

In this section, we will understand the various steps required to configure Dynamics 365 apps. The following diagram outlines the steps required to configure Dynamics 365 apps:

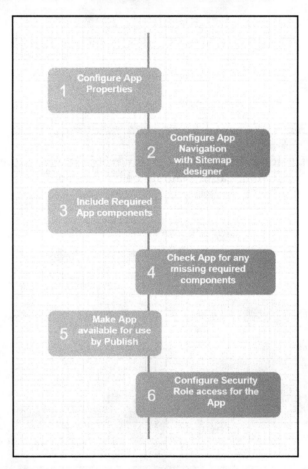

Here are descriptions of each step:

1. **Configure app properties:** App properties such as name, Unique Name, icon, and more, need to be configured as the starting point to configure the app. A detailed description is given in the next section.
2. **Configure App Navigation with Sitemap designer:** Every app can have its own site map. A detailed description is given in `Chapter 1`, *Customize Application Navigation*.
3. **Include Required App components:** App components can consist of artifacts or Entity Assets which need to be included in the app.
4. **Check App for any missing required components:** The app needs to be checked for any missing required components. This can be done by hitting **Validate** before publishing the app.
5. **Make App available for use by Publish:** For users to be able to access the app, it needs to be published. A detailed description is available in the following sections.
6. **Configure Security Role access for the App:** Apps can be secured to allow an only certain set of users to be able to access the app. A detailed description is available in the following sections.

Understanding the app properties and designer interface

Apps have some specific properties which we need to go through before configuring an app. The following properties need to be provided before configuring an app. The following table summarizes the properties:

S. No.	Property name	Property description
1.	Name	This property needs to be provided to give a Unique Name for the app.
2.	Unique Name	Unique Name is auto-populated based on the **Name** property. It contains a prefix which is picked from the publisher prefix. The only part of the Unique Name can be changed (not the prefix as it is picked from the publisher of the solution). A Unique Name can only contain English characters or numbers.

3.	Description	This property contains a short description of what the app is designed to achieve. **Note**: It is recommended you use this property to provide meaningful descriptions for the app, as it will be useful information for ongoing CRM customization and maintenance.
4.	Icon	The default setting for this property is **Use Default App** thumbnail, which is checked. In case you want to use a different web resource for the app icon, clear this checkbox and mention the web resource as an icon for the app. This icon will be displayed in the preview tile of the app.
5.	Client type	This property lets you select the client type behavior for your app. It can be one of the following: • **Web**: This is the classic web browser client interface for Dynamics 365 • **Unified Interface**: This is the new and improved Dynamics 365 web browser client interface with a similar look and feel across PC and mobile devices
6.	App URL suffix	The APP URL property is auto-populated based on the app name specified. An APP URL needs to be unique. The formats are as follows: • **On-premises deployments:** `http://<server>/<org name>/Apps/<App URL>` • **Online deployments:** `https://<server>.crm#.dynamics.com/Apps/<App URL>` **Note**: If cleared, an APP URL is automatically generated with the APP ID.
7.	Use the existing solution to create the app	This property can be utilized to create the app from a list of installed **Solution**. When this option is selected, the **Done** button on the header will switch to **Next**. After selecting **Next**, you can select the available **Solution**. If any site map is configured in the **Solution**, it will also be available for selection. After selecting **Solution,** and optionally site map if it was part of the **Solution**, you can select **Done**. The components that are present in the **Solution** or site map are automatically added to the app.

8.	Choose a Welcome Page	This property lets you select a web resource to be configured as a welcome page for the app. This is a useful property to configure links that will be helpful to users using the app or videos/upgrade instruction links, and more. This link is always visible on a welcome screen when the user opens the app. Users can later select **Do not show this Welcome screen next time** to disable the page, and then the page will not appear the next time the app is opened.

Understanding the App Designer interface and adding components to the app

Now that we understand the app properties from the last section, it is time to configure our first Dynamics 365 app using the Dynamics 365 App Designer, and also understand the interface. The following steps can be taken to create a Dynamics 365 app:

1. Navigate to **Settings** | **My Apps** as shown in the following screenshot:

2. On the **My Apps** screen, you will be able to see a list of already configured apps out of the box, or any other custom apps already configured in your organization:

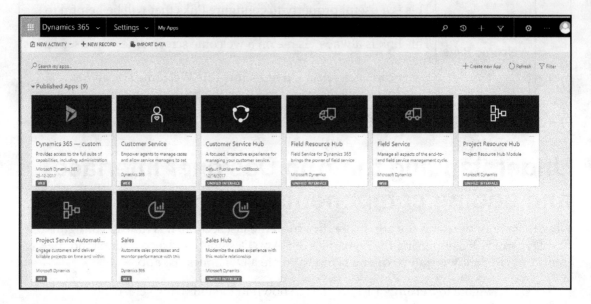

3. On the **My Apps** screen, select the **Create New App button**, available at the top right of the screen, as shown in the following screenshot:

Alternatively, you can also select the **Create New App** tile, available at the bottom of the **My Apps** screen, under the **Apps Being Edited** option on the screen:

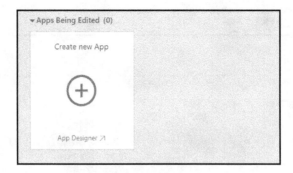

4. The next screen will show the App Designer screen with all the app properties that we described in the last section:

This image shows the App designer screen

5. Choose a meaningful name for the app. In our case, we are creating an app for quickly doing Lead Generation so we will call the app **Lead Generation**. Notice that **Unique Name**, **App URL Suffix**, and **Web URL** properties are automatically generated:

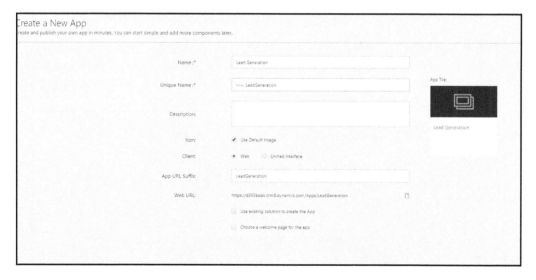

This image shows the Lead Generation

Note: In this step, we keep the default properties for the app. You may wish to override these automatically generated properties.

6. Supply a meaningful description of the app (the URL should be unique):

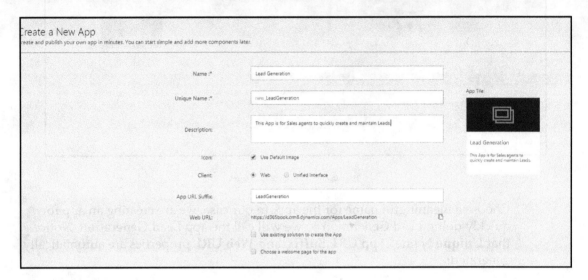

Also, we are going to keep the **Client** type as **Web** (classic CRM web interface).

7. In order to pick a different icon for the app, uncheck the checkbox for **Use Default Image,** and then select a web resource you want to utilize as an **Icon** for the app:

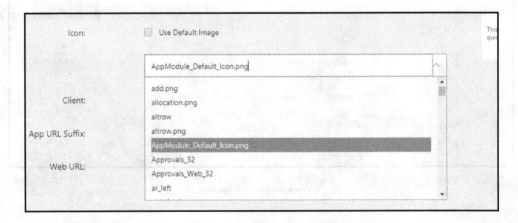

We are going to select **Legacy CRM icon** for this particular app. Notice that on selecting the icon, under the **App Tile** preview towards the right, you can see the preview of the **App Tile**:

8. Optionally, you may choose to **using the existing Solution to create the app** and also **choose a Welcome page for the app**. We will skip the settings for our first Dynamics 365 app and click **Done**, available at the top right of the App Designer screen:

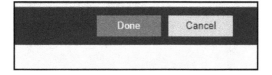

9. After clicking **Done**, the App Designer will navigate to the screen to select the different components.

An app can consist of two distinct types of components, as described in the following table:

S.No.	Component Name	Component Contents
1	**Artifact**	Entity, dashboards, and business process flows
2	**Entity Assets**	Form, view, chart, and more

Let's now understand the layout of the App Designer. The App Designer is split into two distinct areas:

- **Canvas**: Toward the left-hand side of the App Designer, you are presented with a canvas area where you can add app components. The following screenshot gives a sample of the canvas area:

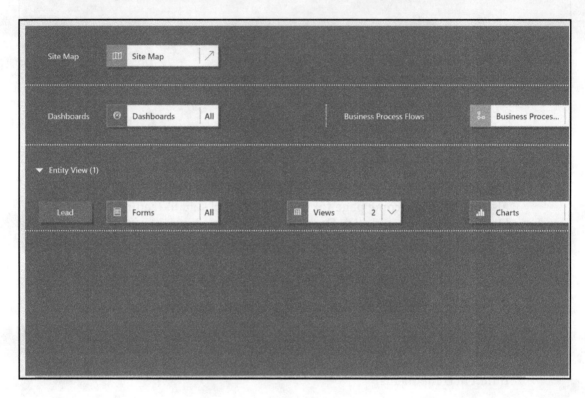

- **Component properties**: Toward the right-hand side of the App Designer, you are presented with an area where you can select the various components and their properties. The following screenshot gives a sample of **Components** and its **Properties** area:

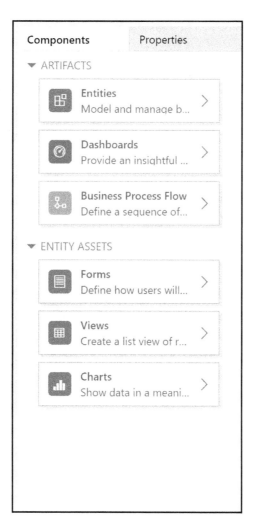

Notice here that the classification of different components is also mentioned in the **Components** area, where the components are grouped into two distinct categories, **ARTIFACTS** and **ENTITY ASSETS**. On the canvas in the App Designer, if you select **Dashboards** or **Business Process Flow**, all the entities under **Dashboards** or **Business Process Flow** are automatically selected by the App Designer. Then, you just need to select the appropriate entity asset under **Entities,** such as **View**, **Form**, and **Chart**.

In our case for our **Lead Generation** app, as no **Site Map** was selected, **Configuration Missing** will be shown in the **Site Map** area:

10. On clicking the arrow icon, on the **Site Map** area in the canvas area of the App Designer, you will be presented with the **Site Map Designer**. The **Site Map Designer** is discussed at length in `Chapter 1`, *Customize Application Navigation*, as per the following screenshot:

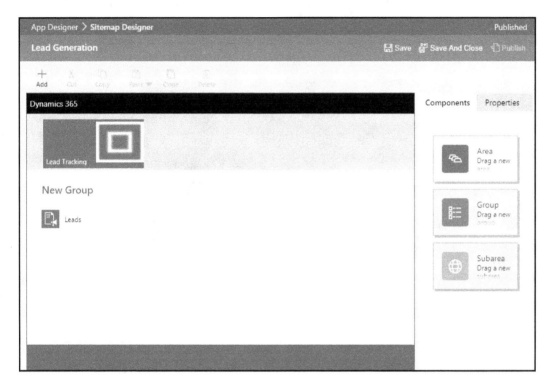

Hit **Save And Close** on the following **Sitemap** editor screen.

Note: For details of Sitemap and Sitemap Designer, please refer to `Chapter 1`, *Customize Application Navigation*.

11. Notice that the **Lead** entity, which was part of the selected site map, is already available in **Entity View** on the App Designer. Similarly, all the components on the selected site map are automatically available on the App Designer:

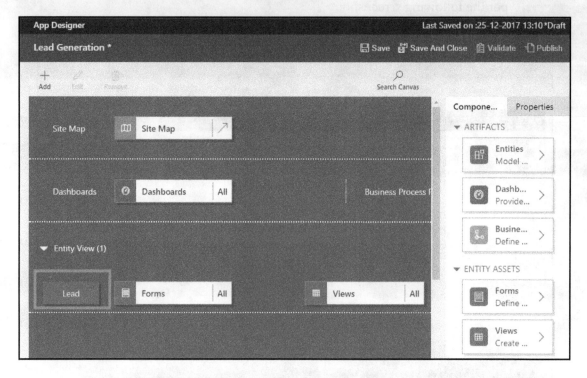

12. Selecting **ENTITY ASSETS** by default, all **Forms** and **Views** for the selected entity are available under **Entity View**. Let's change **Views**. Click on **All** next to **Views** selection and choose the views that you wish to use in this app. Here, only the **All Leads** and **Closed Leads** views are selected:

You may also provide a similar selection of **Forms** and **Charts** and click **Save** on the top right of the screen.

13. Next, let's look at the artifacts side of the screen. Here, you can see that **Site Map**, **Dashboards** and **Business Process Flows** are provided and **All** is selected by default:

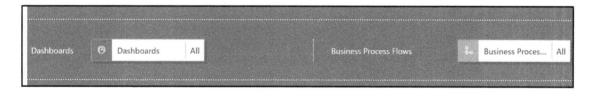

14. We can select the **Business Process Flow** tile and click on the **Area** which says **All**. After doing so, we are presented with the option to select the appropriate **Business Process Flow** available in the current app. As this is the **Lead Generation** app, we only select **Lead to Opportunity Sales Business Process Flow,** which is available in out-of-the-box Dynamics 365:

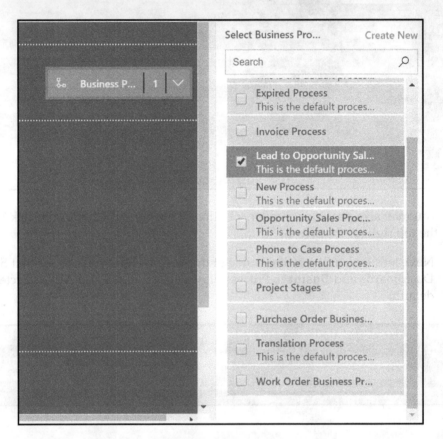

15. As soon as you select a particular **Business Process Flow,** all the entities under it are automatically selected by the App Designer:

16. Next click **Save**. Then click **Validate**, available in the top-right corner of the App Designer:

17. After **Validate**, you might occasionally receive warnings or errors, as shown here:

18. In our case, these are just potential warnings. So, we can skip them; error warnings cannot be skipped through, however. We can publish our app by clicking **Publish**. This will successfully publish the app:

Using the custom app

In the last section, we published a new custom app called Lead Generation. In this section, we will try to use our newly created custom app. Follow these steps to use your newly created custom app:

1. Expand the area under **Dynamics 365** and you should be able to locate the newly published Dynamics 365 app for Lead Generation:

Note: Security considerations will be looked at in the following section of this chapter. Currently, the user has access to the app since it is a system administrator role.

Alternatively, the user can also navigate to **Settings** | **MyApps** and see the app on the list of **Published Apps**:

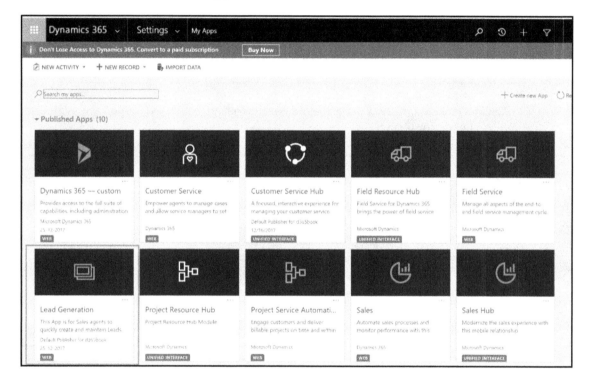

2. Notice that the new app is now launched, and the navigation options in the site map show the site map we had configured earlier:

3. Also, as selected in the **Entity Assets** configuration, only two **Views** are available in the **Leads** for usage:

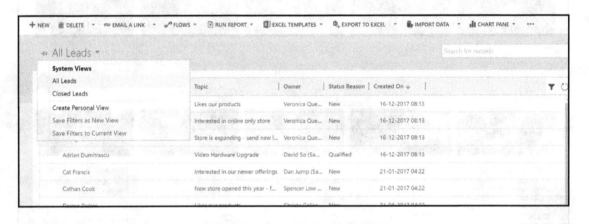

Securing an app

In real-world scenarios, it is often a requirement to give specific app access to a certain set of users only. For this requirement, we can secure apps to be accessible via certain security roles only.

We now wish to edit the Lead Generation app security permissions so that they are only available to sales manager and salesperson security roles. We can do this by enabling app access for certain Security Roles only. Follow these steps to enable app access for certain security roles only:

1. Navigate to **Settings** | **MyApps** and select **More** options under the **Lead Generation** app:

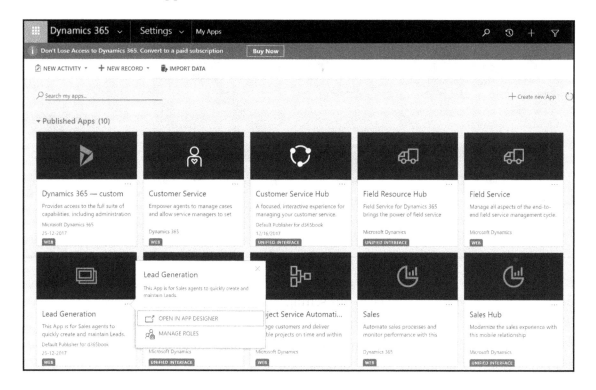

2. Select the **Manage Roles** option. This will launch the **Manage Roles** window on the right side of the screen, where various **Security Roles** can be selected. Select the appropriate roles and click **Save**:

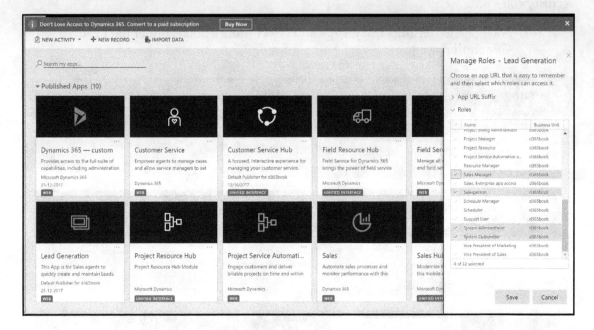

Note: The system administrator and system customizer roles have full access on all apps by default. It is recommended you keep this setting as these security roles will need to maintain or customize apps in future.

Now, Lead Generation App is only available to sales manager and salesperson roles as well as system administrator and system customizer roles.

Editing an existing app

If we wish to edit the layout or customization of any of the artifacts or **Entity Asset** components in an app, we can do this by using the following steps:

1. Navigate to **Settings | MyApps** and select **More** options under the Lead Generation App:

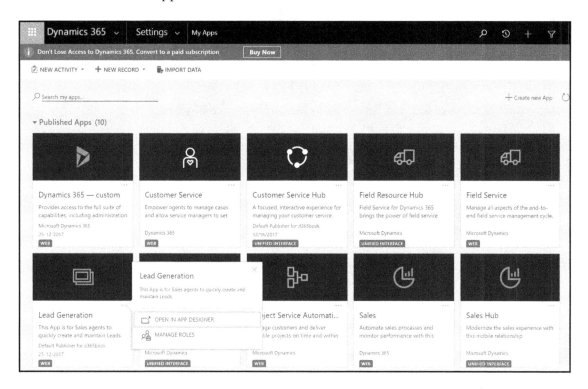

2. Select the **OPEN IN APP DESIGNER** option. This will launch the App Designer window for the app:

Now, the Lead Generation App can be edited as required, and saved. Then, it needs to be validated and published again for changes to be reflected to the users.

Importing and exporting an app

Apps can be packaged from one environment to another as a CRM **Solution** component. To export the Lead Generation App, follow these steps:

1. Navigate to **Settings** | **Solutions** and create a new solution called **Lead Generation**. You may choose to open an existing solution that you are using. On the left-hand side, notice the **Apps** option:

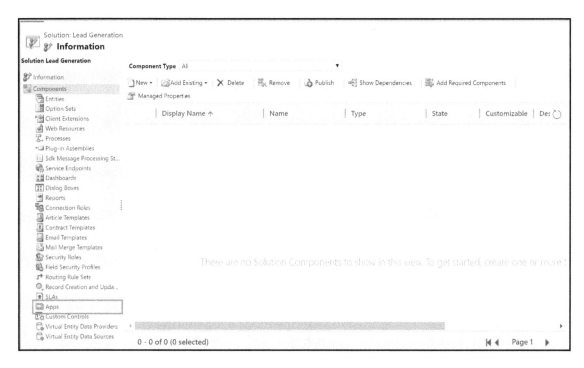

2. Next, select the **Add Existing** app button:

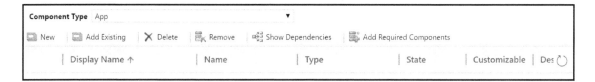

3. Select the **Lead Generation** app and click **OK**:

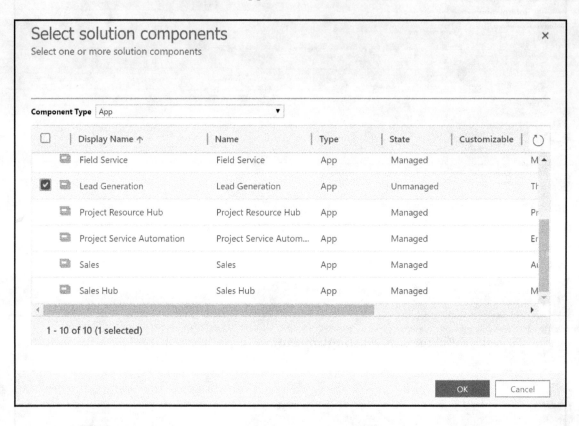

4. If you have not included the custom site map created for the app, you will be prompted to include the required component. Select the **Yes, include required component** option and click **OK**:

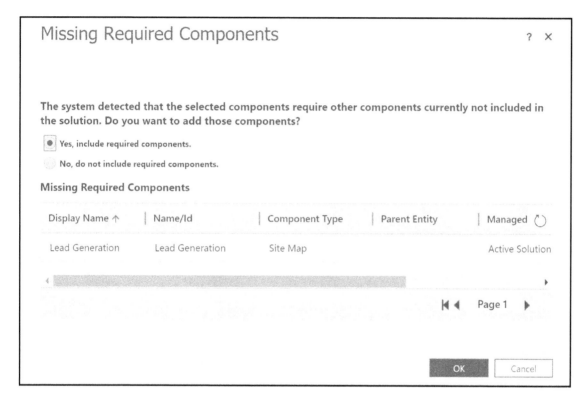

5. The Lead Generation App is now added to the CRM solution. This can now be exported as a CRM solution ZIP file and imported into any other environment.

Deleting an app

Sometimes an app is no longer required in a Dynamics 365 instance and you may wish to delete the app. Follow these steps to delete an app in Dynamics 365:

1. Navigate to the solution containing the app. In our case, we created a **Lead Generation** solution for this purpose. Navigate to **Settings | Solutions** under the **Customizations** area and open the **Lead Generation** solution. Click the **Apps** option from the **Solution** components available on the left-hand side of the screen:

2. Select the **Lead Generation** app and click on the **Delete** button:

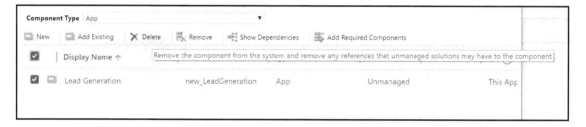

3. You will be prompted to confirm the deletion. Click **Delete**:

 Note: It is recommended you also delete the site map created for the particular app from the CRM instance, otherwise it might cause issues in future if an app is created with a similar name.

4. The app is now removed from the CRM system.

Web browser and OS support for App Designer

App Designer can be used in the following OS and web browser combinations:

- Microsoft Edge on Windows 10
- Internet Explorer 11 on Windows 10 or Windows 8.1
- Internet Explorer 11 Modern on Windows 8.1
- Internet Explorer 10 over Windows 8
- Internet Explorer 10 Modern on Windows 8
- Mozilla Firefox on Windows 8, Windows 8.1, or Windows 10
- Google Chrome on Windows 8, Windows 8.1, or Windows 10
- Apple Safari on MAC OS X

Summary

In this chapter, we saw how apps are introduced as a new and powerful navigation feature in Dynamics 365. We also understood how apps provide the users with quick access to the most relevant options they need to carry out their day-to-day CRM work. Now we can have multiple site maps per app, and built-in App Designer tools in the product itself. We also had a detailed look at the new App Designer and some common operations that can be performed through it.

In the next chapter, we will cover the new Sitemap Designer and how it can be used to create site maps with intuitive drag and drop capabilities.

3

Define Processes Using Visual Process Designer

The Microsoft Dynamics 365 version introduces a new editor for designing Business Process Flows with an improved Business Process Flow designer. Using the Business Process Flow editor, system administrators or system customizers can use a rich graphical editor to create, edit, and configure Business Process Flows. The Business Process Flow editor allows organizations to improve user productivity and the time required to do their day-to-day CRM activities.

In this chapter, we will be covering the following points:

- Overview of Business Process Flow
- Prerequisite privileges required for Business Process Flow
- Basic components of Business Process Flow
- Business Process Flow designer overview
- Create and edit a Business Process Flow
- Overview of a task flow
- Basic components of a task flow

Overview of Business Process Flow

Business Process Flow provides insights into the customer's business stages and also allows for managing fields to be captured in each. It also helps to restrict movements in different stages, based on the required fields to be captured. The end-user finds it more convenient because it is simple to use and provides a visual understanding of the business by means of the Business Process Flows.

Business Process Flow is a guided process for Dynamics 365-end users. It helps to guide end users of CRMs.

It is easy to visualize and appears as a visual element of the entity form. It is a composition of different instruction stages, which helps end users to follow a business flow in the system, without the need for detailed training.

There are two basic components in Business Process Flow from the end-users perspective:

- The first component is a **Stage**, which includes specific instructions, given to users to follow the process
- The second component is a **Step**, which represents fields that should be completed by the end user at a particular stage

A Stage can comprise multiple steps.

Dynamics 365 Business Process Flow makes sure that end users enter data consistently and follow the same steps each time they work with a specific entity or set of entities.

Business Process Flow helps end users to complete their work in a standard way, by following a step-by-step process, completing the fields to be filled at each business stage. In short, Business Process Flows act as a basic guide for the end user with specific flow to capture fields.

You can add common sales and service methodology-related business stages to be mapped via Business Process Flow.

Understanding the Business Process Flow users interface

The following image outlines a Business Process Flow available in Dynamics 365:

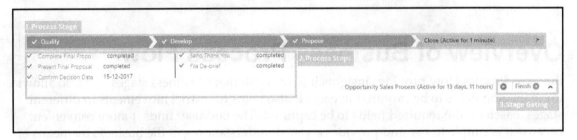

Business Process Flow includes different components, which are required for customization; it includes the following main components:

1. **Stage**:

Stages are like guided labels given at the top of the Business Process Flow to specify what to do:

2. **Step**:

Steps are fields created for the entity used in the stages:

3. **Stage Gating, Set active, Next, Finish**:

At the bottom-right corner of the Business Process Flow, this option helps you go onto the next stage or finish the process:

4. **Workflow**:

Workflow is a type of process used to trigger a specific message in CRM. Business Process Flow has a new feature to be able to trigger workflows while proceeding through different stages.

5. **Conditions**:

Business Process Flow supports conditional branching; conditions are used in a Business Process Flow. These conditions allow adding `if...else` logic into a Business Process Flow in order to move to different stages, based on different field values.

Prerequisites and security roles required for creating a Business Process Flow

Before we start a discussion about the steps required to create a Business Process Flow in Dynamics 365, it is important to understand the prerequisite security privileges, which a user needs before being able to create and edit Business Process Flows. This is particularly important if you wish to give a user or end user the ability to design and use their own Business Process Flow. The following table summarizes the minimum privileges required to create, configure, and activate a Business Process Flow in Dynamics 365:

S. No.	Entity name	Read	Write	Create
1.	Process	Yes	Yes	Yes
2.	Solution	Yes	-	-
3.	Customization	Yes	Yes	-

Solution and customization edit privilege are required, as it is a best practice to create and edit processes from a specific solution.

A detailed look at the security roles areas via CRM screens is given here:

1. Under the **Customization** tab in the Dynamics 365 security role, the **Read**, **Write** and **Create** privileges for the process should be configured as shown:

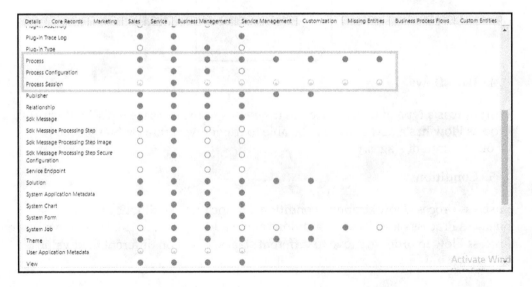

Also, you will need **Miscellaneous Privileges** to activate a process:

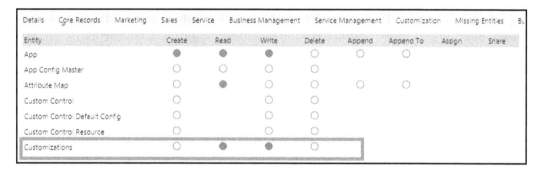

2. Under the **Customization** tab in the Dynamics 365 security role, the **Read** and **Write** privileges for **Customizations** should be configured as shown:

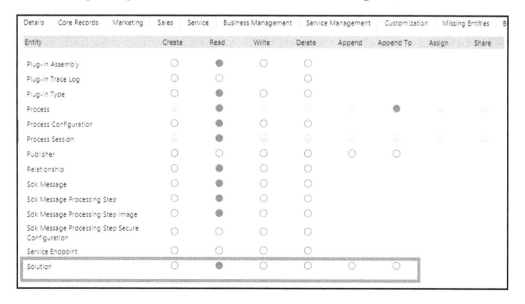

3. Under the **Customization** tab in the Dynamics 365 security role, the **Read** and **Write** privileges for **Customizations** should be configured as shown:

Note: The system administrator and system customizer role already have the required privileges to configure Dynamics 365 Business Process Flow. The previous security privileges need to be configured in case certain security roles other than the mentioned ones need access to create or edit Dynamics 365 Business Process Flow.

To enable Business Process Flow on the Custom entity, a small customization is required. The Business Process Flow checkbox needs to be selected at the Entity configuration. The following figure lists groups of out-of-the-box entities that support Business Process Flow:

Account	Letter	Contact	Quote
Appointment	Marketing List	Email	Recurring Appointment
Campaign	Opportunity	Entitlement	Sales Literature
Campaign Activity	Phone Call	Fax	Social Activity
Campaign Response	Product	Case	Order
Competitor	Price List Item	Invoice	User
Team	Lead	Task	-

Overview of Business Process Flow designer

Now that we are acquainted with the basics of Business Process Flow, it is time to explore the new Business Process Flow editor. The following image shows in detail, the different components available in the new and improved editor. The text following the image outlines the various components available in the Business Process Flow designer:

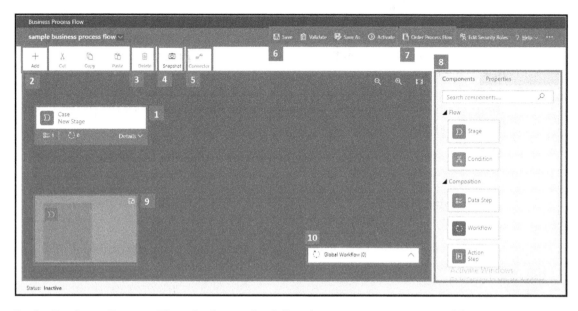

In the Business Process Flow designer, the following components are visible:

1. **Components on canvas**: This stage is created by default when a new Business process flow is created. A customizer can add more components to a canvas and use it.
2. **Add Component button**: To add components on the designer canvas, click on the **Add** button and choose the location where you want to add components.
3. **Delete button**: To remove components from the designer canvas, select the **Component** and use the **Delete** option.
4. **Screenshot button**: This option allows you to take a screenshot of the Business Process Flow designed on the canvas, for documentation purposes.
5. **Connector button**: This option is useful when conditional branching is required, and is used to connect different components.
6. **Save**, **Validate**, **Save as**, **Activate**:
   - **Save**: used to save the current designed Business Process Flow
   - **Validate**: used to validate the process and find out errors in the Business Process Flow
   - **Save as**: used to save the Business Process Flow with a different name
   - **Activate**: activates the Business Process Flow

7. **Order Process Flow**: This option allows you to add sequence numbers on the Business Process Flow. If any entity has more than one Business Process Flow, then this option allows you to select which Business Process Flow is available first to the user.

8. **Add Components and Properties**: This option can also be used to add components onto the canvas. The property tab allows you to set the properties of the components:

   1. **Mini-map**: Mini-map is very helpful for navigating the whole or part of the process.

   2. **Global Workflow**: Global workflows used in the Business Process Flow are listed here or added here.

 Note: The **Edit Security Roles** button can be used to enable different security roles for a particular Business Process Flow.

Creating a Business Process Flow

After understanding Business Process Flow, the following steps explain how to create a Business Process Flow. It is very simple due to a user-friendly UI:

1. Go to **Settings** | **Processes**:

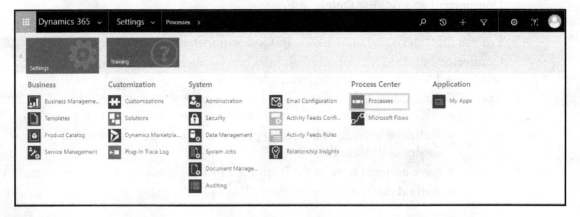

2. On the **Actions** toolbar, click **New**:

3. The **Create Process** dialog box will appear on the screen. Next, complete the required fields as per these specifications:

1. Enter a **Process name** for the Business Process Flow. In this example, we will create a **Phone to case** Business Process Flow example.

2. In the **Category**, specify the process category, and select **Business Process Flow.**

3. Select the entity from the entity list to specify which one you wish to create a Business Process Flow. Here we select the **Case** Entity:

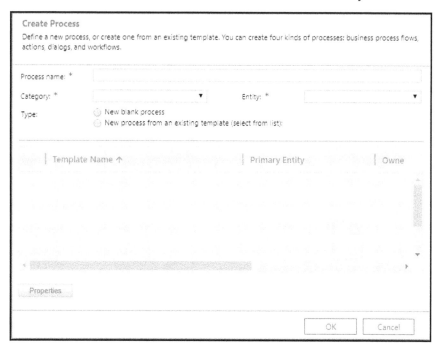

4. Once the new process is created, the Business Process Flow designer opens, with an already-created stage.

5. Drag and drop the **Stage** component from the **Components** tab and drop it on a + sign in the designer area or canvas area.

> 1. To set the properties for a stage, click the stage, and then set the properties in the **Properties** tab on the right side of the screen.
>
> 2. Enter a desired display name.
>
> 3. If desired, select a category for the stage.
>
> 4. Click on the **Apply** button to finalize changes:

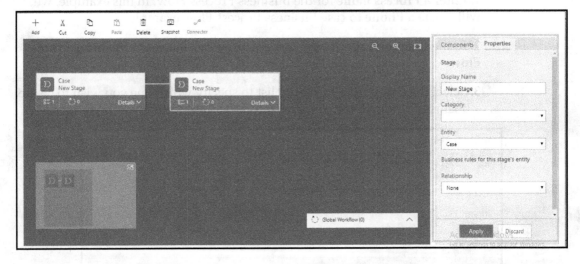

6. To add more components in the Business Process Flow, click on **Components**:

7. Add a stage and steps to the Business Process Flow:

1. Select the **Step** component from **Components**, then drag and drop it to the other stage.

2. Select the step and click on the **Property** tab to set the properties of the step.

3. Add the display name of the step.

4. Select the appropriate field from the list of fields presented in the entity.

5. Select the required checkbox to make the field mandatory.

6. To save and apply changes, click on the **Apply** button:

8. To include a branch (condition) in the Business Process Flow, follow these steps:

1. Select the **Condition** component from the **Components** tab and drag and drop it into the canvas. To connect the stage and condition, drop the **Condition** component on the + sign between the two stages.

2. Select the **Condition** component on the canvas, set the properties of the **Condition** component from the **Properties** tab, and select the **Apply** button to save and apply changes:

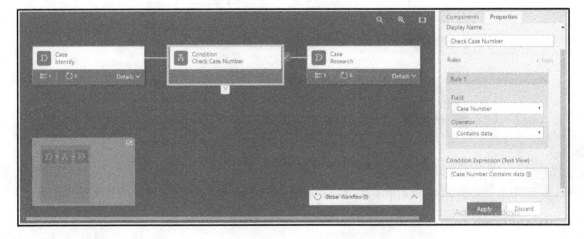

9. To invoke workflow to the Business Process Flow, drag the **Workflow** component to the corresponding stage or Global Workflow:

> 1. Select the **Workflow** component from the component list and drag and drop it onto a stage.
>
> 2. To use the Global Workflow for the process, select the **Workflow** component. Drag and drop it onto the Global Workflow item.
>
> 3. To set the properties of the workflow, click on **Properties**.
>
> 4. Add a **Display Name** for the workflow.
>
> 5. Select the workflow **Trigger** and set it to **Stage Exit**.
>
> 6. Select the workflow to triggers.
>
> 7. To save and apply changes, click on **Apply** button:

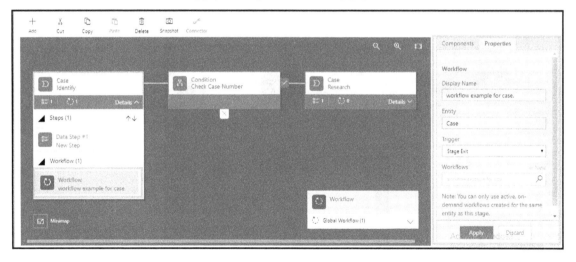

10. Click on the **Validate** button on the action bar, and validate the Business Process Flow:

11. To save, click on the **Save** button on the action bar:

12. To activate the process, click on the **Activate** button on the action bar:

Editing a Business Process Flow

Dynamics 365 allows you to edit an existing Business Process Flow. In this section, we will edit the Business Process Flow already created before, and add an out-of-the-box workflow to the Business Process Flow to send emails:

1. Go to **Settings | Processes**:

2. Select the existing Business Process Flow that you want to edit. Next, click on the **EDIT** button on the action bar:

3. The Business Process Flow designer will open. Expand the first stage of the Business Process Flow and select the **Add** workflow component:

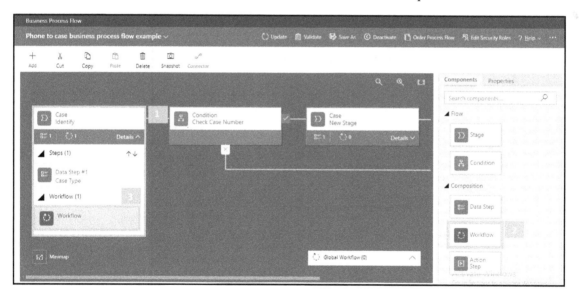

4. Click on the **Workflow** component on the canvas and set its properties. Set the trigger condition to **Stage Exit**, select workflow, and select **Send email workflow**. To save and apply changes on the component, click on the **Apply** button, as shown next:

 Note: Send Email workflow is a pre-configured out-of-the-box workflow to send an email created on a Case entity separately using the standard out-of-the-box workflow editor.

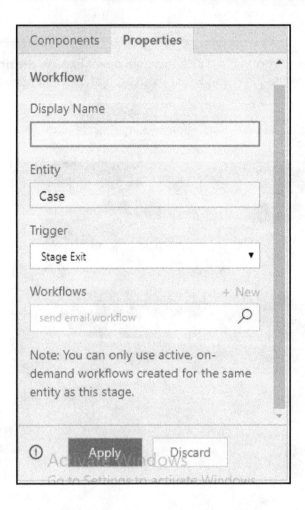

5. Optionally, for adding new fields on the first stage, you need to add a new step component on the first stage and set the property to the subject field from the Case entity:

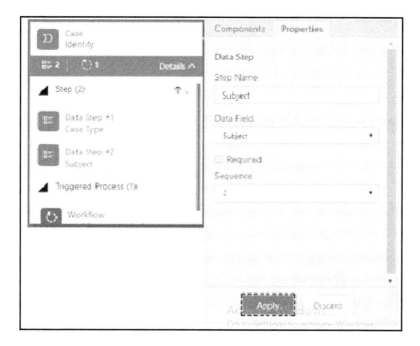

6. To save changes and **Update** the Business Process Flow, click on the **Update** button and close the Business Process Flow designer:

Understanding task flows

Task flows are a variation of Business Process Flows or, as we simply say, task flows are an alternative approach for using business processes on a mobile device. Task Flow has similarities with Business Process Flow, but its features are very different from Business Process Flow. For example, task flows can be executed on different user devices at the same time on the same record. Task Flow also makes data transparent on mobile devices.

There are different features available for use in Task Flow:

- Task Flows are at a user level, meaning each process becomes unique to a user
- Task Flows can be used by different users on the same record, who may get a different result to those users
- Task Flows have editable control from multiple entities
- In Task Flows, conditional branching is more flexible

Components of Task Flow

Consider the following points:

1. **Page**:

   Pages shown in Task Flow are to serve a purpose or to show all the fields on it.

   Pages are designed for mobile devices to occupy a whole screen of a device rather than appear on top of the entity. It just contains fields, labels, and section labels. At least one page is required to be added to the task flow.

2. **Condition**:

   Task Flow conditions are similar to the conditions in a Business Process Flow and are used to support conditional branching in the process. It helps if you add if...else scenarios within a task flow. Conditions are required to add conditional branching between pages. This condition is based on field value inside pages.

3. **Field**:

   Entity fields are used as task flow fields.

4. **Label and section label**:

   Labels and section labels help to add text description on pages and can provide a textual guide to end users.

Creating a task flow

Task flows can be created by following these steps in Dynamics 365:

1. Go to **Settings** | **Processes**:

2. On the **Actions** toolbar, click **New**:

3. Go to the **Create Process** dialog box, and select the **Run process as a task flow** option:

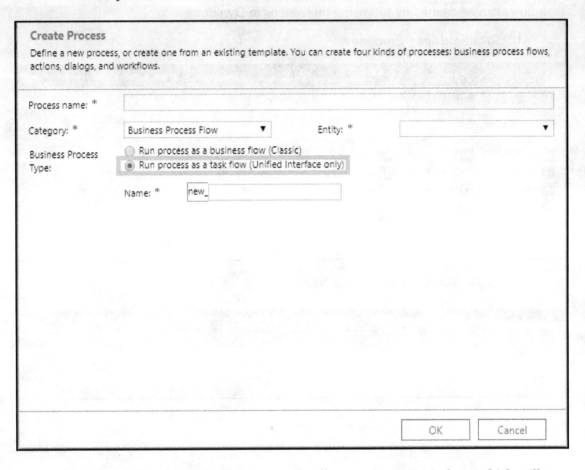

Create Process

Define a new process, or create one from an existing template. You can create four kinds of processes: business process flows, actions, dialogs, and workflows.

Process name: *

Category: *   Business Process Flow ▼   Entity: *   ▼

Business Process   ○ Run process as a business flow (Classic)
Type: ◉ Run process as a task flow (Unified Interface only)

                     Name: *   new_

                                                              OK   Cancel

4. Click on **OK** and Task Flow Designer will open in a new window, which will appear similar to the Business Process Flow designer.
5. Go to the right-hand side of the screen, drag the **Components** tab from page and post which you can drop it on canvas:

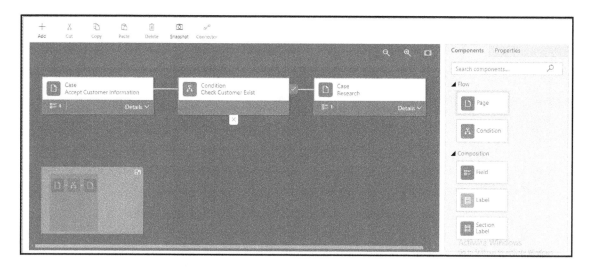

6. To add a name to a page, click on a **Page** in the **Properties** tab, type a new name, and click the **Apply** button:

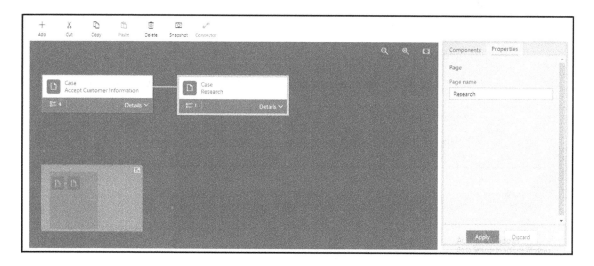

7. To add a branch to the task flow, drag the **Condition** component from the **Components** tab and drop it on the + sign in the appropriate spot:

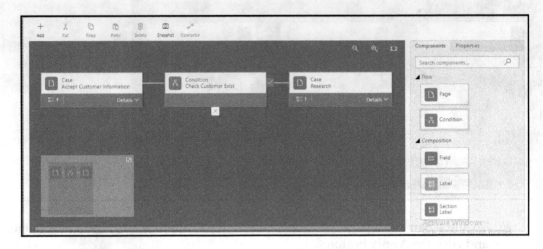

8. To set properties for the condition, click on the **Condition**, and set the properties in the **Properties** tab:

1. Select source entity

2. Select fields from the entity that needs to be checked in the condition

3. Select the operator and the value to be compared

4. Then click on the **Apply** button to save the changes:

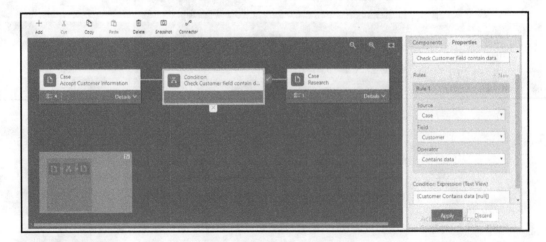

9. If you want to add a field, label, or section label to a page, drag it from the
    Components tab to the appropriate page:

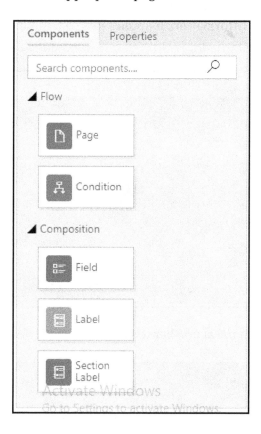

10. To change the properties for one of these items, click on the item, set the properties of the item in the **Properties** tab, and then click the **Apply** button. In our example, we add the customer and contact fields on the first page and add a label, **Customer Information**. It applies to a second page to add **Service Level** field:

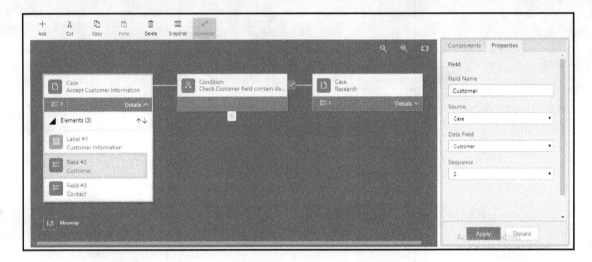

11. Click **Validate** on the action bar to validate the task flow:

12. Click **Save** at the top of the screen, in order to save the process as a draft (as long as a process is a draft, the end user will not be able to use it):

13. To activate the task flow, click **Activate**:

14. To check how the Task Flow is working, go to the Dynamics 365 Mobile App and log in with your credentials:

Summary

In this chapter, we saw how Business Process Flow enhancements are introduced in Dynamics 365. We also had a detailed look at the new Business Process Flow designer and saw some common operations that can be performed through it.

We also had a look at task flows and the Task Flow designer, which can be used to provide an enhanced experience for completing different business stage tasks for users of the Mobile App of Dynamics 365.

In the next chapter, we will cover the new Business Rule designer, and how it can be used to create business rules with intuitive drag and drop capabilities.

4
Define Business Rules Using Business Rule Designer

In the previous chapter, we saw how the new Visual Process Designer can be used to create business process flows using the drag-and-drop capabilities. In this chapter, we will see how the same visual drag-and-drop process designer can be used to create business rules. Business rules were first introduced in Dynamics CRM 2013. Basically, business rules let's define rules such as setting fields to required/not required, show/hide fields, lock/unlock fields, and so on—that is, conditions and actions on our CRM Form/Entity easily through an intuitive interface, for which we had to write either JavaScript or develop plugins earlier. Business rules were enhanced further in a subsequent version of Dynamics CRM. With Dynamics 365, the Business Rules Designer interface has been completely revamped, with capabilities of dragging and dropping components, along with additional features such as Minimap, Snapshot, and so on.

In this chapter, we will be covering the following points:

- Overview of business rules in Dynamics 365
- Understand the different components and how to use them in the new Business Rule Designer
- Implement new recommendation actions introduced in Dynamics 365
- Other features of the Business Rule Designer

Evolution of business rules

As mentioned earlier, business rules were first introduced in CRM 2013. It provided a simple declarative interface through which the system customizer, developer, or a power user can easily create validations and business rules without writing a single line of code. The business rule interface consisted of a set of **conditions, actions** to be taken when those conditions were met, along with a **description** as a convention to understand what the business rule does.

With CRM 2015, many of the limitations of CRM 2013 were addressed. Business rules in CRM 2013 were restricted to run only on the client side. For the server side, writing a plugin or any other custom code was still required. This was addressed in CRM 2015 by adding a new option named **Entity** in **Scope**. The business rule with a **scope** as **Entity** will run both on the client side and server side.

For the Entity scope, if a rule is triggered from forms either during the creation or updating of a record, the rule will first run on the client side and then again on the server side. Therefore, a rule having an action such as Set Sales Amount to Sales Amount + 10 will result in a rule validation failure as it will a create a cyclical reference.

The second biggest update to business rules in CRM 2015 was the support for `if...else` conditions and the possibility of combining multiple expressions in a condition using `AND`/`OR` logic. In CRM 2013, to define a simple rule having an `else` condition, we had to write two business rules.

In business rules, an expression in a condition can only be combined using either `AND` condition or using `OR` condition, but not both.

For example, a rule such as in the Contact form, If **Martial Status** field has value **Married** then make **Spouse/Partner Name** field as **Business Required**, else set its requirement level as `none`. Here, we would have ended up writing two business rules, one for making the **Business Required** field and the other for setting its requirement level as `none`. With the support of `if...else` statements since CRM 2015, we now just need to write a single business rule, shown as follows:

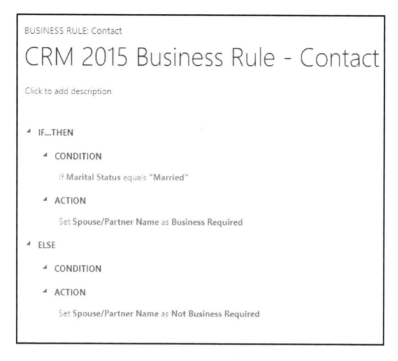

Another update in CRM 2015 was the addition of the new action named **Set default value** for setting the default value of the field.

Different action in CRM 2013. The following screenshot shows different actions that are available in Dynamics 2013:

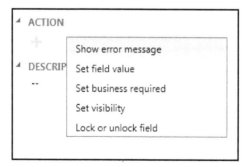

Different action in CRM 2015 (with new **Set default value** action). The following screenshot shows different actions that are available in Dynamics 2015 include the new **Set Default value** action:

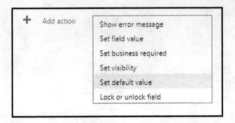

CRM 2015, along with the action of setting a default value for a field, also brought the feature of clearing the value of a field through business rules.

The next release, CRM 2016, added the ability to invoke a business rule based on business process flow properties. Shown as follows, we have defined both the Business Process rule and active stage rule in the conditions; that is, if **Business Process** equals **Opportunity Sales Process** and **Active Stage** is **Propose**. The following screenshot shows the usage of business process flow while defining business rule:

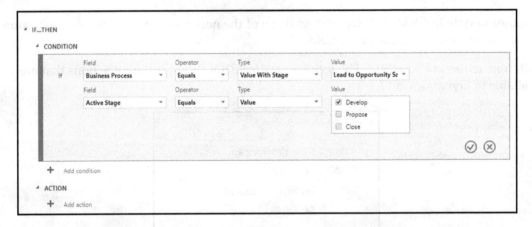

Similar to the active stage rule, we could define a condition based on the selected stage rule in CRM 2016.

Creating business rules based on business process flows is detailed at https://msdn.microsoft.com/en-us/library/mt639372.aspx.

With the December 2016 update for Dynamics 365, we now have a newly updated editor for defining business rules, a new action called Recommendation, along with some new features.

In this section, we covered the journey of business rules from CRM 2013 to CRM 2016. Now, let us have a look at the new Business Rule Designer and all the components inside Dynamics 365 in detail.

Getting to know the new Business Rule Designer

To have a quick look at the new designer, open any entity for customization and select **Business Rules** on the left navigation and click on the **New** button. This will open up the new Business Rule Designer introduced in Dynamics 365 with a completely new look and feel. The new designer allows us to add a component such as conditions and actions using the drag-and-drop feature:

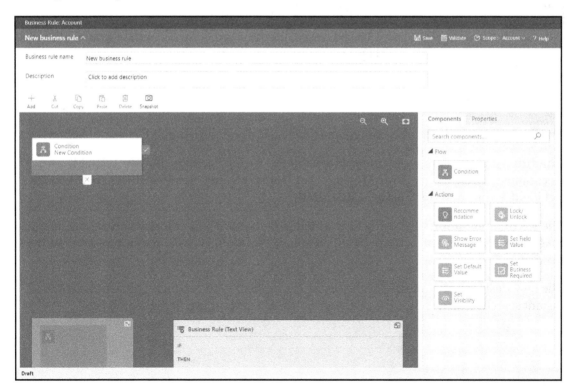

The key point to remember here is that the business rules are still the same fundamentally; it is only the editor for it that has been updated. We still have the same options available for **Scope** that we had; that is, **Entity**, **All Forms,** and the individual forms for that entity:

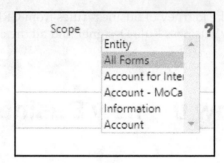

Let us pause and do a quick recap of the Scope:

Scope type	Description
Entity	The business rule runs on all forms of the **Entity** including **Quick Create** and server-side.
All Forms	The business rule runs on all forms of the Entity including **Quick Create**.
Specific Form (information, account, and so on)	The business rule runs only on that specific form of the **Entity**.

The Business Rule Designer's components are basically grouped into **Flow** and **Actions**.

Condition components come under **Flow** and the various actions that are available are **Recommendation, Show Error Message, Set Default Value, Set Visibility, Lock/Unlock, Set Field Value,** and **Set Business Required.**

The **Recommendation** is a new action added in Dynamics 365, using which we can suggest that the user perform an activity based on some condition. We will cover it in detail in the up coming sections.

The new designer also allows for the searching of these components. The search is of type instant search, which shows the result while we are still typing in the search box.

For example, typing in **set** in the search box shows the actions with set in their names in the drop-down, and also filters the visible components:

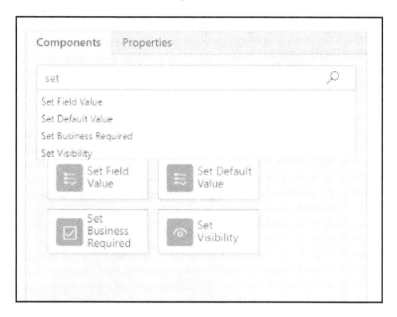

Every component—that is **Condition** and **Action**, has its specific set of properties. Before we look at the properties of each of these components, let us see how we can add these components in the Business Rule Designer canvas.

Specifying conditions using condition components

While creating a new business rule, the business rule designer opens with a single condition already added.

To add more conditions, we can click on the **Add** button on the toolbar and select **Add Condition**:

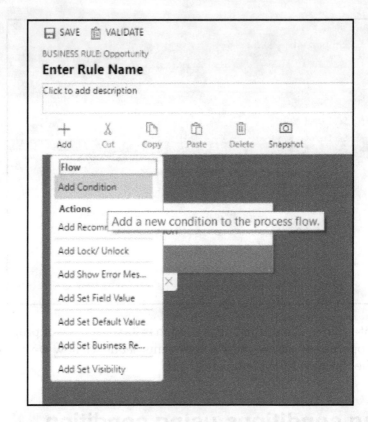

The other option is to drag and drop the condition component from the **Components** tab into the designer canvas. Selecting the condition in the designer will show the properties specific to the condition component in the **Properties** tab:

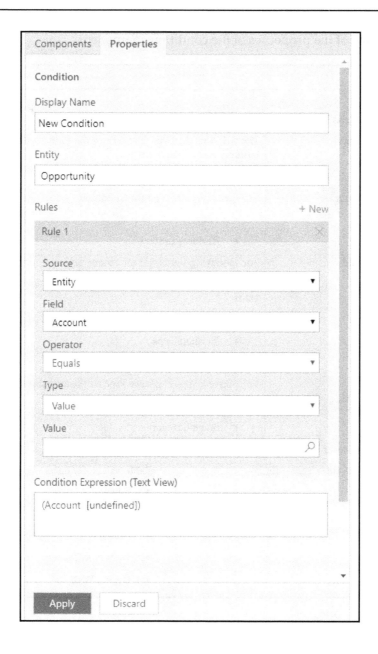

Let us look at some of the properties of the condition component.

CONDITIONS			
Condition			
	Display Name	For specifying a label for the Condition.	
	Entity	The field that displays the name of the Entity against which business rule is being written.	
Rules	A collection of rules.		
	Source	For specifying the type for Condition • Entity • Business process	
	Field	For specifying field type for Source Selected. For source type – Entity it displays all the attributes of that entity. • Account • Account Type • Account Close Date ... For source type – Business Process the available options are • Process Name • Stage Category	
	Operator		
	For source type – Entity	Available values for operator are • Equals • Does not Equal • Contains • Does Not Contain • Begins With	

Clicking on **+ New** adds a new rule to the rules section. For example, **Rule 2** in the following image:

The following image shows the **Rule Logic** and the **Condition Expression (Text View)** property inside the properties tab. The **Apply** button applies the condition and the **Discard** button can be used to **undo** the last action performed, similar to the *Ctrl + Z* command:

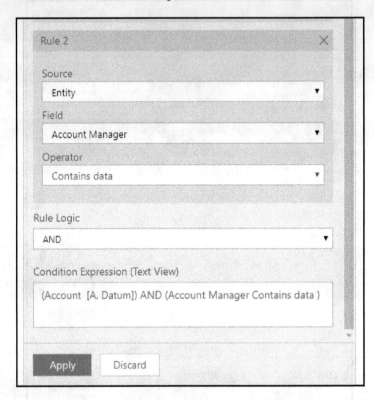

Now, let us have a look at the properties of the different type of actions available for business rules.

Taking actions for conditions using action components

An action can be added in the same way as a condition, by clicking on the **Add** button on the toolbar and selecting the action that we want to add. The action can also be added by dragging it from the **Components** tab and associating it to a condition, shown as follows. Here, we have dragged the **Show Error Message** action from **Components** tab and linked it to our existing **New Condition:**

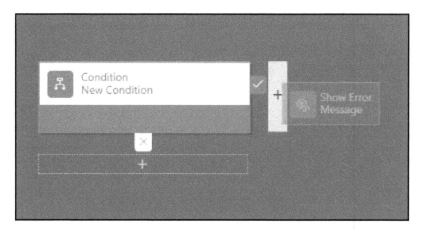

This adds the **Show Error Message** action to the condition:

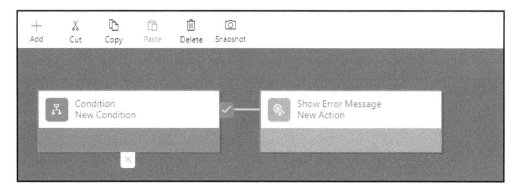

Let us now have a look at the properties of all the different actions available:

- **Lock/Unlock**: This action can be used to define whether a field needs to be locked or unlocked:

This is how the locked field **Probability** will display inside the opportunity form:

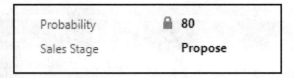

- **Show Error Message**: This action can be used to show the error message on a particular field:

This is how the error message shows up inside opportunity form. Hovering over the red cross icon shows the error message:

- **Set Field Value**: The Set Field Value action can be used to define a value for a field. The value can be set using the following options. Based on the field's data type, the options will vary:

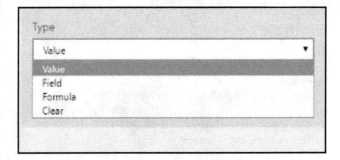

- **Value**: This can be used to specify the field's value directly
    - **Field**: This can be used to specify the field's value to another field's value
    - **Formula**: This can be used to specify the field's value by applying a formula (this option is available for the **Date Time**, **Whole Number**, and **Decimal fields**)
    - **Clear**: This clears the field's value (this option is not available for the boolean and option set fields)

For example, we can use the **Set Field Value** action to define a rule that sets the estimated close date to be 100 days from the day the opportunity is created using formula, shown as follows:

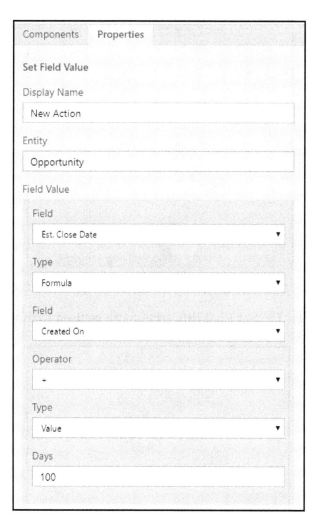

- **Set Business Required**: The **Set Business Required** action can be used to set a field to be either **Business Required** or non-mandatory:

- **Set Visibility**: The **Set Visibility** section can be used to show or hide the field:

- **Recommendation**: As we saw earlier, **Recommendation** is a new action introduced in Dynamics 365. The different properties of **Recommendation** are:

Recommendation		
	Recommendation Name	For specifying the name of the recommendation action.
	Entity	The field that displays the name of the Entity against which business rule is being written.
	Field	Specifies the field on which we want to set the recommendation.
	Recommendation Title	Specifies the title for the Recommendation dialog box.
	Recommendation Details	Specifies the description for the Recommendation inside the Recommendation dialog box.

Recommendation is a special type of action, which itself has an **Actions** inside it:

This **Actions** is of type **Set Field Value**:

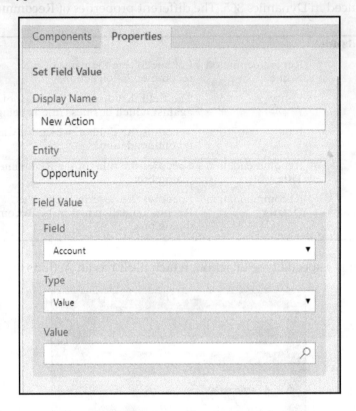

It is the same **Set Field Value** action that we covered earlier. To see all the components in action, let us implement a recommendation business rule.

Recommendation in action

Now we have some basic understanding of different properties of the recommendation action and the different components of the Business Rule Designer, let us implement a scenario to see them in action. The scenario we will implement would be, for an example, if the **Sales Stage** selected is **Propose**, we would recommend the user to set the probability as 80.

Let us implement it step by step.

There are four ways of creating a new Business Rule in CRM:

- At **Field** Level:
    1. Open the **Entity** for customization
    2. Click and open the field
    3. Select **Business Rule** in the left navigation and click on **New** to create a new business rule:

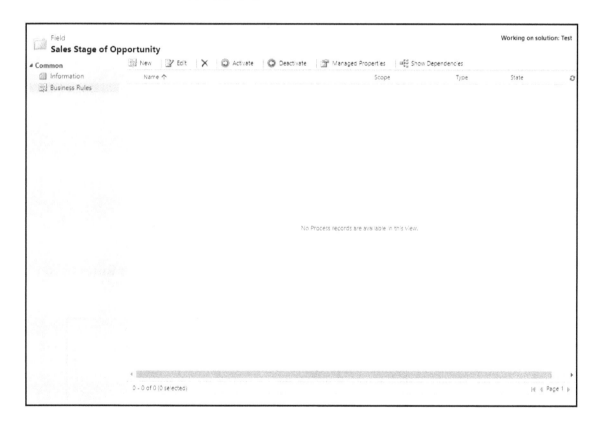

- At Entity level:
    1. Open the **Entity** for customization
    2. Select **Business Rule** in the left navigation and click on **New** to create a new business rule:

- From form:
    1. Open the form for customization. Click on the **Business Rules** ribbon button:

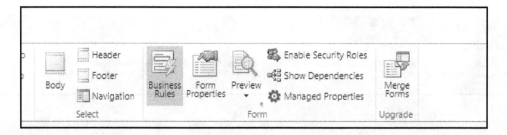

    2. This opens the **Business Rule Explorer** on the right panel of the form, which lets us create a new business rule by clicking on the **New Business Rule** button:

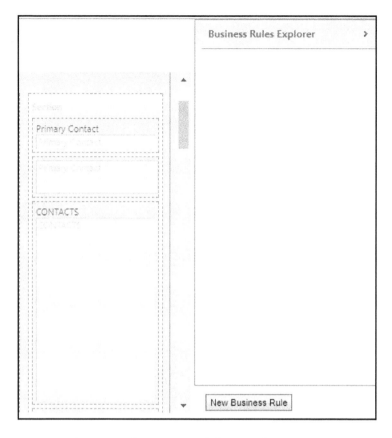

3. Another way that we can define the business rule from within the Form is by opening the form for customization, double-clicking on any of the fields or selecting any of the fields, and clicking on the **Change Properties** ribbon button to open the **Field Properties** dialog box. We can then select the **Business Rule** tab and click on **New** to create a new business rule.

4. Coming back to our scenario, let's select **Opportunity** entity for customization and create a new business rule with the following details:

Rule name	Recommendation for Sales Stage.
Description	Recommend probability to be 80 for Sales Stage - Proposed.

5. Select the condition component and define the rule *When Sales Stage equals to Propose*, shown as follows, in the **Properties** tab:

6. Click on **Apply** to apply the condition
7. Next, we need to add a **Recommend Action** to this condition
8. Either click on the **Add** button on the toolbar or drag the **Recommendation** action from the **Components** tab:

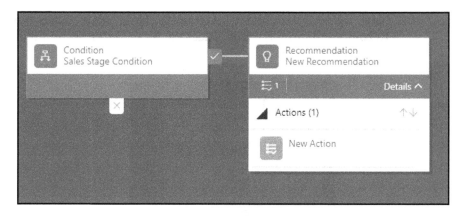

9. Select the **Recommendation** action and define its properties, shown as follows, and click on **Apply**:

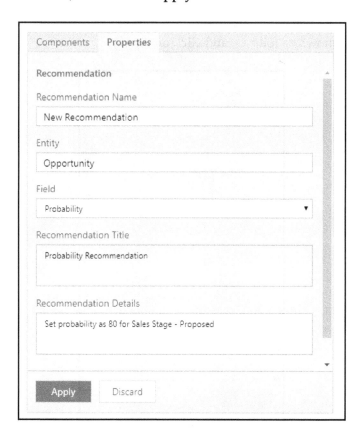

10. Next, we need to define the **Action** (Set Field Value) that is part of **Recommendation**. For this, select the **New Action** section within **Recommendation**:

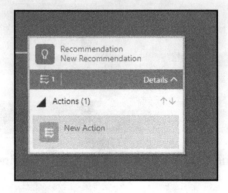

11. We will define the action as `Set probability field value as 80`, shown as follows, and click on **Apply**:

This is how our final rule will look inside the designer canvas. Click on **Save** to save the rule; it will also validate the rule for any errors. We can also click on **Validate** to validate our rule at any point, while we are still defining it:

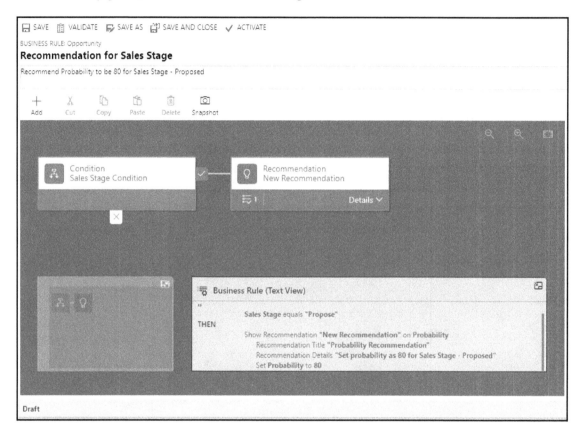

On successful validation, we will get a **Validation Successful** message.

In the case of any error, the Validate will show the error message, shown as follows, highlighted in red. We can check the properties tab to figure out the cause of the error. Before we can save and publish the business rule, we need to fix all the errors:

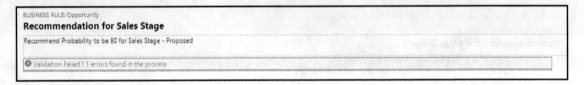

Next, we need to click on **Activate** to activate the rule.

To see the business rule in action, we need to open the opportunity record and set the value of sales stage to **Propose**:

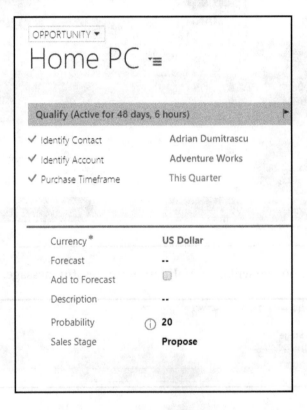

This shows the information icon next to the **Probability** field. Clicking on it opens the **Recommendation** box with the recommendation title and details that we set earlier:

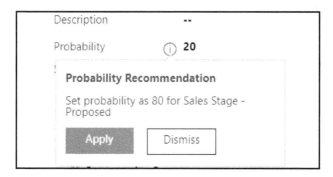

We can click on the **Dismiss** button to close the recommendation dialog box. Clicking on **Apply** will update the probability value to **80**, as we had defined it in the **Set Field Value Action**, shown as follows:

So, now we have implemented our Recommendation rule. Now, let us cover other additional features of the Business Rule Designer in the next section.

Additional features of Business Rule Designer

Apart from the provision of creating rules, there are some additional features introduced in the new Business Rule Designer, let us have a quick look at those new features.

Cut, copy, and paste the component

The toolbar within the Business Rule Designer gives the option to cut, copy, paste, and delete the component.

To cut or copy the component, select the component and press the **Cut** or **Copy** button in the toolbar. Or, we can also use our keyboard shortcuts (*CTRL + C* or *CTRL + X*) to copy or cut:

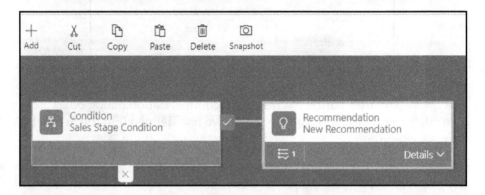

Clicking on **Paste** (or *CTRL + V*) shows the different area with the + symbol where the copied component can be added:

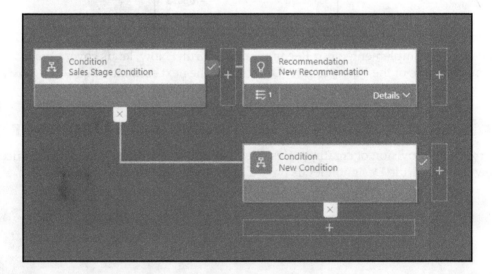

Clicking on + adds the copied component to that specific location.

Deleting the component

To delete the component, just select the component and click on the **Delete** button (or press *CTRL + X*) on the toolbar. This will open a **Confirm Deletion** dialog box.

Clicking on **OK** on the **Confirm Deletion** dialog box removes the component.

Taking a snapshot of the business rule

Clicking on the **Snapshot** button on the toolbar saves the current state of the business rule as an image file:

The file is saved with the name of the business rule with the `.png` extension.

Set zoom level and Fit to Canvas for ease of readability

We can set the zoom level of the Business Rule Designer by clicking the - and + lenses. The third option is for Fit to Canvas, which makes the business rule definition auto-adjust to fit the Business Rule Designer canvas:

Navigating easily using Minimap

The Business Rule Designer canvas also has Minimap component that gives a mini view of the designed business rules:

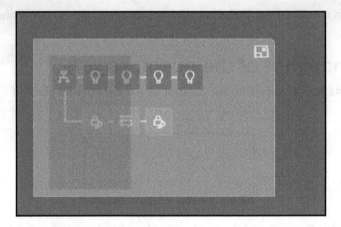

It also allows to easily navigate inside the designer canvas. Using Minimap, we have easily scrolled to the bottom-right corner of our business rule definition inside the designer where we have the **Lock/Unlock** action component, shown as follows:

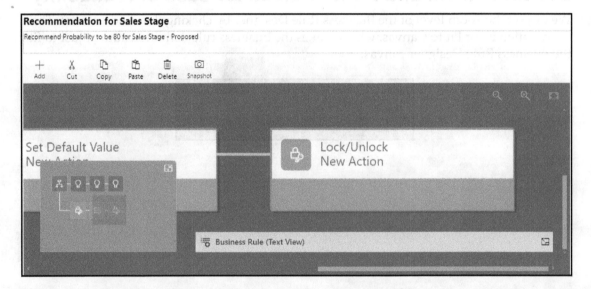

Using Business Rule (Text View) to read through the business rule

The **Business Rule (Text View)** component inside the designer canvas displays the text view of the rule defined.

For the Recommendation rule that we defined earlier:

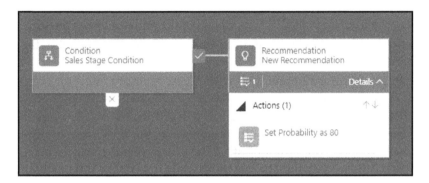

The **Business Rule (Text View)** will show the following content:

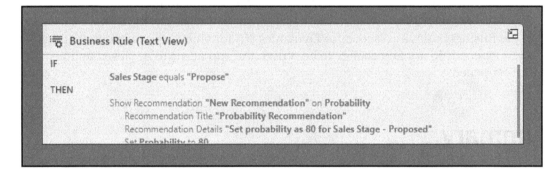

A few key points about business rules

The following are important points regarding business rules that we need to consider before we decide on using them:

- We cannot use the business rule to hide tabs and sections of a form.
- The `OnChange` event of the field will not be triggered if that field's value is set using a business rule.
- There is a limitation of 10 `if...else` conditions in a business rule.
- The business rule will not run if it references a field that is not in the form. It will not show any error message.
- The business rule, if not defined with Scope as Entity, will run only during the load of the form and when the value of a field changes. It will not run on save of the form.
- Business rules run in order of their activation. So, if we have multiple interrelated business rules defined for an Entity, the business rule that was activated first will run first followed by the other business rule in order of their activation.
- If we have both JavaScript and business rules defined for a specific field, JavaScript will be executed first.
- Business rules don't support whole number fields with the TimeZone, Duration, or Language formats.
- Business rules are cached for Dynamics 365 for tablets app, when that app is opened. So, for any change to be reflect, the app needs to be closed and re-opened.

Summary

In this chapter, we covered how business rules have evolved starting from CRM 2013 to Dynamics 365. We have an entirely new designer that makes it more intuitive to write and define business rules. We also had a detailed look at the new Recommendation action that was added in Dynamics 365 along with a host of new features.

In the next chapter, we will look at Microsoft PowerApps and how it can be used to create custom business apps.

5
Creating Custom Business Apps

PowerApps is a service that allows you to create, manage, and use custom business apps across the platform. It connects to the existing system and data source of customer securely allows customizer to build apps without writing a code. It is possible to make those apps available for web and mobile users instantly by publishing them.

In this chapter, we will be covering the following points:

- Overview of PowerApps
- Privileges required to configure and create PowerApps
- Connectors in PowerApps
- Understanding the PowerApps design interface
- Creating a PowerApps using data from Dynamics 365
- Running PowerApps on mobile and tablet devices
- Data connection service in PowerApps
- Creating an app using a data connection service
- Creating an entity in a data connection service
- Customizing the PowerApps

Overview of PowerApps in Dynamics 365

PowerApps is a service that securely makes a connection with the data source, such as Azure, Dynamics 365, or Office 365, and minimizes the security concern of the organization about the data. Any user can design in PowerApps without writing a code. It is very convenient to publish these PowerApps.

From an employee's perspective, PowerApps provides agility to work in the following ways:

- Provides the ability to create an app quickly
- Provides the ability to create an app that works on every device
- Provides Microsoft Office's experience on the app
- Provides use of built-in **Connection** to make a connection with PowerApps for a cloud service such as Dynamic 365 or Office 365

From a developer's perspective, PowerApps provides the following features:

- Inclusion of Azure service into PowerApps, increasing performance and speed at user end
- Ease of creating additional data connection and API of any existing business system
- Reliability and robustness in management of organization data security

PowerApps accelerates working and takes less time to build apps. This is very effective and efficient for those users who are beginners to designing apps. It allows you to deliver content of cloud-to-mobile devices directly.

PowerApps saves a tremendous amount of development time, and also allows connection of cloud data sources with minimum configuration.

Prerequisite for designing PowerApps

It is very simple to design in PowerApps. Before that, we will discuss the configuration and designing process of PowerApps. Complete the following steps for the designing process:

1. Create Office 365 instance with a Dynamics 365 subscription
2. Sign in to the PowerApps website with your Office 365 login ID
3. Make sure your user has Office 365 Global Administrator Role

Connectors in PowerApps

PowerApps is capable of getting data from the cloud. To do so, first, the connectors should be created. Connectors specify a data source of PowerApps. Transferring data from the cloud to PowerApps is very simple and secure. There is no need to worry about any kind of encryption to make data secure.

The PowerApps connector supports many services, such as online or on-premises data. There are two types of connectors available in PowerApps:

- **Standard connectors**: These are known as standard connectors because PowerApps provides support for many services such as Dynamics 365, SharePoint, and Excel. There are many connectors that support PowerApps.

- **Custom connectors**: The custom connector is only created when there is any need to connect PowerApps with custom service; for example, custom service design by developers to fetch data from local data servers to PowerApps.

Some types of connectors work only with a specific data source; for example, a tabular data source, such as SharePoint or Excel. Some connectors are designed to work with the collaboration of function-based data sources, such as Outlook, Facebook, and Twitter. When data is fetched from these data sources, PowerApps has its own different functions for interaction with the data. However, function-based data needs to do more work with PowerApps than tabular data.

The following is a list of connectors that are available in PowerApps:

10to8 Appointment Scheduling	Computer Vision API	Inoreader	Pivotal Tracker
Act!	Content Conversion	Insightly	Planner
Adobe Creative Cloud	Content Moderator	Instagram	Plivo
Adobe Sign	DB2	Instapaper	PostgreSQL
Amazon Redshift	Disqus	Intercom	Power BI
Apache Impala	DocFusion365 - SP	JIRA	PowerApps Notification
AppFigures	DocuSign	JotForm	Project Online
Approvals	Dropbox	LeanKit	Redmine
Asana	Dynamics 365	LinkedIn	RSS
AWeber	Dynamics 365 for Financials	LiveChat	Salesforce
Azure AD	Dynamics for Operations	LUIS	SendGrid
Azure Application Insights	Dynamics NAV	Mail	Service Bus
Azure Automation	Easy Redmine	MailChimp	SFTP
Azure Blob Storage	Elastic Forms	Mandrill	SharePoint
Azure Cosmos DB	Event Hubs	Medium	Skype for Business
Azure Data Lake	Eventbrite	Microsoft Forms	Slack
Azure Event Grid	Excel	Microsoft StaffHub	SmartSheet
Azure Event Grid Publish	Face API	Microsoft Teams	SMTP
Azure File Storage	Facebook	Microsoft Translator	SparkPost
Azure Log Analytics	File System	MSN Weather	SQL Server
Azure Log Analytics Data Collector	Flic	Muhimbi PDF	Stripe

Azure Queues	FlowForma	MySQL	SurveyMonkey
Azure Resource Manager	FreshBooks	Nexmo	Teamwork Projects
Azure Table Storage	Freshdesk	Notifications	Teradata
Basecamp 2	Freshservice	Office 365 Bookings	Text Analytics
Basecamp 3	FTP	Office 365 Groups	Todoist
Benchmark Email	GitHub	Office 365 Outlook	Toodledo
Bing Maps	Gmail	Office 365 Users	Trello
Bing Search	Google Calendar	Office 365 Video	Twilio
Bitbucket	Google Contacts	OneDrive	Twitter
Bitly	Google Drive	OneDrive for Business	TypeForm
Bizzy (H3 Solutions, Inc.)	Google Sheets	OneNote (Business)	UserVoice
Blogger	Google Tasks	Oracle Database	Video Indexer
Box	GoToMeeting	Outlook Customer Manager	Vimeo
bttn	GoToTraining	Outlook Tasks	Visual Studio Team Services
Buffer	GoToWebinar	Outlook.com	WebMerge
Calendly	Harvest	PagerDuty	WordPress
Campfire	HelloSign	Parserr	Wunderlist
Capsule CRM	HipChat	Paylocity	Yammer
Chatter	HTTP with Azure AD	Pinterest	YouTube
Cognito Forms	Informix	Pipedrive	Zendesk
Common Data Service	Infusionsoft	Pitney Bowes Data Validation	-

PowerApps is designed to support external data sources stored in the cloud; for example, get data from Excel file stored on OneDrive also there is another data source such as calendar, emails and so on, sooner notifications will be supported for the data source.

Managing data for PowerApps

Using data in PowerApps is not a great challenge with the help of connectors, but using data from the cloud may result in an input of massive amount of data coming into the app. This is not good for either the user or the system itself. It is very important to make an efficient and effective app to manage the data, because fetching data is like getting the useful information required for the app user. This is required to reduce memory, processing power, and for network bandwidth of PowerApps. It will also improve response time and performance of the PowerApps by getting useful data.

To encounter a problem with bulk data, **delegation of data** is used by PowerApps. A delegation of data only provides the data that is useful to the users for the user app. This sorting of data saves lots of network traffic. It means PowerApps will process data before it loads the device.

Delegation is nothing but applying a formula to data before sending it over the network. Delegation is only supported by tabular data sources.

The following is a list of data sources with information as to whether they support delegation:

Data source	Support delegation
Common Data Service	Yes
SharePoint	Yes
SQL Server	Yes
Dynamics 365	Yes
Salesforce	Yes
Dynamics 365 for Operations	No
Dynamics 365 for Financials	No
Dynamics NAV	No
Google Sheets	No

PowerApps achieves delegation with the help of delegable function. The following list specifies some delegation functions and data sources supported by connections:

Functions	Data Source				
	Common Data Service	SharePoint	SQL Server	Dynamics 365	Salesforce
Average	No	No	Yes	No	No
Filter	Yes	Yes	Yes	Yes	Yes
LookUp	Yes	Yes	Yes	Yes	Yes
Max	No	No	Yes	No	No
Min	No	No	Yes	No	No
Search	Yes(Onlu Support String)	No	Yes	Yes	Yes
Sort	Yes	Yes	Yes	Yes	Yes
SortByColumns	Yes	Yes	Yes	Yes	Yes
Sum	No	No	Yes	No	No

The following list specifies filter and lookup delegable predicate for each data source:

	Common Data Service	SharePoint	SQL Server	Dynamics 365	Salesforce
Not	Yes	No	Yes	Yes	Yes
IsBlank	No	No	Yes	Yes	No
TrimEnds	No	No	Yes	No	No
Len	No	No	Yes	No	No
+, -	No	No	Yes	No	No
<, <=, =, <>, >, >=	Yes	Yes (only =)	Yes	Yes	Yes
And (&&), Or (||), Not (!)	Yes(Operators only)	Yes (except Not (!))	Yes	Yes	Yes
In	No	No	Yes	No	Yes
StartsWith	No	Yes	No	No	No

Fetching on-premises data for PowerApps

It is possible to use on-premises data for PowerApps. Gateways are used to connect on-premises data with PowerApps. Gateways are bridges between data available in on-premises servers with PowerApps. Gateways are capable of making a connection with the on-premises data source using the following connections:

- Filesystem
- DB2
- SharePoint
- Informix
- SQL Server
- Oracle

PowerApps designer

PowerApps designer is used to manage PowerApps. This designer contains the following components, which are being used to design PowerApps:

Screens: Screens are the containers for the different controls of PowerApps. The screen is nothing but the visual front end of an application designed for user interaction. In PowerApps, managing the screen is simple.

Following types of screens are available in PowerApps:

- Blank
- Scrollable screen
- List screen
- Form screen

Controls: To design the PowerApps, different UI elements are required. These UI elements are also known as controls.

The following list specifies controls for the PowerApps designer:

1. Text control:
    - Label
    - Text input
    - HTML text
    - Pen input

2. Controls:
    - Button
    - Drop-down
    - Date picker
    - List box
    - Checkbox
    - Radio
    - Toggle
    - Slider
    - Rating
    - Timer

3. Gallery:
    - Vertical
    - Horizontal
    - Flexible height
    - Blank vertical
    - Blank horizontal
    - Blank flexible height

4. Data table
5. Forms:
    - Edit
    - Display
    - Entity form

6. Media:
    - Image
    - Camera
    - Barcode
    - Video
    - Audio
    - Microphone
    - Add picture

7. Charts:
    - Column chart
    - Line chart
    - Pie chart

Creating PowerApps using Dynamics 365 data

It is a simple and reliable option to create PowerApps. In this section, we will discuss how to create PowerApps; however, we will also look at how to configure Dynamics 365 in PowerApps. PowerApps is capable of retrieving data from the cloud, including Azure and Dynamics 365. It is very easy to publish PowerApps on the web and on mobile platforms.

To create PowerApps, follow these steps:

1. Log into Office 365 instance, and select the **Explore all your apps** option:

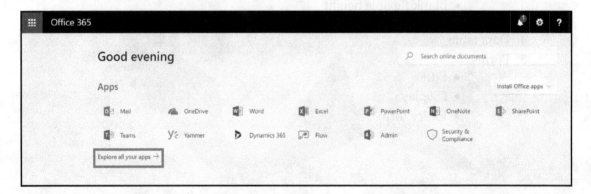

2. Select the **PowerApps** option.

3. You will be logged into the PowerApps section, or you can directly log into PowerApps using this link: `https://web.powerapps.com/`. Use the same credentials for Office 365 instance as with the the PowerApps login:

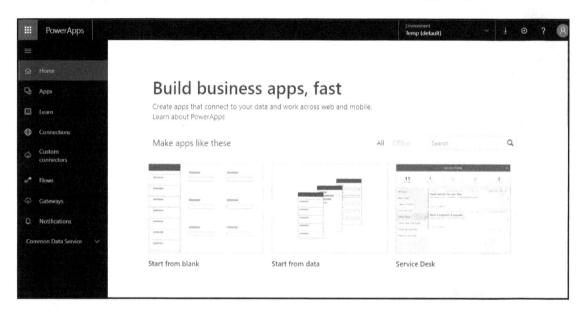

4. The Navigation section is presented at the left side of the screen. To create an app, first create a connection. Select **Connections** from Navigation.

5. PowerApps will redirect you to the **Connections** section. Here, to add a new connection, click the **New connection** option that appears on the upper-right corner:

6. A list of connections will appear on the screen, as shown in the following screenshot. Select **Dynamics 365** from the list of connections:

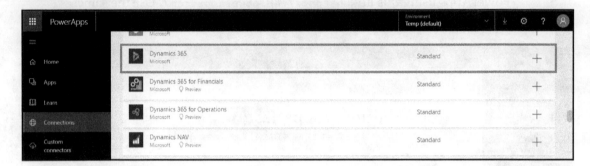

7. A confirmation dialog box will appear on the screen. Click on the **Create** button:

8. Now, check the **Connections** section; you will notice the **Dynamics 365** connection will appear on the screen, as shown in the following screenshot:

Creating a PowerApps for case entity

The first step of pulling data from the cloud is completed by creating a connection. After creating a connection, the next step is to create a PowerApps. There are two ways to create a PowerApps—either you create a PowerApps from scratch using the PowerApps designer, or generate the PowerApps automatically.

The following steps will be used to create a PowerApps:

1. Sign in to `https://web.powerapps.com/` using your Office 365 credentials.
2. Select **Apps** from Navigation:

3. Select the **Create an app** button:

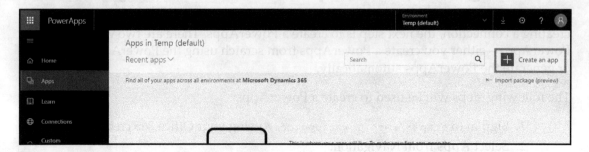

4. Select the **Dynamics 365 Phone layout** option under **Start with your data**:

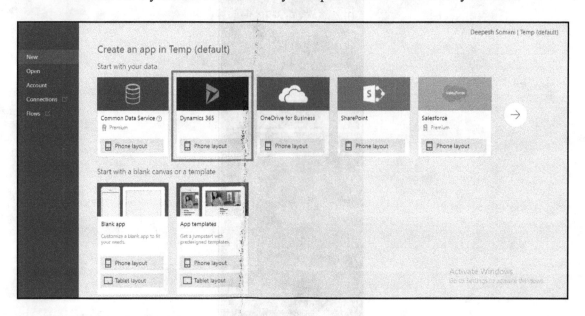

5. Click on **Connections** to see the list of all **Connections**. After selection of **Connections**, **datasets** will appear in a dataset list corresponding to the **Connections**:

6. Select the appropriate dataset corresponding to **Connections**:

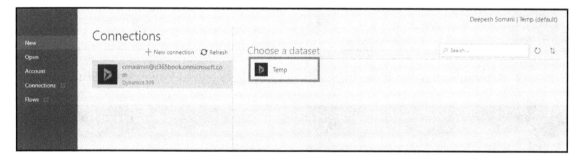

7. A list of tables will be open, corresponding to **datasets**.

8. Select the **Cases** table from the list and click the **Connect** button:

9. After this step, the PowerApps site will redirect you to **PowerApps Studio**:

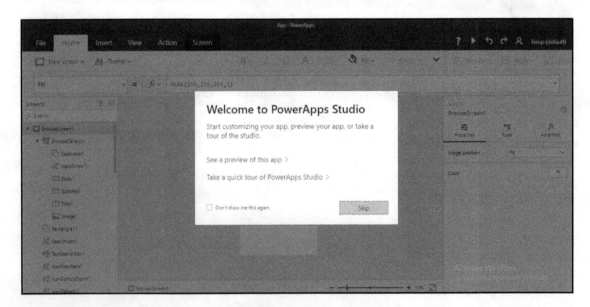

10. To customize the app, first select a screen from the screen list created by the default app. To select screen of the app to navigate to the left side of the PowerApps studio:

11. PowerApps creates three screens, as per the data received from the case record (please refer to the screen mentioned in Step 10 for reference):
    - **BrowseScreen1**: This default screen appears when a user starts the app. The app is shown here.
    - **DetailScreen1**: This screen appears when an item is selected on the browse screen.
    - **EditScreen1**: This screen appears when clicking on an item to edit it.

12. To run PowerApps, click on **run**, or preview the app at the upper-right corner:

13. After the preview, save the app by selecting the **File** option:

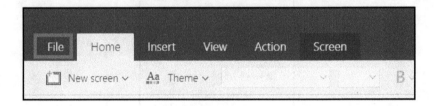

14. Click on **Save**. Enter a name for the app, and select a location to store the app:

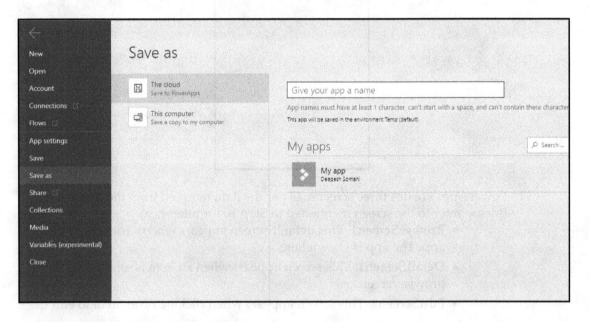

Running PowerApps on a mobile or tablet device

1. Install **PowerApps** on a mobile or tablet device.
2. Sign in with your Office 365 credentials.
3. Select **App** from the list of apps:

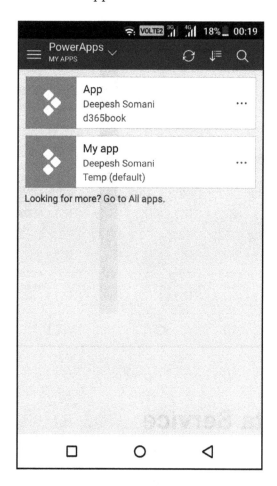

4. Open the selected **App**.

5. PowerApps will start running:

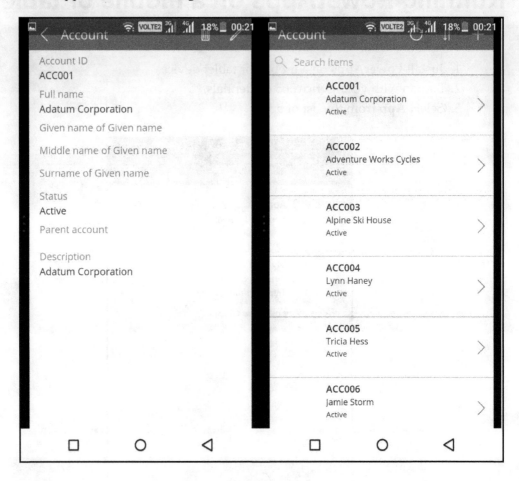

Common Data Service

The common Data Service is an Azure-based cloud storage service designed to gather data from multiple applications and make it centralized to users. It is referred to as a common data model, which contain data entities. Data entities contains data fields, which store data. Entities are similar to a table of the data source. PowerApps generates a good app from the Common Data Service.

Here are the following advantages of using the Common Data Service:

- Importing of data into custom or standard entities
- Creation of custom entities that will support different scenarios and applications
- Capability to add custom fields to the standard entity
- Capability to collaborate custom and standard entities into the app
- Increase productivity by add-ins to access data from Microsoft Excel and Outlook
- Use of role-based security for custom and standard entities to achieve security
- Capability to use predefined data pick list, such as country, and salutation

Every entity includes a set of records that users can delete, read, update, and create. It is possible to create relationships between entities. This is as simple as using lookup.

Entities in the Common Data Service are custom and standard. These entities are responsible for securing storage of data. Following are the benefits of entities:

- **Simple to manage**: All data, that is, data and metadata, is stored in the cloud.
- **Simple to share**: Efficient and easy to share the data between multiple users.
- **Simple to secure**: Data is securely stored so that users can see it only if you grant them access. Role-based security allows you to control access to entities for different users within your organization.
- **Simple metadata**: All data and relationships are easily stored on PowerApps.
- **Productivity tools**: Entities are easily available over productivity tools such as Microsoft Excel and Outlook.
- **Picklists**: Easy-to-use pick lists of predefined data.

There are two types of entity in the Common Data Service:

- **Standard entity**: Standard entity is provided by the Common Data Service. These entities are provided by default.
- **Custom entity**: Custom entities are like extensions provided in the Common Data Service. These custom entities are created when there is a need to add new data to the Common Data Service.

Entities include fields. Each field has a name, data type, display name, and few easy validations. Data types can be text, date, number, and more. There are three types of fields:

- System fields
- Standard fields
- Custom fields

System fields: System fields are the most important fields. These fields cannot be changed or deleted. System fields present all entities either standard or custom. The following fields are important system fields.

- Created Record Date
- Created By
- Modified Record Date
- Last Modified By

Custom fields: When system or custom entity needs extra an data field, then it is possible that we have to add a custom field in those entities.

Standard fields: Each standard entity contains standard fields.

It is also possible to create relationships between lookups. Lookups data type is used to represent the relationship between entities.

Creating PowerApps using Common Data Connection

We have seen Common Data Connection-related things. To understand Common Data Connection, the following steps will help to create Common Data Connection:

1. Go to the PowerApps website, and create a new connection. Select **Common Data Service**:

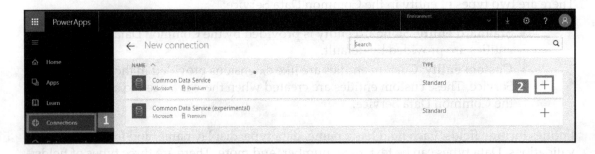

2. Select the **Create** button on the **Common Data Service** dialog:

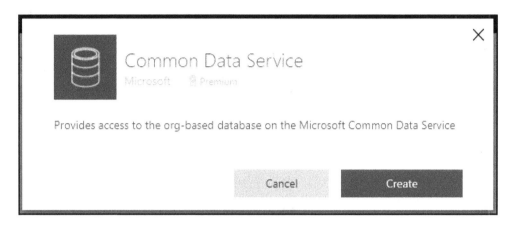

3. Authenticate using your Office 365 credentials.
4. Check Common Data Connection by navigating to PowerApps Navigation.
5. Create a new app by clicking on the **App** section in Navigation. Create a new app, using the **Common Data Service**:

6. Select the **Account** entity from the **Choose an entity** list, and click on **Connect**:

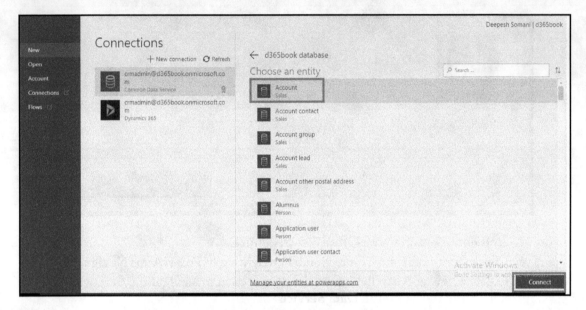

7. Automatic PowerApps will be generated from the **Account** data:

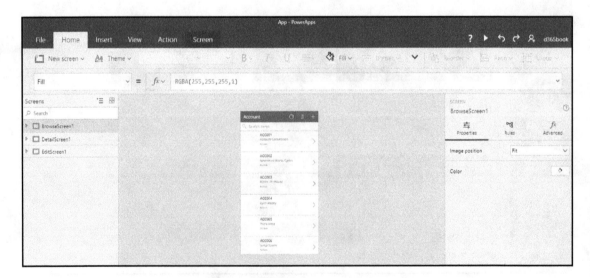

8. Click on the **Preview** button to run the app:

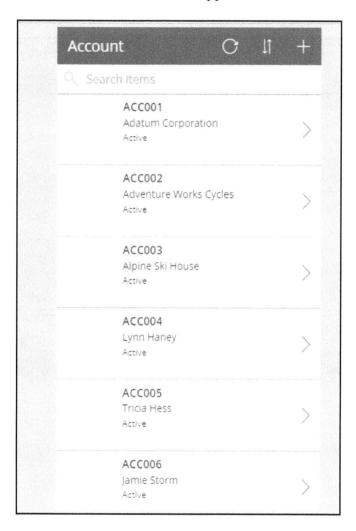

9. Select the **File** option from the menu bar. Click on the **Save as** option, then specify location and name of an **App**:

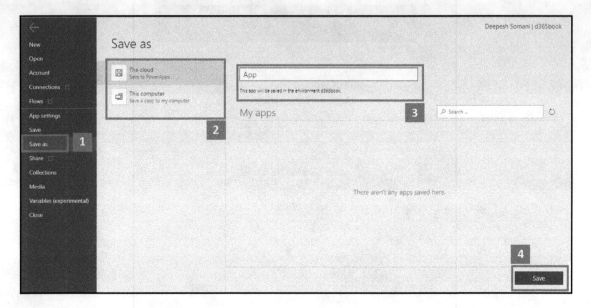

Creating a custom entity

The following steps will specify how to create a custom entity:

1. Go to www.powerapps.com, then on the left Navigation panel, expand the **Common Data Service** section, and then select **Entities**:

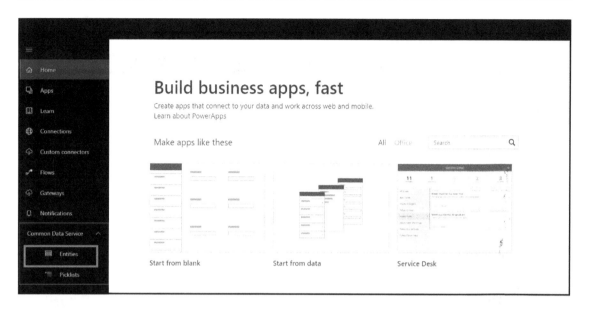

2. Select the **New entity** button. Fill all required fields on the **New entity** dialog box:

3. The entity will be created, and will display all fields:

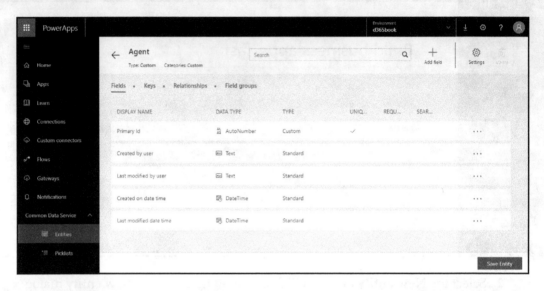

4. There are different sections to add for an entity, including **Fields**, **Keys**, **Relationships**, and **Field group**.
5. To add a **Field**, select the **Field** section, then select the **Add Field** button. The **Add field** form will open.
6. Complete the required information, and click on the **Add Field** button:

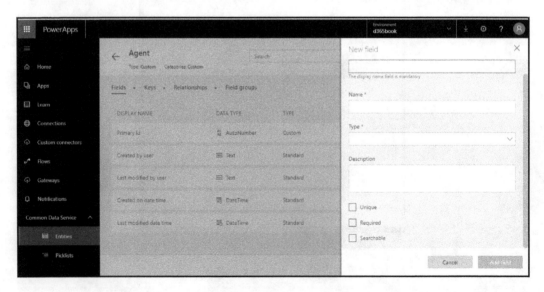

7. To add a relationship, follow the same steps and then click on the **Relationship** section. Select the **add** button and fill to **Add relationship** specify related entity:

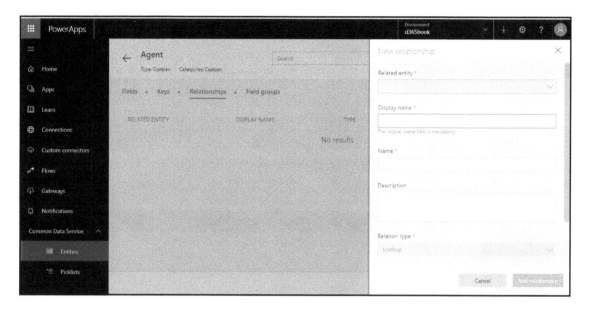

8. Do all the changes, and click on the **Save Entity** button:

Customizing PowerApps

PowerApps provides feasibility for customization. It is possible to change the appearance, theme, and controls of an app easily from the PowerApps designer. The following customizations are possible in PowerApps.

For this purpose, we will use create an app in the last section:

1. Edit screen size and orientation:

1. Open the recently created **App** for last section **Account App**. Go to **Apps** in the Navigation pane of the PowerApps website.
2. Select the . . . symbol at the end of the **App** ribbon. Click on the **Edit on the web** option:

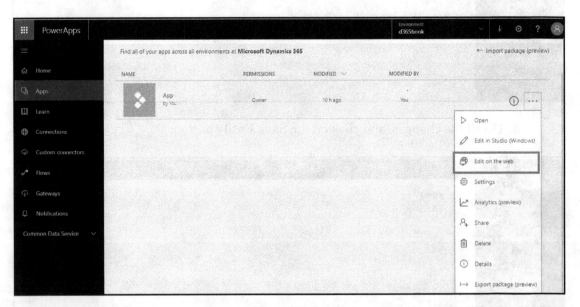

3. The PowerApps designer will open in a new tab:

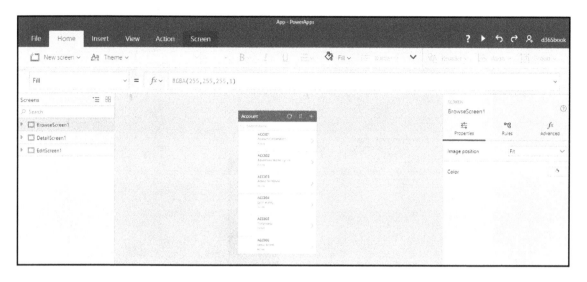

4. Select the **File** option on the menu bar.
5. Then click on the **App settings** option:

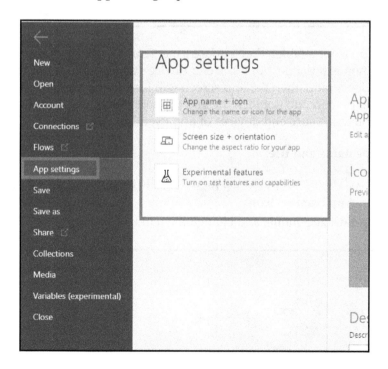

6. In the **App settings**, select **Screen size + orientation**. Set **Orientation** to Portrait, then to save changes, click on the **Apply** button:

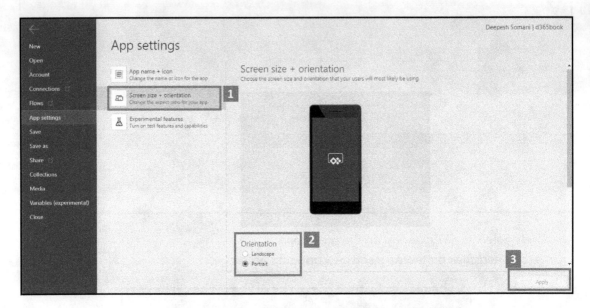

7. If the app is for a tablet, then choose aspect ratio. Locking of aspect ratio and orientation is possible, but if the end device's aspect ratio is not matched with an app's aspect ratio, then the app screen will look inappropriate on the end device. As good practice, do not lock the app's aspect ratio and orientation of PowerApps until you make sure end devices of app users are the same.

2. Edit PowerApps name and tile:

1. Now, to change the app name, go to the **File** menu and select **App settings.**
2. Click on **App Name + Icon**.
3. Click on **Edit app name**, and change the name of the app:

4. The PowerApps site page will be redirected to an app **Setting** page; you can change app settings from this section. Click on the **Edit app name** option and a Change app name dialog will appear onscreen change name of an app:

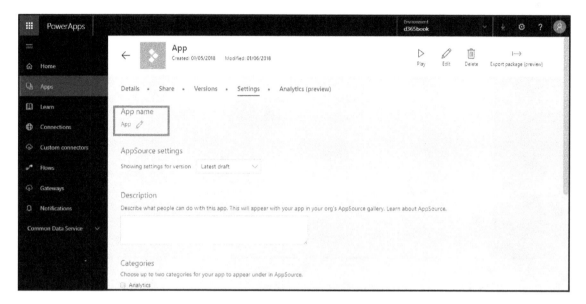

5. Rename app and **Save changes**:

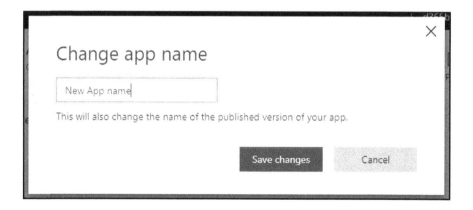

6. Editing of app tile and symbol is also allowed in PowerApps:

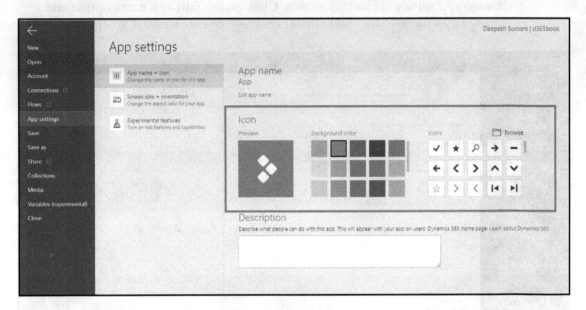

7. Now, click on the **Save** option from Navigation, then click on **Save** app. It will show an option to **Publish** the app. Click on the **Publish** this version button, and publish the app:

3. Add screen on PowerApps:

The process of designing an app includes adding a screen. To add a multiscreen in an app, follow these steps:

1. On an App in PowerApps designer, select the **Home** button on the menu and click on **New screen**. Choose the appropriate screen for the app, or select **Blank** screen:

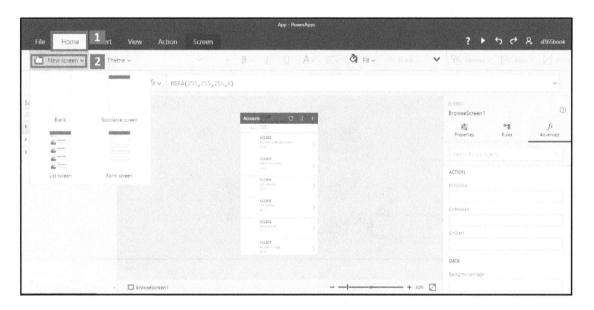

2. To rename the screen name, click on the **Screen** option in the left Navigation pane, then select **Rename**, or right-click on **Properties** and then rename the screen. Give it the name, `Account Source`:

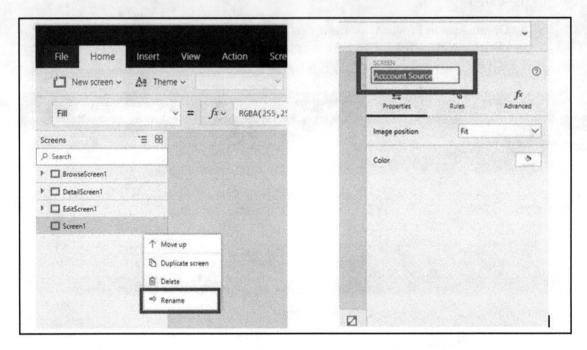

3. After adding the screen, add Navigation on **DetailScreen1**. Select **DetailScreen1**, then click on the **Insert** button on the menu:

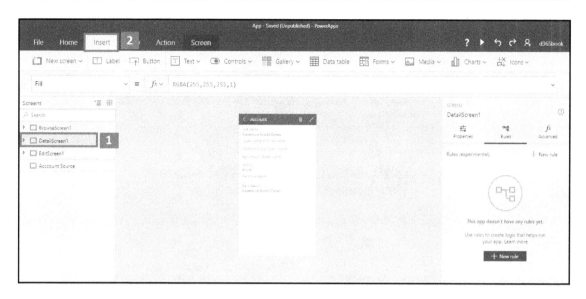

4. Select **Icons**, and add a forward icon on the screen, as demonstrated in the following screenshot. If necessary, change the color of the forward arrow from the property:

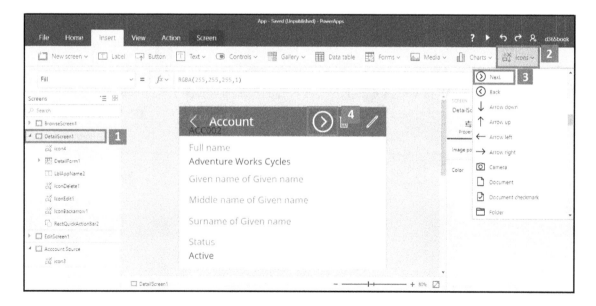

5. After adding the screen, add Navigation on **DetailScreen1**. Select **DetailScreen1** then click on the **Insert** button on the menu:

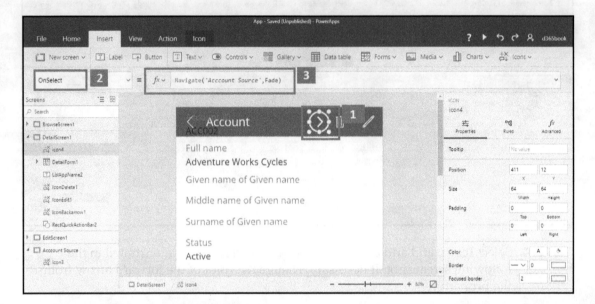

6. Select **Icons** and add a forward icon on the screen. If necessary, change the color of the forward arrow from property:

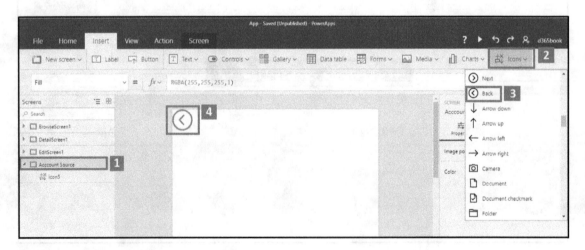

7. Select and adjust the **Icon**. Select the **Action** tab while **Icon** is selected. On Navigation, select **OnSelect** and set its property to **Navigate**, as shown in the following screenshot:

8. Select the **Account Source** screen, and add a backward arrow on the screen:

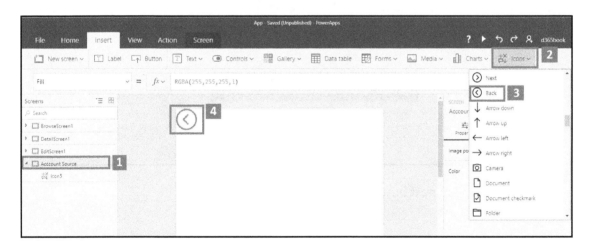

9. Set the **Action** of the icon as shown in following image:

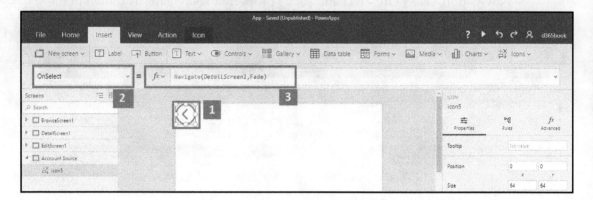

10. Now click on the **Preview** button to run and test the app:

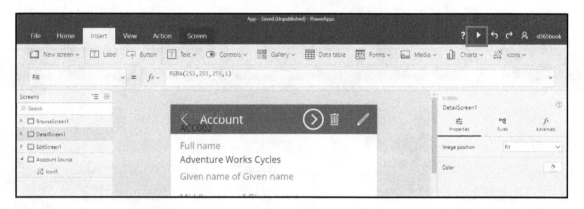

11. Click on the **next** button of the app:

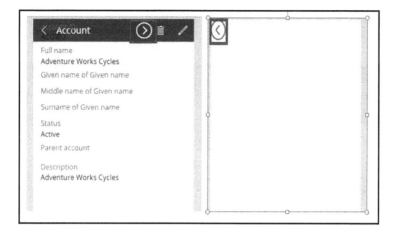

4. Add and configure controls in PowerApps:

Controls are UI elements on screen that make an app more interactive. The following steps are for adding and configuring controls on screen. In the last section, a blank screen had added to the app. The following steps will continue to add controls in the same app used in the previous section:

1. Open the app in PowerApps designer and select **Screen**:

2. Select the **Insert** option from the menu bar. Click on **Label** this action will add a label on screen:

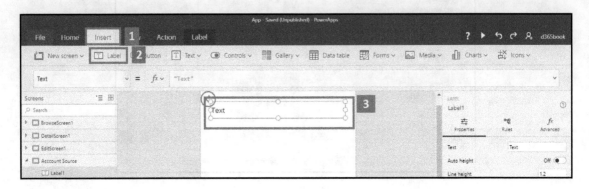

3. To change the property of a newly-added label, select **Label** on the screen, then click on the **Property** tab on the right-hand side. Change the name of the label to `Account Detail Label`, and the text to `Account Detail`. Resize the label by dragging its edges:

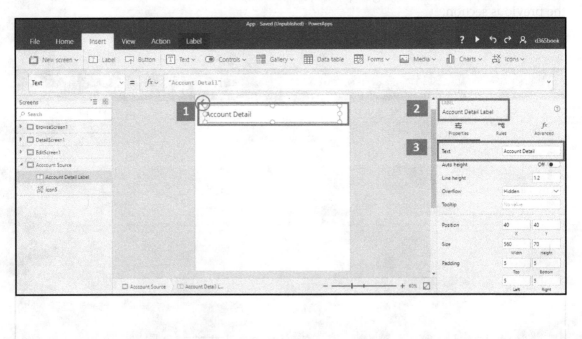

4. To configure control, select **Label** and click on the **Home** button in the menu bar. All configuration options will be available to use:

5. Change the color of the label by selecting **Fill**, and then selecting the appropriate color:

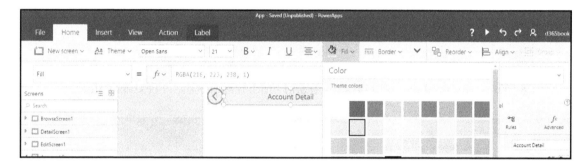

6. Add a checkbox on screen, and another label:

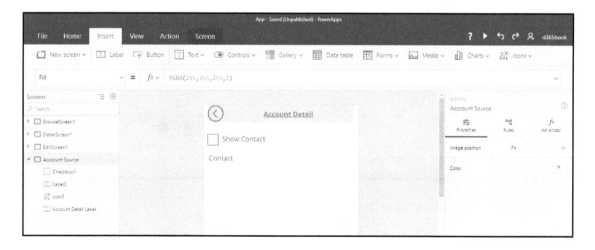

7. Check the visibility of the contact label to off from the property, and set the following property for the label:

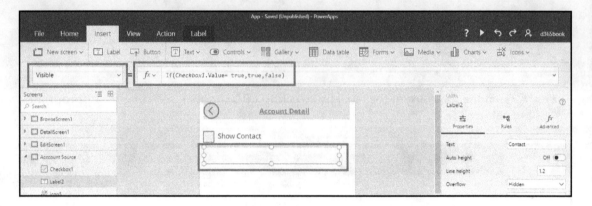

8. The `Contact` label will be shown and hidden as per the checkbox value:

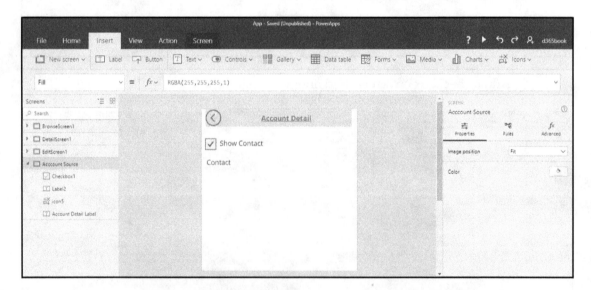

9. Save and publish changes.

5. Add list and data source in PowerApps:

PowerApps supports the adding of multiple connections. We will continue the app designing from the last section to add a different data source, and add a list using **Gallery** control:

1. Open the app in PowerApps designer, and select the **Account Source** screen:

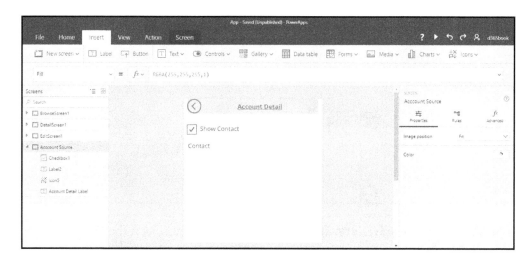

2. Select the **Insert** button, and click on **Gallery** to add the gallery's **Vertical** layout:

3. Adjust **Gallery** and the **Visible** condition, as shown in the following screenshot:

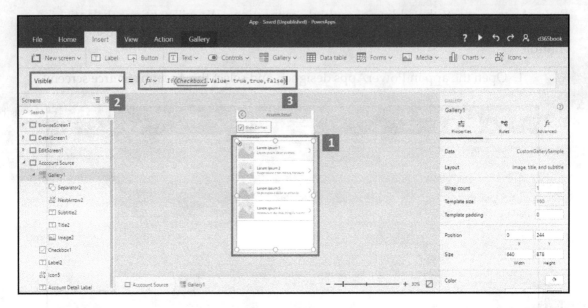

4. Add data to the **Gallery**. First, select **Gallery**, then click on the **Properties** tab. Select **Custom data source** if the data source has not been added, then Add the data source:

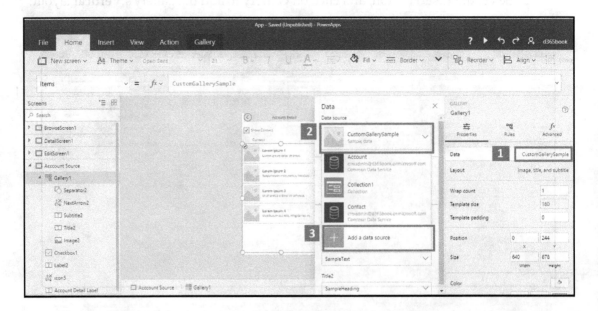

5. Select a connection from the list of connections, or create a new connection, then click on **Connection**. In this example, select **Common Data Service**:

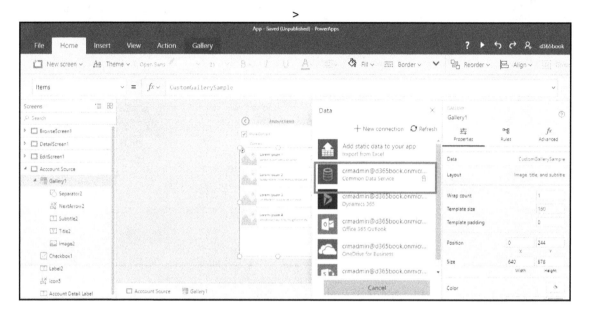

6. Select **Contact** from the entity list, then click on the **Connect** button:

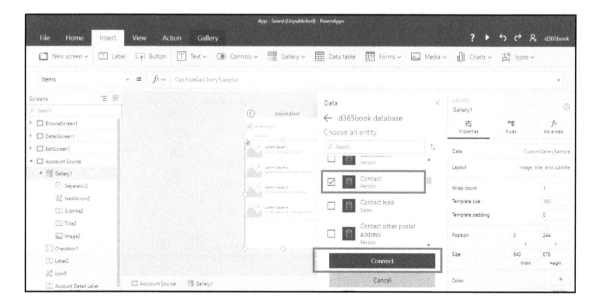

7. Select the **Contact** data source:

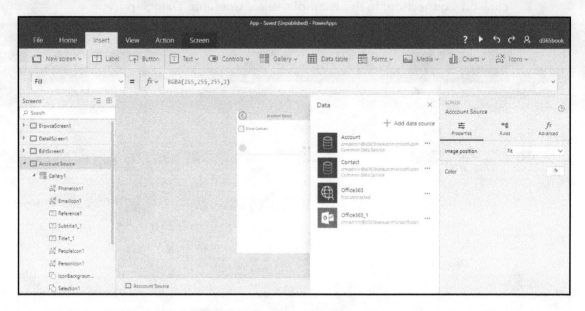

8. All contacts will appear in **Gallery** control:

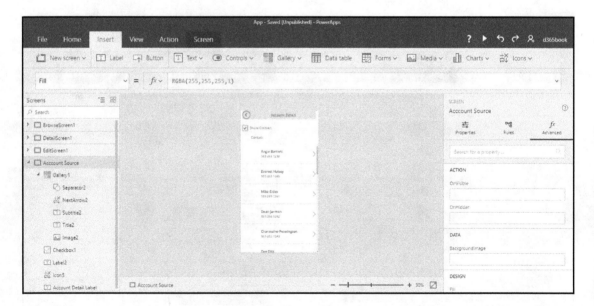

Summary

In this chapter, we have seen all the PowerApps features. We have also implemented and configured PowerApps Connections, and Data Source. We have also created and configured different PowerApps, by using Dynamics 365 data and the Common Data Service data.

6
Automate Business Processes Using Microsoft Flow

In the previous chapter, we learned how we can use Microsoft PowerApps to easily create custom business apps. In this chapter, we will learn about Microsoft Flow, which can be defined as a cloud-based service that enables users to build workflows that automate different tasks and processes across multiple applications and services.

In this chapter, we will be covering the following points:

- What is Microsoft Flow?
- Microsoft Flow in the context of Dynamics 365
- Automating processes using Microsoft Flow
- The differences between Dynamics Workflow and Microsoft Flow

Getting to know Microsoft Flow

As described earlier, Microsoft Flow is a cloud-based service that allows us to create automated workflows between different applications and services. The list of applications and services we can use with Microsoft Flow is constantly expanding. Currently, Microsoft Flow supports more than 170 service connectors, which includes popular applications like Dynamics 365, Office 365 Outlook, OneDrive for Business, SharePoint, Twitter, and Facebook.

For a full list of the available connectors in Microsoft Flow, visit the following link:
`https://flow.microsoft.com/en-us/connectors/`

If this is not enough, we can also build our own connector for our RESTful API that uses JSON.

Create custom connectors in Microsoft Flow at `https://flow.microsoft.com/en-us/documentation/register-custom-api/`

Apart from cloud-based services, we can also connect to on-premise data sources. To connect to on-premise data sources like SharePoint, SQL Server, Oracle, and so on, we can create an on-premise data gateway.

Manage an on-premise data gateway in Microsoft Flow at `https://flow.microsoft.com/en-us/connectors/`

Microsoft Flow comes with predefined templates. Templates are prebuilt flows around popular services and scenarios, which we can start using immediately. We can use existing templates to create a flow or if a particular scenario is not covered by existing templates, we can create our own flow from scratch—that is, create one from the beginning.

For a full list of templates in Microsoft Flow, go to the following link:
`https://flow.microsoft.com/en-us/templates/`

Some of the most popular templates available are:

- **Save Office 365 email attachments to OneDrive for business**
- **Send myself a reminder in 10 minutes**
- **Get a push notification when I receive an email from my boss**

These templates are divided into categories such as approval, button, collect data, email, mobile, notifications, and so on. The templates can also be sorted by **Name**, **Popularity**, and **Published Time**, as shown in the following screenshot:

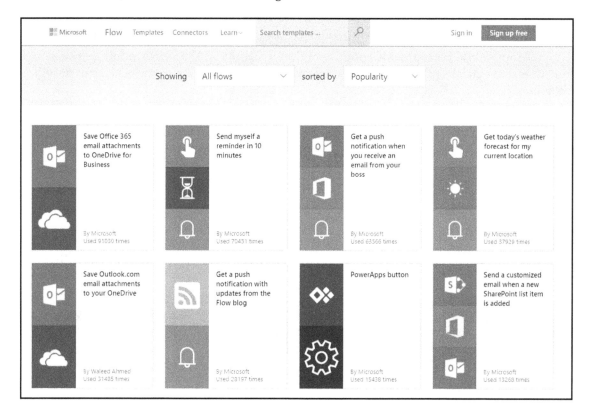

To create a flow, we need to sign in using an existing Microsoft account (either work, school, or personal) or else we need to Sign Up first.

Go to Microsoft Flow's home page (`https://flow.microsoft.com`) and click on **Sign in** or **Sign up free**:

 Microsoft Flow doesn't support email addresses that end with `.gov` and `.mil`.

Choosing the right Microsoft Flow plan

Before we dive further into creating a flow, let's first understand what features are offered by different Microsoft Flow plans. Basically, there are two Microsoft Flow plans—a free plan and a premium plan.

The free plan, **Flow Free**, includes unlimited flow creation, 750 runs per month (per user), and 15-minute checks (if a flow is triggered in less than 15 minutes after its last run, it will be queued).

Flow Plan 1, which is paid, comes with unlimited flow creation, 4,500 runs per month, and 3-minute checks. It also includes premium connectors such as Salesforce, Common Data Service, Adobe Creative Cloud, and others.

 Check out the full list of premium connectors here: https://flow.microsoft.com/en-us/connectors/?filter=category= premium

Following are some of the premium connectors, such as **Salesforce**, **DB2**, and **DocuSign**, amongst others:

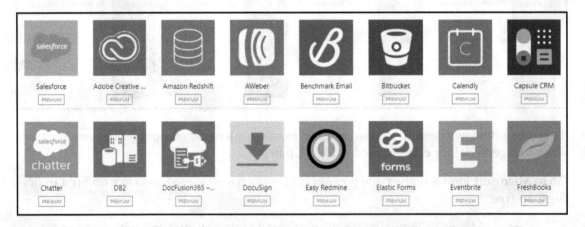

Flow Plan 2 comes with unlimited flow creation, 15,000 runs per month, and 1-minute checks, along with premium connectors. A 90-day free trial is available for **Flow Plan 1** and **Flow Plan 2**.

Apart from the above plans, there are Dynamics 365 plans, as well as Office 365 plans, that include Microsoft Flow. These plans come with unlimited flow creation, 2,000 runs per month, and a flow frequency of 5 minutes. However, they don't include premium connectors. Following are the two plans that come with Dynamics 365 applications:

Microsoft Flow for Dynamics 365 Plan	Microsoft Flow Plan 2
• Dynamics 365 Enterprise Sales • Dynamics 365 Enterprise Field Service • Dynamics 365 Enterprise Marketing • Dynamics 365 Enterprise Customer Service • Dynamics 365 Enterprise Project Service Automation • Dynamics 365 Enterprise Operations • Dynamics 365 Business Edition Financials	• Dynamics 365 Enterprise, Plan 1 • Dynamics 365 Enterprise, Plan 1 • Dynamics 365 Business Edition Plan.

Understanding the different components of a Flow

We've covered the differences between the different plans for Microsoft Flow, which can help us in deciding the right plan for us. Now let's understand the different components within a flow.

The different components of a flow are:

- **Services**: Services can be defined as the different applications that Microsoft Flow connects to, such as Twitter, SharePoint, Facebook, and so on. These services can act as sources as well as destinations within a Flow. Following is a list of a few of the services that come with Microsoft Flow. Currently, there are 160 services supported, and the list keeps growing.

- **Triggers**: Triggers are the starting point of the flow. They can be a manual trigger from a button in Microsoft Flow that needs to be manually initiated by the end user, or they can be automated, scheduled to run at a specific time or started from another application or service. A trigger can also be vent-based; when an event occurs in the service, it will trigger the flow. For example, a lead record being created in CRM or a new item being added in SharePoint's list can be the trigger. The following is a list of triggers specific to Dynamics 365:

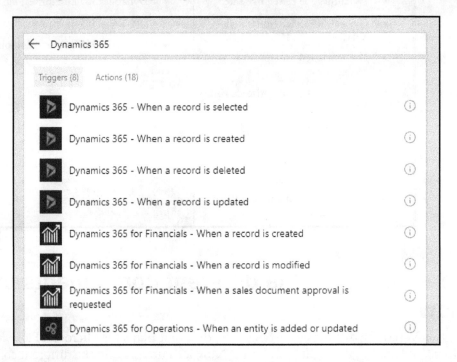

- **Actions**: Actions define the steps to be taken when a flow is triggered or, in other words, the output of the workflow execution. Actions could be things like sending an email, creating a record, posting on social media such as Twitter or Facebook, and so on. The following is a list of actions that are specific to Dynamics 365:

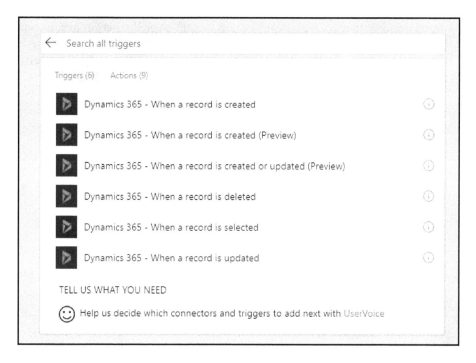

- **Conditions**: Conditions can be used to put `if/then` branch logic inside Flow. They basically include the **Yes** path and No path that a flow can take based on the output of the condition:

- **Loops and switch**: Using loops, we can iterate over the action and execute it multiple times, or only once, when a specific condition is met. This can be done using **Apply to each** or **Do-Until** steps in the action. Similarly, the **Switch** step can be used to specify a switch case like logic within an action:

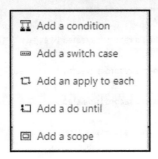

The following image shows a blank **Switch** step having an **Apply to each** and a **Do Until** step:

 We can submit our suggestions regarding new connectors and triggers to be added through the Flow Ideas portal:
https://powerusers.microsoft.com/t5/Flow-Ideas/idb-p/FlowIdeas

In this section, we covered what Microsoft Flow is, which different plans offered, and the basic components that comprise a Flow. In the next section, we will cover what Microsoft Flow offers from a Dynamics 365 context.

Understanding Microsoft Flow in the context of Dynamics 365

Microsoft Flow comes with prebuilt templates for Dynamics 365, such as Create Dynamics 365 leads from Excel Table, Notify your team about new opportunities, and so on. The following are some of the popular templates specific to Dynamics 365.

> For a full list of Dynamics 365 templates, go to the following link:
> https://flow.microsoft.com/en-us/connectors/shared_
> dynamicscrmonline/dynamics-365

The following table lists the different triggers available for Dynamics 365:

Triggers (4)		
• **When a record is selected**		
• **When a record is created**		
• **Delete a record is deleted**		
• **When a record is updated**		
Required Parameters	Organization Name	Specifies the name of the organization to be connected.
	Entity Name	Specifies the name of the entity.

At the time of writing this chapter (November 2017), Microsoft has also added two new triggers and four new actions for Dynamics 365 that are in the preview as version 2. These newer versions of triggers and actions will continue to get the latest features. Having a separate version helps to test new features without disrupting the existing flow that uses the existing version.

A new trigger has been added, which gets invoked for both the creation and the update of an entity's record. The newer version of both the trigger and action support option sets as user localized strings wherein the existing still works on integers as option set values.

List of Actions that available for Dynamics 365:

ACTIONS (5)		
• **Create a new record**		
Required Parameters	Organization Name	Specifies the name of the organization to be connected.
	Entity Name	Specifies the name of the entity.
	Record Item	Specifies the record to be created.
• **Delete a record**		
• **Get record**		
Required Parameters	Organization Name	Specifies the name of the organization to be connected.
	Entity Name	Specifies the name of the entity.
	Item Identifier	Specifies the identifier for the record to be deleted.
• **List Records**		
Required Parameters	Organization Name	Specifies the name of the organization to be connected.
	Entity Name	Specifies the name of the entity.
Optional Parameters	Filter Query	Specifies the OData filter for the records to be retrieved.
	Order By	Specifies OData order by for the records returned.
	Top Count	Specifies the total number of records to be retrieved.
	Expand Query	Specifies if the related entities to be included. Default is none.
• **Update a record**		
Required Parameters	Organization Name	Specifies the name of the organization to be connected.
	Entity Name	Specifies the name of the entity.
	Record Identifier	Specifies the identifier for the record to be updated.
	Record Item	Specifies the record to be updated.

The following is the new Triggers and Actions that have been added to Dynamics 365:

Triggers:

- **When a record is created (preview)**: Triggers a flow when a record is created in Dynamics 365 with option sets exposed as strings
- **When a record is created or updated (preview)**: Triggers a flow when a record is created or updated in Dynamics 365 with option sets exposed as strings

Actions:

- **Create a new record (preview)**: Creates a new record for an entity with option sets exposed as strings
- **Get record (preview):** Retrieves the specific record for an entity with option sets exposed as strings
- **List records (preview)**: Retrieves records for an entity with option sets exposed as strings
- **Update record (preview)**: Updates an existing record for an entity with option sets exposed as strings

In Dynamics 365, we need to enable **Change Tracking** for custom entities for Microsoft Flow to track any update to or deletion of that entity's record. By default, change tracking is enabled for OOB entities. For a custom entity, go to **Settings** | **Customizations** | Open the **Entity for Customization** | Check **Change Tracking** checkbox in the **Data Services** section in the **General** tab.

Creating a Dynamics 365 Flow

We can create a flow from Microsoft Flow's home page (`https://flow.microsoft.com/`) or, inside Dynamics 365, we can go to **Settings** | **Microsoft Flows** to create a flow.

We can also create a flow using the **Create a flow** or **See your flows** menu option from **Flows** flyout menu on the ribbon, as shown in the following screenshot:

The following screenshot shows the new Flows menu added to Form's ribbon:

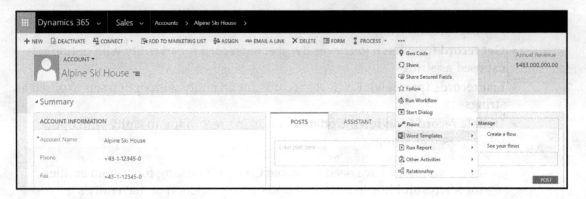

Let's implement a sample flow to see all the components in action.

We will be implementing the following scenario:

- **Scenario**: On creation of a lead record in Dynamics 365 with Rating as High, add a new row with the details of the lead record in an Excel file inside OneDrive, create a follow-up task in Wunderlist, and finally send a notification in the Microsoft Flow mobile app.
- **Trigger**: When a lead record is created in Dynamics 365.
- **Condition**: If the value for Rating field is High in the lead record created.
- **Action**: Insert a row in Excel, create a task in Wunderlist, and send a notification.

1. Go to the Microsoft Flow home page (`https://flow.microsoft.com/`), log in using your Microsoft account, go to **My Flows** and click on **Create from blank**.
2. Specify the flow name and search for Dynamics 365 in the search box, which filters the list of triggers and actions specific to Dynamics 365. In the result, we need need to select the **Dynamics 365- When a record is created** trigger:

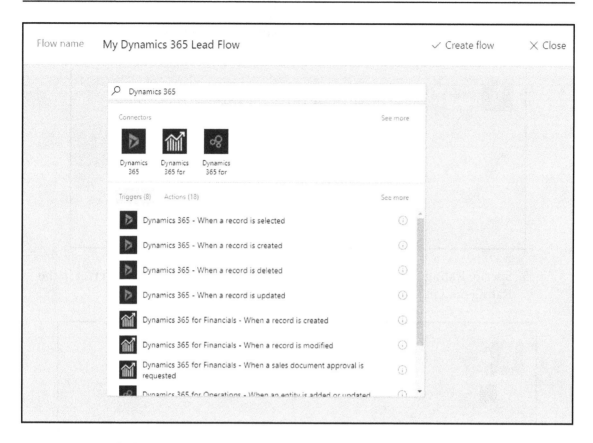

3. Specify the **Organization Name** of the CRM to connect to and select Leads in the **Entity Name**:

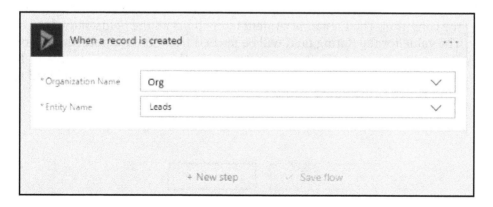

4. Click on **New Step**, followed by **Add a condition** to add a condition:

5. Specify **Rating** as equal to 1, that is, the OptionSet value for option **Hot** in the **Rating** field in Lead, as shown in the following screenshot:

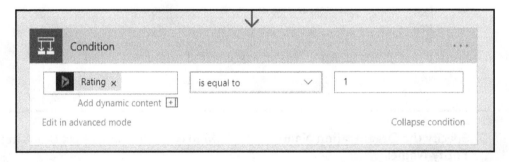

6. Search for the Rating field in the **Dynamic content** tab's search box to add it to the condition. The **Dynamic content** tab will list all the fields of the lead entity. The value for the Rating field will be fetched from the lead record created in Dynamics 365 when the flow executes, hence the term dynamic content. The dynamic content will basically hold the details of the newly created lead record at runtime when the flow executes:

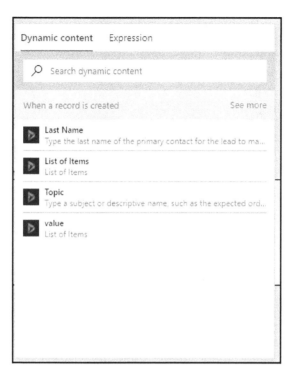

7. The condition block has an associated **If yes** and an **If no** path. Click on **Add an action** in **If yes** path to add an action:

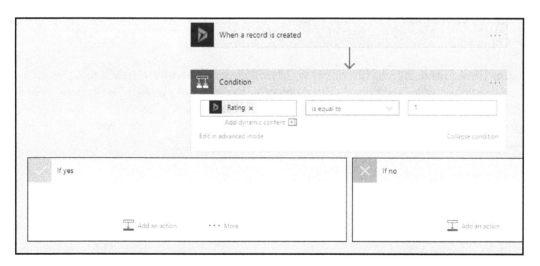

8. Search and select **Excel - Insert row** action:

9. If required, sign in to your OneDrive account and authorize Microsoft Flow. Inside the `One Drive` folder, select the Excel file along with the table to which you want to save the lead details. The following screenshot shows the existing lead table in our Excel file, to which we will be adding a new row with details of the lead record:

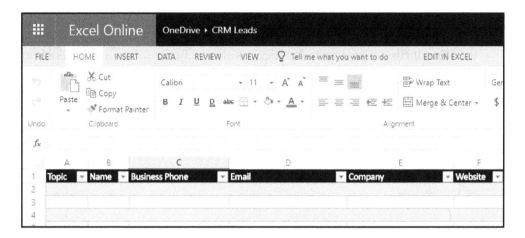

10. Map each of the columns with corresponding fields (dynamic content) in the **Insert row** action, as shown in the following screenshot:

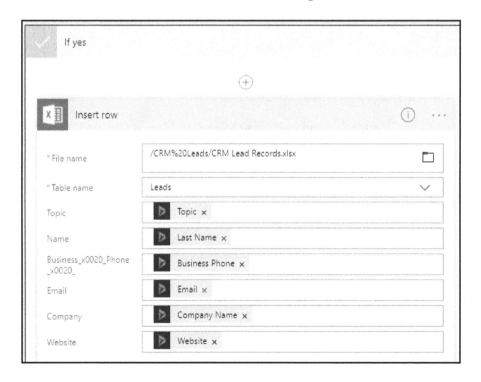

11. For our Next Action, add a new Action that creates a task in Wunderlist. To do this, click on **Add an action** inside the **Insert row** action added earlier and select the **Wunderlist - Create a task** action, as shown in the following screenshot:

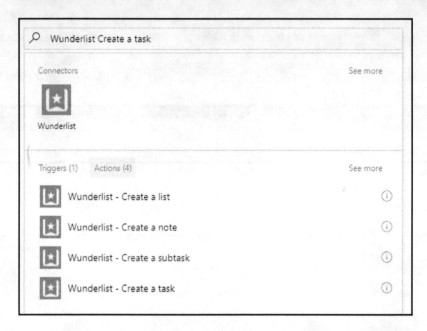

12. Sign in to Wunderlist and authorize Microsoft Flow if required. Specify the details as shown in the following screenshot:

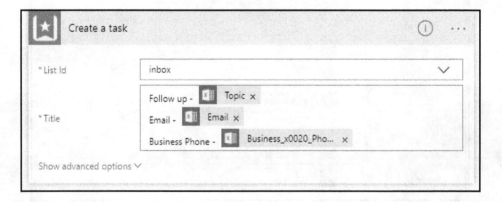

13. For sending a push notification to the Microsoft Flow Mobile App, click on **Add an action** in our flow and select **Notifications - Send me a mobile notification** action, as shown in the following screenshot:

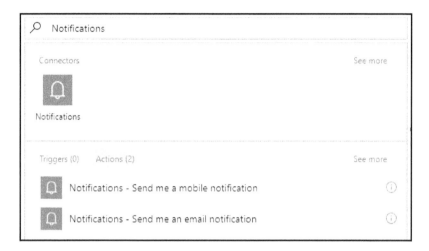

14. Specify the details as shown in the following screenshot:

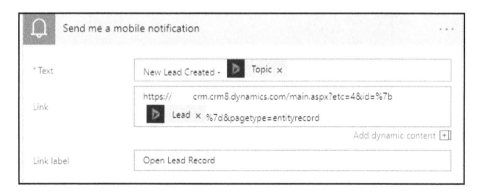

16. Click on **Create flow** to create the flow.

17. To test our Flow, let's create a lead record with Rating as Hot and specify the other details as shown in the following screenshot:

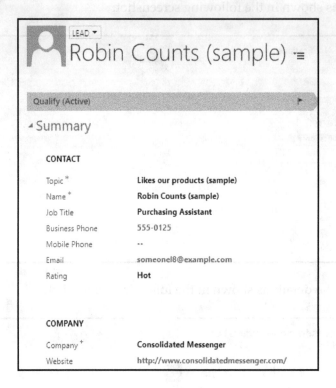

17. To check the status of the Flow, select **My Flows** in Microsoft Flow's home page and click on the Flow we created:

18. Clicking on **See all** options in the **RUN HISTORY** gives all the details of Microsoft Flow's run history:

19. Clicking on the Succeeded row will show us the execution details of the steps. In our case, all the steps are successful, as indicated by the green checkmark:

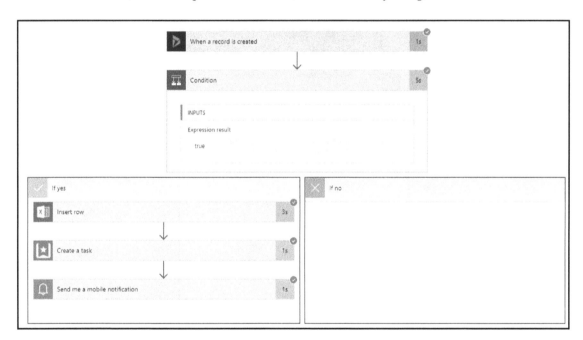

Now let's check the output of each of the actions in their respective application:

1. **Insert Row in Excel Action**: This action has added a new row to our Excel with details of the lead record created:

2. **Create a task in the Wunderlist Action**: This action has added a new to-do task in the inbox of Wunderlist:

3. **Send me a mobile notification in the Microsoft Flow Mobile App Action**: This action has sent a notification regarding the lead record created inside the Flow Mobile app:

The Microsoft Flow mobile app is available for Android, iOS, and Windows Phone. Using a mobile app, we can create a flow from a template, monitor flow activity, and manage our flows: `https://flow.microsoft.com/en-us/documentation/mobile-create-flow/`

This completes the creation and testing of our Dynamics 365 Flow. Now, to share this Flow with another user, we can add that user as an owner:

1. Go to **My Flows** | Select the **Flow** | Click on **Invite another Owner**:

2. Specify the new owner:

 We can also submit our flow as a template to the gallery of templates for Microsoft Flow: `https://flow.microsoft.com/en-us/documentation/publish-a-template/`

In this section, we saw different templates, triggers, and actions specific to Dynamics 365. We also created a custom Dynamics 365 flow. In the next section, we will compare Flow with Dynamics 365 Workflow, which will help us to choose one over the other.

Dynamics 365 Workflow versus Microsoft Flow

There are certain scenarios which can be implemented using either Dynamics Workflow or Microsoft Flow. Following are a few points we can consider when deciding.

If a scenario can be implemented within Dynamics 365 using Workflow, then Workflow is the better choice. This is because we can easily manage and monitor it from within CRM, through System Jobs. For managing and monitoring a flow, we need to go outside CRM and do the same from within Flow's portal.

Workflow can run both synchronously and asynchronously. Workflow will trigger immediately when conditions are met. So, in scenarios where we want immediate action to be taken, Workflow is a better choice. Moreover, Workflow is solution-aware, so it can move easily from one environment to another.

Microsoft Flow is a better fit in scenarios where we want to seamlessly integrate with third-party applications and services such as Twitter, Facebook, Yammer, and so on. To implement this within Workflow would require development effort, that is, writing a custom workflow activity.

With Workflow, we are restricted to email notifications; however, with Flow, we can send notifications in the form of SMS, push notifications to Flow's Mobile App, and email notifications from an account other than the Dynamics 365 User through Gmail, Hotmail, and so on, without writing a single line of code.

Microsoft Flow supports the approval scenario through approval specific actions, as shown in the following screenshot. An approval request can go to users other than Dynamics 365 Users:

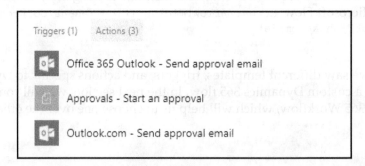

Microsoft Flow has Dynamic 365, List records Action, which can be used to retrieve the records of an entity. We can use it to find a list of records of an entity matching a specific condition and can then act upon it. This can also be used to design a flow which either updates or deletes the child records when a parent record is updated or deleted. Normally, to implement such a scenario, we would have to write a custom workflow activity or plugin inside CRM. With Microsoft Flow, we can achieve this without writing a single line of code:

Deleting all the child records when a parent record is deleted in Dynamics 365 using Microsoft
Flow: `https://debajmecrm.com/2017/02/21/dynamics-crm-365-flows-us`
`ing-microsoft-flows-generic-framework-to-delete-all-child-`
`records-when-a-parent-record-is-deleted-in-dynamics-365/`

In Dynamic Workflow, to implement schedule jobs we would end up using either wait or time out condition, which could impact on the performance of the system. On the other hand, Microsoft Flow supports the **Recurrence** trigger, which can trigger an event to run at regular, customized time intervals:

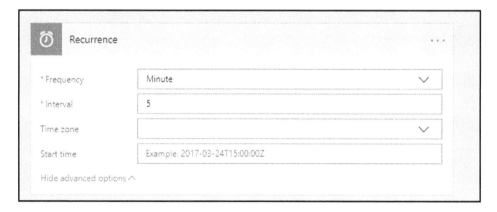

In short, there are no clearly defined boundaries when it comes to choosing one over the other, as both have their own share of benefits and shortcomings.

Summary

In this chapter, we covered how Microsoft Flow can be used to write workflows that can seamlessly integrate with multiple applications and services, and without even a single line of code. We also had a detailed look at Microsoft Flow in the context of Dynamics 365 and learned how to write a simple flow that integrates multiple applications.

In the next chapter, we will look at Web APIs and how we can consume them to create apps that integrate with Dynamics 365.

7
Develop Apps using Web API

Web API is a new feature, introduced for the first time for Dynamics CRM 2016. You can use Dynamics 365 Web API with different programming languages, multiple platforms, and devices. Web API in Dynamics 365 uses **Open Data Protocol** (**OData**), also known as OData version 4. As Dynamics 365 Web API is built on open standards, it is not necessary to use any assemblies.

With Dynamics 365, **Organization Data Service** was deprecated and was replaced with Web API. The main purpose of the API is to provide parity with organization services and try to reduce as many constraints as possible.

The following are the characteristics of Web API:

- It implements OData version 4.0 for building and consuming RESTful APIs over rich data sources such as DOC, HTML, and PDF
- It supports a wide variety of programming languages such as .Net, C++, Java, Python, devices, and platforms
- Request and response have JSON format

Getting started with Dynamics 365 Web API (client-side JavaScript)

Dynamics 365 Web API can be called and accessed using JavaScript. You can use Web API with HTML web resources, form scripts, and ribbon commands to perform various operations on data.

Web API is very convenient to use with JavaScript as it returns results in the form of JSON objects that can be easily converted to JavaScript objects.

In Dynamics 365, Web API is used mainly with HTML web resources and in Single Page Applications.

JavaScript web resources

The main benefit of using Web API in JavaScript web resources is that you will not need to authenticate because web resources are a part of the application and can be accessed by authenticated users only. You can directly write a code for Web API operations in the JavaScript web resource, and perform operations.

Single Page Applications

Single Page Applications are capable of making Dynamics 365 Web API calls. They consists of many JavaScript libraries that are running on browsers, which authenticate the Dynamics 365 API using **Cross-Origin Resource Sharing (CORS)**.

While using JavaScript in a Single Page Application, the adal.js library is used to allow the user to authenticate and to access Dynamics 365 from a hosted web app. You must also integrate an authorization header that contains an authentication token.

Further on, in this chapter, we will look through some examples that use Web API for performing CRUD operations using web resources.

Dynamics 365 Web API uses XMLHttpRequest object to perform operations.

Working with XMLHttpRequest in Dynamics 365 Web API

XMLHttpRequest (XHR) is a native object supported by all browsers, which enables AJAX techniques for making web pages dynamic.

We will look at a very simple example that uses a Web API and XMLHttpRequest object.

The following is the Web API code that will fetch all the opportunities:

```
var req = new XMLHttpRequest();
req.open("GET", Xrm.Page.context.getClientUrl() +
"/api/data/v8.2/opportunities()", true);
req.setRequestHeader("OData-MaxVersion", "4.0");
req.setRequestHeader("OData-Version", "4.0");
req.setRequestHeader("Accept", "application/json");
```

```
req.setRequestHeader("Content-Type",
"application/json; charset=utf-8");
req.setRequestHeader("Prefer", "odata.include-annotations="*"");
req.onreadystatechange = function() {
  if (this.readyState === 4) {
    req.onreadystatechange = null;
    if (this.status === 200) {
      var result = JSON.parse(this.response);
      var opportunityid = result["opportunityid"];
    } else {
    Xrm.Utility.alertDialog(this.statusText);
    }
  }
};
req.send();
```

In the preceding code, you will notice that after initializing a new `XMLHttpRequest` object, you need to open it before sending or setting any properties for it. The parameters of an `open` method are an HTTP request method (`GET`, `PUT`, `POST`, `DELETE`, and so on), a URL, and a Boolean parameter that indicates whether the operation is to be performed asynchronously.

Web API URL and versions

A Web API URL consists of the following:

- **Protocol**: A protocol in HTTP request can be `http://` or `https://`.
- **Base URL**: A base URL is nothing but the URL of your current organization that can be retrieved using the function—`Xrm.Page.context.getClientUrl()`.
- **Web API path**: Web API path in Dynamics 365 is API/data.
- **Version**: It is the version of Web API for Dynamics 365. The latest version is 9.0.
- **Resource**: A resource can be the name of the entity, function, or an action you want to perform.

The URL used in the preceding example is `Xrm.Page.context.getClientUrl() + "/api/data/v8.2/opportunities()`.

HTTP request also supports various **HTTP methods** described as follows:

- `GET`: It is used for retrieving data; the status code for a successful call is `200 OK`
- `POST`: It is used for the creation of new records
- `PATCH`: It is used for updating or performing `upsert` operations on entity records
- `DELETE`: It is used for deletion of records
- `PUT`: It is used when updating individual properties of an entity record

For HTTP Request, various HTTP headers are also used that are described as follows:

Dynamics 365 supports only JSON format. So, these following headers can be used with Dynamics 365 Web API.

For every request, you must include the `Accept` header value of `application/json`, which returns body, even in the case of no response. If there is an error, it will be returned in JSON format. Your code can work without this header, but it is a best practice to use it with your request.

You must always include headers, `OData-Version` and `OData-Max-Version` set to a value of 4.0. The current version of OData is 4.0, but to avoid ambiguity about OData versions in future, you should have these headers included in your request.

The properties that do not include any recent changes may include cached data. So, to override browser caching of Web API requests, you must include the `If-None-Match:` `null` header in the request body.

After getting a basic idea about Web API in Dynamics 365, we will move toward performing various operations using Web API. We will also learn how to create, retrieve, update, and delete an entity record using a Web API request. We will also go through associate and disassociate request examples.

Therefore, at least the following HTTP headers should be included:

- `Accept: application/json`
- `OData-MaxVersion: 4.0`
- `OData-Version: 4.0`
- `If-None-Match: null`

Querying data using Dynamics 365 Web API

While retrieving data from Dynamics 365, you can set various criteria for the data you need and can apply various filters for retrieving specific data. For this, we will look at an example for querying data, using Web API from Dynamics 365:

1. In this example, we will use `$set` and `$top` system query options to return the `firstname` property of the first five contacts:

```
Request: GET [Organization URI] /api/data/v9.0/contacts?
$select=firstname&$top=5
Accept: application/json
OData-MaxVersion: 4.0
OData-Version: 4.0
```

The response to the preceding request will be as follows:

```
{
  "@odata.context":  "https://biocondev3.crm8.dynamics.com
  /api/data/v9.0/$metadata#contacts(firstname)",
  "value": [
  {
    "@odata.etag": "W/"684628"",
    "firstname": null,
    "contactid": "ade1d0f5-28ed-e711-a95e-000d3af27347"
  },
  {
    "@odata.etag": "W/"679541"",
    "firstname": null,
    "contactid": "fa420510-85ec-e711-a95f-000d3af27534"
  },
  {
    "@odata.etag": "W/"679547"",
    "firstname": "C",
    "contactid": "94cd4c79-85ec-e711-a95f-000d3af27534"
  },
  {
    "@odata.etag": "W/"679575"",
    "firstname": null,
    "contactid": "e8f5339f-88ec-e711-a95f-000d3af27534"
  },
  {
    "@odata.etag": "W/"681230"",
    "firstname": null,
    "contactid": "fc71e9b9-a2ec-e711-a95f-000d3af27534"
  }
  ]
```

```
            }
```

2. In the next example, we will look at how to limit the number of entity records
   returned for any request. The maximum number of records that can be returned
   is 5,000. You cannot retrieve more than 5,000 records in Dynamics 365:

```
Request: GET [Organization
URI]/api/data/v9.0/accounts?$select=nameHTTP/1.1
Accept: application/json
OData-MaxVersion: 4.0
OData-Version: 4.0
Prefer: odata.maxpagesize=3
```

The response to the preceding request will be as follows:

```
{
"@odata.context":
"https://biocondev3.crm8.dynamics.com/api/data/v9.0/$metadata#conta
cts(firstname)",
"value": [
{
"@odata.etag": "W/"684628"",
"firstname": null,
"contactid": "ade1d0f5-28ed-e711-a95e-000d3af27347"
},
{
"@odata.etag": "W/"679541"",
"firstname": null,
"contactid": "fa420510-85ec-e711-a95f-000d3af27534"
},
{
"@odata.etag": "W/"679547"",
"firstname": "C",
"contactid": "94cd4c79-85ec-e711-a95f-000d3af27534"
}
]
}
```

3. Now, we will see how to apply system query options to query data using
   Dynamics 365 Web API. The first query option is appended after [?] and every
   proceeding option is separated using [&]. Query options are case sensitive.

In the next query, we will select the `firstname` and `lastname` of a contact whose age is less than 50:

```
GET [Organization
URI]/api/data/v9.0/contacts?$select=firstname,lastname&$top=3&$filter=age
lt 50
```

The standard filter operators used in Dynamics 365 Web API are as follows:

Operator	Description	Example
Comparison operators	-	-
Eq	Equal	`$filter=age eq 50`
Ne	Not equal	`$filter=age ne 50`
Gt	Greater than	`$filter=age gt 50`
Ge	Greater than or equal	`$filter=age ge 50`
Lt	Less than	`$filter=age lt 50`
Le	Less than or equal	`$filter=age le 50`

The logical operators are as follows:

Operator	Description	Example
Logical operators	-	-
And	Logical and	`$filter=age lt 50 and age gt 20`
Or	Logical or	`$filter=contains(firstname,'(sample)') or contains(firstname,'test')`
Not	Logical negation	`$filter=not contains(firstname,'sample')`

The grouping operators are as follows:

Grouping operators	-	
( )	Precedence grouping	`(contains(firstname,'sample') or contains(firstname,'test')) and age gt 50`

Standard query options

The OData string query functions supported by Web API are as follows:

Function	Example
Contains	$filter=contains(firstname,'(sample)')
Endswith	$filter=endswith(firstname,'Inc.')
startswith	$filter=startswith(firstname,'a')

Order by query:

You can order the records in ascending or descending order. The following example shows how to order records:

```
GET [Organization
URI]/api/data/v9.0/contacts?$select=firstname,age,&$orderby=age
asc,firstname desc&$filter=age ne null
```

Now, after learning to query using Dynamics 365 Web API, we will go through CRUD operations. We will look through some examples of performing these operations.

CRUD operations using Dynamics 365 Web API

We will look at some basic examples for creating, updating, retrieving, and deleting an entity.

Create an entity

The following is a code for Web API that creates a new record for the `entity` account. For that first, we will create a JSON object and set the required properties:

```
//Creates a JSON object for an Entity to be created.
var entity = {};
//Sets the properties for entity.
entity.accountnumber = "AC1009348YU";
entity.name = "Shree Technosoft";
entity.telephone1 = "9978759612";
var req = new XMLHttpRequest();
req.open("POST", Xrm.Page.context.getClientUrl() +
"/api/data/v8.2/accounts", true);
req.setRequestHeader("OData-MaxVersion", "4.0");
req.setRequestHeader("OData-Version", "4.0");
req.setRequestHeader("Accept", "application/json");
```

```
req.setRequestHeader("Content-Type", "application/json;
charset=utf-8");
req.onreadystatechange = function() {
  if (this.readyState === 4) {
    req.onreadystatechange = null;
    if (this.status === 204) {
      var uri = this.getResponseHeader("OData-EntityId");
      var regExp = /\(([^)]+))\)/;
      var matches = regExp.exec(uri);
      var newEntityId = matches[1];
    } else {
      Xrm.Utility.alertDialog(this.statusText);
    }
  }
};
req.send(JSON.stringify(entity));
```

Retrieving list of entity records

Next, we will retrieve a list of accounts from Dynamics 365 using a Web API request. The following is the code for retrieving a list of entities:

```
var req = new XMLHttpRequest();
req.open("GET", Xrm.Page.context.getClientUrl() +
"/api/data/v8.2/accounts?$select=accountid,accountnumber,accountrat
ingcode,telephone1", true);
req.setRequestHeader("OData-MaxVersion", "4.0");
req.setRequestHeader("OData-Version", "4.0");
req.setRequestHeader("Accept", "application/json");
req.setRequestHeader("Content-Type", "application/json;
charset=utf-8");
req.onreadystatechange = function() {
  if (this.readyState === 4) {
    req.onreadystatechange = null;
    if (this.status === 200) {
      var results = JSON.parse(this.response);
      for (var i = 0; i < results.value.length; i++) {
        var accountid = results.value[i]["accountid"];
        var accountnumber = results.value[i]["accountnumber"];
        var accountratingcode = results.value[i]
        ["accountratingcode"];
        var telephone1 = results.value[i]["telephone1"];
      }
    } else {
      Xrm.Utility.alertDialog(this.statusText);
    }
  }
};
```

```
req.send();
The response for the above code will be as below:
{
    "@odata.context":    "https://demoorg3.crm8.dynamics.com/api/
    data/v8.2/$metadata#accounts
    (accountid,accountnumber,accountratingcode,telephone1)",
    "value": [
    {
        "@odata.etag": "W/"671215"",
        "accountid": "9252cd68-e9e3-e711-a95e-000d3af27163",
        "accountnumber": "DR567821X",
        "accountratingcode": 1,
        "telephone1": null
    },
    {
        "@odata.etag": "W/"677922"",
        "accountid": "e771ecea-edea-e711-a95f-000d3af27534",
        "accountnumber": "DR9888900RR",
        "accountratingcode": 1,
        "telephone1": null
    },
    {
        "@odata.etag": "W/"707246"",
        "accountid": "2de6ad4f-0ef1-e711-a95e-000d3af278ae",
        "accountnumber": "AC1009348YU",
        "accountratingcode": 1,
        "telephone1": "9978759612"
    },
    {
        "@odata.etag": "W/"684666"",
        "accountid": "493d50f5-28ed-e711-a95e-000d3af27fd9",
        "accountnumber": "DR7845699AS",
        "accountratingcode": 1,
        "telephone1": null
    }
    ]
}
```

These retrieved objects can be easily converted to JavaScript objects. These objects can be assigned to a JavaScript array and can be used for further operations.

Update an entity record

Now, we will update an `entity` record. For updating a record, you will need to pass the GUID of the record you want to update and also a JSON object that consists of fields to be updated. Here, we will update `email` and `city` for an account record:

```
var entity = {};
entity.emailaddress1 = "contact@shreetech.in";
entity.address1_city = "Mumbai";
var req = new XMLHttpRequest();
req.open("PATCH", Xrm.Page.context.getClientUrl() +
"/api/data/v8.2/accounts(2de6ad4f-0ef1-e711-a95e-000d3af278ae)",
true);
req.setRequestHeader("OData-MaxVersion", "4.0");
req.setRequestHeader("OData-Version", "4.0");
req.setRequestHeader("Accept", "application/json");
req.setRequestHeader("Content-Type", "application/json;
charset=utf-8");
req.onreadystatechange = function() {
  if (this.readyState === 4) {
    req.onreadystatechange = null;
    if (this.status === 204) {
      //Success - No Return Data - Do Something
    } else {
      Xrm.Utility.alertDialog(this.statusText);
    }
  }
};
req.send(JSON.stringify(entity));
```

Delete an entity record

For deleting an `entity` record, you will need to pass the GUID of the record to be deleted. The following is the code to delete an account `entity` record from Dynamics 365:

```
var req = new XMLHttpRequest();
req.open("DELETE", Xrm.Page.context.getClientUrl() +
"/api/data/v8.2/accounts(2de6ad4f-0ef1-e711-a95e-000d3af278ae)",
true);
req.setRequestHeader("Accept", "application/json");
req.setRequestHeader("Content-Type", "application/json;
charset=utf-8");
req.setRequestHeader("OData-MaxVersion", "4.0");
req.setRequestHeader("OData-Version", "4.0");
req.onreadystatechange = function () {
  if (this.readyState === 4) {
    req.onreadystatechange = null;
```

```
        if (this.status === 204 || this.status === 1223) {
          //Success - No Return Data - Do Something
        } else {
          Xrm.Utility.alertDialog(this.statusText);
        }
      }
    };
    req.send();
```

Impersonation in Dynamics 365 Web API

When you want to execute business logic on behalf of another user, then you will need to use impersonation. Sometimes, there are some processes or business logic on behalf of a particular Dynamics 365 user that has the appropriate security role of that user; for such requirements, impersonation is very useful.

In the code, whenever you need to create a record on behalf of another user, you will use this feature. For that, you will need two user accounts. To use impersonation you will need to add one header named MSCRMCallerID with a GUID value that is equal to the user's system user ID as shown in the next request.

Please refer to the following code:

```
Request
POST [Organization URI]/api/data/v9.0/contacts HTTP/1.1
MSCRMCallerID: 9ba9f608-514e-49fd-81cd-84537a31f68e
Accept: application/json
Content-Type: application/json; charset=utf-8
OData-MaxVersion: 4.0
OData-Version: 4.0
{"name":"Contact created using impersonation"}
```

Retrieving metadata using Web API

Microsoft Dynamics 365 is a metadata-driven application, where you will need to query metadata for some scenarios and specific requirements. Dynamics 365 Web API supports querying metadata. We will use the EntityDefinitions entity to retrieve the metadata of the contact entity.

The following is the request to query metadata:

```
GET
[OrgURL]/api/data/v8.2/EntityDefinitions(LogicalName='contact')/Att
ributes"
Following is the Sample code for querying metadata for Contact
Entity:
var req = new XMLHttpRequest();
//Opens request
req.open("GET", window.parent.Xrm.Page.context.getClientUrl() +
"/api/data/v8.2/EntityDefinitions(LogicalName='contact')/Attributes
", true);
//Sets request Headers
req.setRequestHeader("OData-MaxVersion", "4.0");
req.setRequestHeader("OData-Version", "4.0");
req.setRequestHeader("Accept", "application/json");
req.setRequestHeader("Content-Type", "application/json;
charset=utf-8");
req.setRequestHeader("Prefer", "odata.include-annotations="*"");
//Function to detect ready state change
req.onreadystatechange = function () {
  if (this.readyState === 4) {
    req.onreadystatechange = null;
    //Check if request completed successfully
    if (this.status === 200) {
      var result = JSON.parse(this.response);
      var index = 1;
      for (var i = 0; i < result.value.length; i++) {
        //Gets schemaname from response.
        var schemaName = result.value[i].SchemaName;
      }
    }
    else {
      Xrm.Utility.alertDialog(this.statusText);
    }
  }
};
 req.send();
});
```

Updates for Web API in Dynamics 365 in version 9.0

Now, in the newly released version 9.0 for Dynamics 365, there are many remarkable changes made to querying data and performing various operations using Dynamics 365 Web API. With the new release, we will not need to create any requests for using Web API, instead, you will use built-in and pre-defined functions for using Web API.

Using Web API in the new Dynamics 365 version is very simple and easy. Now, Dynamics 365 has a new library `Xrm.WebApi` and performs CRUD operations using Web API. This library provides functions to perform operations, which we will look through in the following examples and sample code.

Create an entity record

Here is a sample code to create a new contact using the `Xrm.WebApi.createRecord()` function:

```
function createContact() {
  // contact data object
  var entity = {};
  entity.firstname = "Mark";
  entity.lastname = "Andrew";
  entity.telephone1 = "7845687845";
  entity.address1_city = "California";
  // create record
  Xrm.WebApi.createRecord("contact", entity).then(
  function success(result) {
    console.log("Contact Created Successfully !!");
  },
  function (error) {
    console.log(error.message);
  }
 );
}
```

Update an entity record

In the following example, we will be updating a record contact by adding a new attribute `email`:

```
function updateContact() {
  // contact data object
  var entity = {};
  entity.emailaddress1 = "mark@gmail.com";
  //get contact id
  var contactId = "DC1F674E-55F1-E711-A95F-000D3AF27163"
```

```
// update contact record
Xrm.WebApi.updateRecord("contact", contactId, entity).then(
function success(result) {
  console.log("Contact Record Updated");
},
function (error) {
  console.log(error.message);
}
);
}
```

Delete an entity record

The following is the sample code to delete a contact record:

```
function deleteContact() {
  var contactId = "DC1F674E-55F1-E711-A95F-000D3AF27163";
  Xrm.WebApi.deleteRecord("contact", contactId).then(
  function success(result) {
    console.log("Contact deleted");
  },
  function (error) {
    console.log(error.message);
  }
  );
}
```

Retrieving records

In the new version, you can directly use fetch XML to retrieve multiple records from Dynamics 365 using Web API. In the following example, we will use fetch an XML query to fetch/retrieve contacts for a selected account. The following is the sample code for retrieving records from Dynamics 365:

```
function retrieveMultipleContacts(executioncontext) {
  var formContext = executioncontext.getFormContext();
  var contactId = formContext.data.entity.getId();
  var fetchContacts = "<fetch version='1.0' output-format='xml-
  platform' mapping='logical' distinct='false'>" +
  "<entity name='contact' >" +
  "<attribute name='fullname' />" +
  "<attribute name='telephone1' />" +
  "<attribute name='contactid' />" +
  "<order attribute='fullname' descending='false' />" +
  "<filter type='and'>" +
  "<condition attribute='parentcustomerid' operator='eq'
  uitype='account' value ='" + accountId + "' />" +
```

```
"</filter>" +
"</entity >" +
"</fetch > ";
Xrm.WebApi.retrieveMultipleRecords("contact", "fetchXml= " +
fetchContacts).then(
  function success(result) {
  for (var i = 0; i < result.entities.length; i++) {
    console.log(result.entities[i]);
  }
},
 function (error) {
   console.log(error.message);
  });
}
```

Summary

In this chapter, we saw how to work on Single Page Applications, XMLHttpRequest in Dynamics 365 Web API, Web API URL and versions, and Standard Query Options, and also saw how to work on CRUD operations using Dynamics 365 Web API. In the next chapter, we will cover Azure integration with Dynamics 365, configure Azure integration with Dynamics 365, and write Azure-aware plugins and different listener applications.

8

Leverage Azure Extensions in Dynamics 365

In the previous chapter, we learned how we can consume the new REST Web API endpoint in Dynamics 365 to perform various operations and how to use it to develop custom business applications. In this chapter, we will learn how Dynamics 365 natively supports integration with Microsoft Azure. This chapter assumes a basic understanding of fundamentals of the Microsoft Azure.

 For Microsoft Azure reference—`https://docs.microsoft.com/en-us/ azure/fundamentals-introduction-to-azure` and `https://azure. microsoft.com/en-in/training/`

Microsoft Azure can be defined as a cloud computing platform or collection of cloud-based services that developers and IT professionals can use to build, test, deploy and manage applications through various data centers across the globe. Microsoft Azure provides **Infrastructure as a service (IaaS)**, **Platform as a service (PaaS)** and **Software as a service (SaaS)**.

With **IaaS,** we are basically referring to Azure virtual machines, that is servers hosted on the cloud. The cloud computing service provider, Microsoft in this case, manages the infrastructure and we need to pay for using the resources. Here we have complete control and are responsible for managing operating systems, middleware and applications running there. We can also deploy Dynamics 365 On-premises in Microsoft Azure virtual machines.

With **PaaS**, we have a complete development and deployment environment available to us inside the cloud, which we can use to build, deploy, and manage our applications in the cloud. We pay for the cloud services that we are using. Here, we only manage our applications and services, and the cloud service provider manages everything else.

With **SaaS**, we basically connect and use software or cloud-based apps over the internet. Here, we just need to pay for the cloud-based app that we are going to use. The cloud service provider manages everything, be it underlying infrastructure, middleware, application software and so on. We just need to connect to these apps, mostly using a web browser over the internet to use them. Dynamics 365 Online falls under SaaS.

In this chapter, we will be covering the following points:

- Understanding Azure Integration with Dynamics 365
- Configuring Azure Integration with Dynamics 365
- Writing Azure-aware plugins and different listener applications

Understanding Azure integration with Dynamics 365

Microsoft Azure Service Bus is the main component in Microsoft Azure Stack that enables us to connect Dynamics 365 with Microsoft Azure. Through Azure Service Bus we can pass the details of an operation performed inside Dynamics 365 to multiple applications that are listening to it and can read and process that information.

Introduction to Microsoft Azure Service Bus

Azure Service Bus can be defined as a cloud messaging service that runs in Microsoft's Azure Data Center. Azure Service Bus enables us to connect different applications, services or devices that are hosted in the cloud or on-Premises inside the firewalled networks. It can be used to connect different **line-of-business** (**LOB**) applications, tablets, phones or even any household appliances or sensors. This Azure Service Bus supports two different communication mechanisms: brokered messaging (queues, topics, and subscriptions) and relay service.

The Azure Service Bus brokered messaging capabilities include queues and topics that can be created and hosted in Microsoft's Azure Data Center. An application can connect to the queue or topics created and send messages to them. These messages will be stored durably. Receiving applications can then connect to them and can receive and process the messages. The sending applications and the receiving applications can either be hosted in the cloud or can be on-premises. Queues provide unidirectional asynchronous communication where the publisher publishes a message and the subscriber receives the message. Each message is received by a single subscriber. Topics also provide unidirectional asynchronous messaging infrastructure where a publisher publishes a message and receivers receive the message like a queue. The main difference is that the same message can be received by multiple subscribers, who can optionally specify some criteria so that they only receive the messages that match the rules specified. As they provide one-way asynchronous communication through a broker, that is there is no direct connection between senders and receivers, it is not suitable for scenarios where we want both sender and receiver to exchange messages or directly connect to each other, or want synchronous communication between them. To address this Azure Service provides relays.

The Azure Service Bus relay service provides bi-directional synchronous communication capabilities between applications, unlike queues and topics. The relay service allows us to expose an endpoint in the cloud that serves as a proxy for our services hosted on the cloud or on-premises services. Any client with internet access can then make calls to this endpoint, which are relayed back to the service hosted behind the firewall or any other application listening for the messages. This provides a very reliable and cost-effective way for organizations to expose service.

Azure Service Bus documentation
: `https://docs.microsoft.com/en-us/azure/service-bus-messaging/`.

Understanding Dynamics 365 and Azure Service Bus

In the previous section, we covered the basics of Azure Service Bus, in this section we will look at how Dynamics 365 is integrated with Azure Service Bus.

The following diagram shows how Dynamics 365 works along with Azure Service Bus to connect to applications that can be in the cloud or hosted behind the firewall:

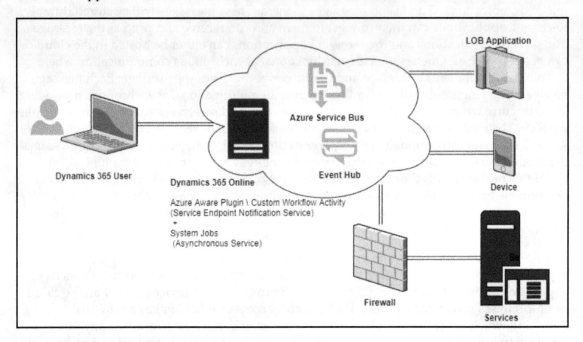

Here is a step-by-step explanation for the same:

1. A Dynamics 365 user performs an operation inside CRM, like creating a lead record, updating an opportunity and so on.
2. This triggers the execution of registered Azure-aware OOB (out of the box) plugins or custom Azure-aware plugins or workflow activity, which then notifies the asynchronous service system job.
3. Once the asynchronous service receives the notification, it handles the posting of data context of the request message to the Azure Service Bus. The posting is performed through a system job. Dynamics 365 User can check the status of the system job inside Dynamics 365 Web application, (**Settings** | **System Jobs**).
4. Microsoft Azure Service Bus then relays the execution context to Microsoft Azure Service Bus listener applications. The Azure Service Bus also manages the authorization. Dynamics 365 that posts the data to Service Bus and any listener application that reads it, are authorized by using **either Access Control Service (ACS)** or **Shared Access Signature (SAS)**.

Azure Service Bus: Authentication and Authorization—`https://docs.` `microsoft.com/en-us/azure/service-bus-messaging/service-bus-` `authentication-and-authorization`.

5. Microsoft Azure Service Bus listener applications that are registered on an Azure Service Bus solution endpoint can read and process the Dynamics 365 execution context posted by Azure Service Bus.
6. The Azure Service Bus then sets the status of the related system job as completed.

SAS Authorization was introduced in CRM Online 2016 Update 1 and performs better than ACS. SAS is the recommended authorization method for Dynamics 365. Refer here for updating a service endpoint from ACS to SAS Authorization—`https://msdn.microsoft.com/en-us/library/` `mt728940.aspx`.

Understanding the Azure-aware plugin

As we saw earlier, we can register an Azure-aware plugin against a particular event inside Dynamics 365, which then passes this execution context to Azure Service Bus, which in turn relays it to the listener applications. Here, we can either use the OOB Azure-aware plugin or we can write our own custom Azure-aware plugin or custom workflow activity.

With Dynamics 365 Online Version 9.0, we can use Webhooks as an alternative to Azure Service Bus to send data about the events to a web application—`https://docs.microsoft.com/en-us/dynamics365/` `customer-engagement/developer/use-webhooks`.

For the OOB Azure-aware plugin, we need to first register the new service endpoint through the plugin registration tool:

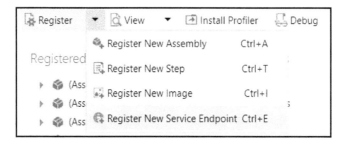

Inside service endpoint registration, we need to specify a connection to Azure Service Bus to which we want to pass the plugin events:

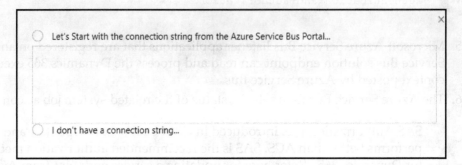

The service endpoint holds the authorization information about the Azure Service Bus such as Service Bus Namespace address and SAS Key. After successful registration, we can then add a plugin step to the service endpoint added, the way we do for our usual plugin assemblies.

This Azure-aware OOB plugin executes in full trust. However, there are certain limitations with the OOB Azure-aware plugin, such as it can only run asynchronously, cannot call CRM SDK Method, and cannot write trace statements for logging, or auditing purposes.

Apart from the OOB Azure-aware plugin that Dynamics 365 provides, we can also create our own custom Azure-aware plugin or custom workflow activity.

The `IServiceProvider` passed to the `Execute` method of IPlugin contains an instance of `IServiceEndpointNotificationService`. We can call its `Execute` method to post the execution context to Azure Service Bus. The `Execute` method needs an entity reference of the service endpoint; we can grab the service endpoint ID from the plugin registration tool. Adding this code to invoke the endpoint notification service makes our Plugin **Azure aware**:

```
public class AzureAwarePlugin : IPlugin
{
public void Execute(IServiceProvider serviceProvider)
{
// set the Service Endpoint Id
var serviceEndpointId = "[ServiceEndpointGuid]";

// Obtain the execution context from the service provider.
IPluginExecutionContext context = (IPluginExecutionContext)
serviceProvider.GetService(typeof(IPluginExecutionContext));
```

```
// Extract the notification service for posting execution context
IServiceEndpointNotificationService notificationService =
(IServiceEndpointNotificationService)
serviceProvider.GetService(typeof(IServiceEndpointNotificationServi
ce));
// Call the Execute method.
var response = notificationService.Execute(new
EntityReference("serviceendpoint",
new Guid(serviceEndpointId)), context);
}
}
```

The custom Azure-aware plugin executes in partial trust mode in the sandbox. The benefit of writing a custom plugin is that we can call CRM SDK methods and can also receive a response from the listener applications in case of two-way relay service. Additionally, the plugin can be registered as either synchronous or asynchronous.

 For Azure-aware plugins, it is recommended to register them to run asynchronously for best system performance.

Understanding different contracts between Dynamics 365 and an Azure solution

The following are the different types of contract that can be defined while registering a new service endpoint through the plugin registration tool:

Queue:

For a queue contract, a message queue needs to be created in Azure Service Bus. The listener application waits for the message to be posted by Service Bus in the queue. When the message is available in the queue, the listener application can read and process the message. The listener application doesn't need to be actively listening in the case of a queue contract.

One-way:

In the case of a one-way contract, the listener application needs to be actively listening. The post to the Service Bus fails if there is no active listener and the status of the system job is set to "Failed" after the system job runs out of retries.

The listener application needs to implement the `IServiceEndpointPlugin` interface's `Execute` method along with `WS2007HttpRelayBinding`, to which `RemoteExecutionContext` is passed from the Azure Service Bus.

Two-way:

The two-way contract is similar to a one-way contract, the only difference is that in the case of the two-way contract a message of type string can be returned back to the custom plugin workflow activity that posted the message to Azure Service Bus from the listener application.

The listener application needs to implement `ITwoWayServiceEndpointPlugin` interface's `Execute` method along with `WS2007HttpRelayBinding`, to which `RemoteExecutionContext` is passed from the Azure Service Bus.

REST:

A REST contract is similar to a two-way contract. Here, the listener application needs to implement the `IWebHttpServiceEndpointPlugin` interface's `Execute` method, along with `WebHttpRelayBinding`, to which `RemoteExecutionContext` is passed from the Azure Service Bus.

Topic:

Topics are similar to queues. However, with topics, one or more listeners can subscribe to receive messages from the topic. The messages are filtered and routed to the subscriber via the corresponding subscription from the topic.

Event Hub:

Microsoft Azure event hubs provide telemetry services on a very large scale. They are typically used for large-scale application telemetry and Internet of Things scenarios. Several devices or applications can send telemetry messages to the event hubs. The messages can be in thousands or millions per second to be read and processed. Creating an event hub solution application is similar to writing an Azure Service Bus listener application. Here, we first start by creating an event hub in Microsoft Azure just as in Azure Service Bus. Next, we need to specify the event hub connection string while registering the Dynamics 365 service endpoint through the plugin registration tool. We will talk in more detail about it later on in the chapter.

 To write listener applications for the above contracts, we need to use Azure SDK Version 1.7 or later—`https://azure.microsoft.com/en-in/downloads/`.

Now, as we have a basic understanding of the Azure Extensions available inside Dynamics 365, we will implement a simple business scenario in the next section to see it in action.

Configuring Dynamics 365 and Azure Service Bus integration

Let us take a simple scenario for implementation which will help us in understanding how to configure Azure Extensions inside Dynamics 365 and how to write different listener applications for different contract types. The listener application is basically a third-party application which needs to get notified whenever an event occurs in Dynamics 365. The listener application and the Dynamics 365 are two separate disconnected applications.

Scenario: On creation of a lead record in Dynamics 365, pass its information (execution context) to the listener application through Azure Service Bus. The listener application can then read and process that information.

Let us walk through all the steps in detail:

1. Log in to an Azure Management portal `https://portal.azure.com` using an existing account or create a free account
   at `https://azure.microsoft.com/en-us/free/`

2. Search and Add a new Service Bus service in the portal. Provide the required details and click on **Create namespace** to create the Service Bus namespace. The name that must be specified needs to be unique across the entire data center. This creates a URI for the Service Bus namespace which can be used to access it over the internet. This Service Bus namespace acts as a container for the communication mechanisms such as relay service and brokered messaging (queues and topics):

3. Next, we would create a queue to which we would be posting the message from Dynamics 365. Open the Service Bus and click on the **+ Queue** button to create a queue with the required details:

4. Provide the details as shown here and click on the **Create** button to create the queue:

5. For the Queue created, select **Shared access policies** and click on **Add** to create a new shared access policy. As the name suggests, send rights are required for sending messages to a listener at a namespace, similarly, listen rights will be required by a listener application to begin listening on a namespace. Manage rights would be required to create a queue, delete a queue, create a subscription, enumerate topics, subscriptions and so on. Here, we have selected the **Send** and **Listen** checkbox while adding the SAS policy as we are going to use the same policy for both sending and listening. We can also create two separate policies, one for the sender and another for the listening application. Click on **Create**, to create a new SAS policy:

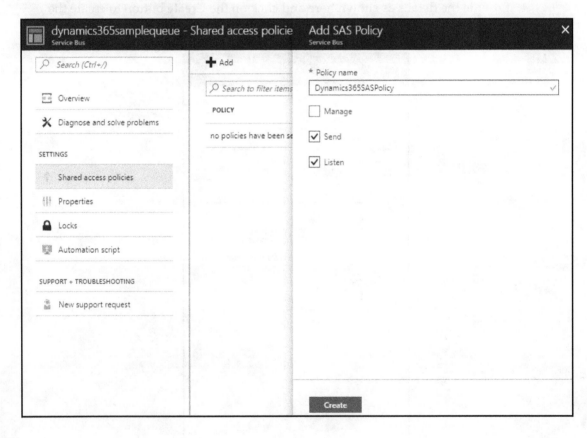

Rights required for **Service Bus Operations** (**SAS**) are detailed here—https://docs.microsoft.com/en-us/azure/service-bus-messaging/service-bus-sas#rights-required-for-service-bus-operations

6. Select the shared access policy created and copy its primary connection string.
7. Back in Dynamics 365, we need to register a service endpoint through the plugin registration tool. Select **Register New Service Endpoint** in the plugin registration tool.

Download the latest Microsoft Dynamics 365 SDK from—https://www.microsoft.com/en-us/download/details.aspx?id=50032

8. Paste the connection string into the **Register New Service Endpoint** dialog box and click **Next**:

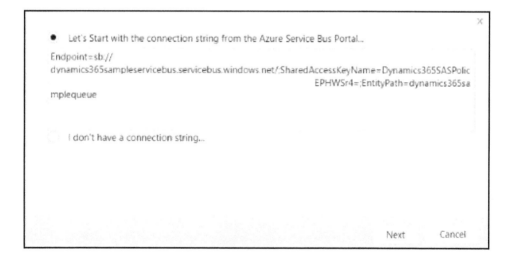

9. This auto-populates the **Service Endpoint Registration** details. Click on **Save**:

Service Endpoint Registration

Configure a connection to Azure Service Bus to which plug-in events can be sent.

Name	dynamics365samplequeue dynamics365sampl
NameSpace Address	sb://dynamics365sampleservicebus.servicebus
Designation Type	Queue ⌄
Queue Name	dynamics365samplequeue
Message Format	.NETBinary ⌄
Authorization Type	SASKey ⌄
SAS Key Name	Dynamics365SASPolicy
SAS Key	••••••••••••••••••••••••••••••••••
User Information Sent	None ⌄
Description	

Save   Cancel

This adds the service endpoint in the plugin registration tool. Next, we register a new step for create message on the Lead entity. Set **Execution Mode** to **Asynchronous**. If we try setting it as **Synchronous** we will get the following alert **Only asynchronous steps are supported for Service Endpoint plug-ins** as OOB Azure-aware plugin only supports asynchronous execution mode:

10. Now let us create a lead record inside Dynamics 365 to trigger the plugin:

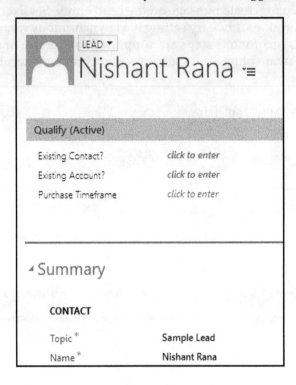

11. Go to **Settings** | **System Jobs**, a corresponding system job would have been created which shows the status of the message posted to Azure Service Bus from the asynchronous service:

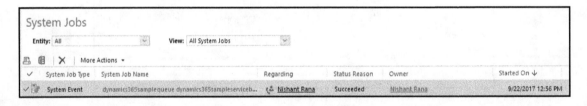

12. Back in our queue, we can see a new message added to **ACTIVE MESSAGE COUNT**:

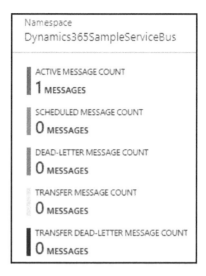

In next section, we will create listener applications to read the data posted to Azure Service Bus from Dynamics 365.

Writing a queue listener

Let us create a simple queue listener to read the message passed to queue:

1. Open Visual Studio and select **Project Type** as **Console Application**.
2. Install the following NuGet Package in the project—`WindowsAzure.ServiceBus`. It provides a client library for Microsoft Azure Service Bus operations.
3. Add a reference to the `Microsoft.Xrm.Sdk` assembly or install the following NuGet Package – `Microsoft.CrmSdk.Core` assemblies.
4. Specify the same connection string that was defined for the service endpoint in the plugin registration tool.

5. We need to create a `QueueClient` object using the connection string and get the remote execution context using the `BrokeredMessage` received. Next, we are retrieving the value for the topic field, the name of the entity and the message on which the plugin was fired from the `RemoteExecutionConext` and writing it to console as shown as follows:

```
// set the connection string of the Shared Access Policy created
for the Queue
var connectionString =
"Endpoint=sb://[namespace].servicebus.windows.net/;SharedAccessKeyN
ame=[KeyName];SharedAccessKey=[KeyValue];EntityPath=[QueueName]";

// create the Queue Client object
var client =
QueueClient.CreateFromConnectionString(connectionString);

while (true)
{
Console.Write("Press [Enter] to retrieve a message from the
queue.");
string line = Console.ReadLine();
Console.WriteLine("Waiting for a message from the queue... ");
try
{
// get the message from the Queue Client
BrokeredMessage brokeredMessage = client.Receive();

// if message recieved
if (brokeredMessage != null)
{
// get the Remote Execution Context passed from the Azure Service
Bus
RemoteExecutionContext context =
brokeredMessage.GetBody<RemoteExecutionContext>();

// cast to Entity object
Entity entity = (Entity)context.InputParameters["Target"];

// get the lead's topic attribute value
var leadTopic = entity.Attributes["subject"].ToString();

// output to console
Console.WriteLine(string.Format("   Entity Name = {0}, Message Name
= {1}, Lead's Topic = {2}",
context.PrimaryEntityName, context.MessageName, leadTopic));
```

```
// marks message as processed and deleted
brokeredMessage.Complete();
}
}
catch (TimeoutException ex)
{
Console.WriteLine(ex.Message);
continue;
}
catch (FaultException ex)
{
Console.WriteLine(ex.Message);
continue;
}
}
```

6. On running our application, we can see the following details passed as `RemoteExecutionContext` to the queue in the output:

```
Press [Enter] to retrieve a message from the queue.
Waiting for a message from the queue...
    Entity Name = lead, Message Name = Create, Lead's Topic = Sample Lead
Press [Enter] to retrieve a message from the queue.
Waiting for a message from the queue...
```

The sample application, when run, will read the message in the queue and print the details in the console.

Here, the **Message Time to Live** property of the queue defines the time span the message will remain in the queue, if not processed. After which it is will be either removed or dead lettered, that is, moved to another secondary sub-queue named dead letter queue. The dead letter queue holds the messages that were not delivered or processed.

Azure Service Bus dead letter queue—https://docs.microsoft.com/en-us/azure/service-bus-messaging/service-bus-dead-letter-queues.

The **Lock Duration** property of the queue specifies the number of seconds for which a message will be locked by a receiver once it receives it. This specifies the time the listener application has to process the message. If not processed, the message will be available to be received by another receiver.

Writing a topic listener

Let us continue with our previous scenario of the creation of a lead record and update it to use topics instead of queues:

1. Log in to Azure Portal to create a topic in Azure Service Bus by clicking on **+Topic**.
2. Add the required details and click on the **Create** button:

3. Inside **Topic**, create a new shared access policy and copy its primary connection string. This connection string will be used while registering a new service endpoint in the plugin registration tool as shown here:

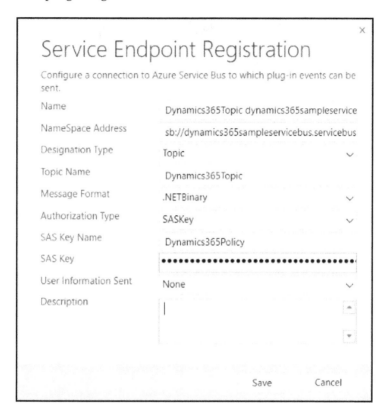

4. Add a new step to this registered service endpoint for it to be triggered by the **Create** of the lead record in Dynamics 365.

5. Now let us go back to our created topic. Click on the **+ Subscription** button inside **Topic** to add a new subscription. Specify required details as shown here and click on **Create**:

6. This creates a new subscription inside **Topic**. We can create multiple subscriptions and each subscription will receive a copy of the message that has been posted to the Azure Service Bus.

7. The following is the sample code for our topic listener application. Here instead of a QueueClient object, we would be using a SubscriptionClient object to read and process the context passed:

```
// set the connection string of the Shared Access Policy created
for the Subscription
// along with name of the Topic and Subscription
```

```
var connectionString =
"Endpoint=sb://[namespace].servicebus.windows.net/;SharedAccessKeyN
ame=[KeyName];SharedAccessKey=[KeyValue];EntityPath=[TopicName]";

var topic = "[topic]";
var subscriptionName = "[subscription]";

// create the Subcription Client object
var client =
SubscriptionClient.CreateFromConnectionString(connectionString,
topic, subscriptionName);

while (true)
{
Console.Write("Press [Enter] to retrieve a message from the
topic.");
string line = Console.ReadLine();
Console.WriteLine("Waiting for a message from the topic... ");
try
{
// get the message from the client
BrokeredMessage brokeredMessage = client.Receive();

// get the Remote Execution Context passed from the Azure Service
Bus
RemoteExecutionContext context =
brokeredMessage.GetBody<RemoteExecutionContext>();

// cast to Entity object
Entity entity = (Entity)context.InputParameters["Target"];

// get the lead's topic attribute value
var leadTopic = entity.Attributes["subject"].ToString();

// output to console
Console.WriteLine(string.Format("  Entity Name = {0}, Message Name
= {1}, Lead's Topic = {2}",
context.PrimaryEntityName, context.MessageName, leadTopic));

// marks message as processed and deleted
brokeredMessage.Complete();
}
catch (TimeoutException ex)
{
Console.WriteLine(ex.Message);
continue;
}
catch (FaultException ex)
```

```
{
Console.WriteLine(ex.Message);
continue;
}
}
```

8. Now, let us go back to Dynamics 365 and create a lead record to trigger our plugin:

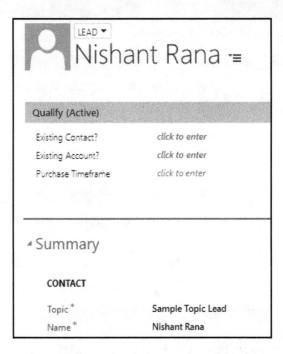

9. Inside our topic, we can see that all the subscriptions created for that topic have received the message:

NAME	STATUS	MESSAGE COUNT
Dynamics365Subscription	Active	1
Dynamics365Subscription1	Active	1

10. Running our subscription listener, we get the expected output:

```
Press [Enter] to retrieve a message from the topic.
Waiting for a message from the topic...
   Entity Name = lead, Message Name = Create, Lead's Topic = Sample Topic Lead
Press [Enter] to retrieve a message from the topic.
```

Until now we have covered how to write a listener application for queues and topics, in the next section we will cover writing listener applications for one-way, two-way and REST contracts.

Writing a one-way listener

Let us walk through all the steps required for writing a one-way listener:

1. Continuing with the same scenario, first, we need to register our service endpoint. For this, create a new shared access policy for the Azure Service Bus namespace. Go to shared access policies settings for the Azure Service Bus and click on **Add** to create a new policy with send and listen rights and copy its primary connection string.

2. Paste the copied connection string in the **Register Service Endpoint** dialog box of the plugin registration tool.

When we create an Azure Service Bus namespace, a policy called `RootManageSharedAccessKey` is automatically created. It has an associated pair of primary and secondary keys that grant send, listen, and manage rights to the Service Bus namespace. It is recommended you create additional policies instead of using this default policy which has all the permissions.

3. Update the value for properties in **Service Endpoint Registration** as shown here:

- **Namespace Address**: Replace `sb` with `https`
- **Designation type**: `OneWay`
- **Path**: `MyPath`

The following screenshot shows the **Service Endpoint Registration** dialog box populated with the appropriate values:

4. Register a step, on the **Create** of the lead record for the service endpoint registered and trigger it by creating a lead record inside Dynamics 365.
5. Go to **Settings** | **System Jobs** and check the corresponding system job created.
6. Here the system job will fail with the following message:

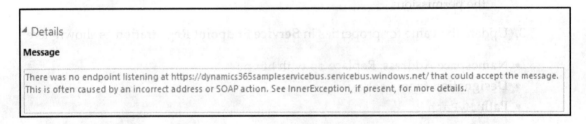

7. As we discussed earlier, for the relay service, an active listener is required, unlike queues or topics.

8. In our one-way listener application, we need to implement the `IServiceEndpointPlugin` **interface and use** `WS2007HttpRelayBinding`.

9. In the following, we are self hosting the service in a console application:

```
[ServiceBehavior]
class AzureExample : IServiceEndpointPlugin
{
static void Main(string[] args)
{
// get the shared access key name
// shared access key value
// service bus endpoint from the Shared Access Policy Connection
String.
var sharedAccessKeyName = "[keyName]";
var sharedAccessKey = "[keyValue]";
var serviceBusEndPoint =
"https://[serviceBusNameSpace].servicebus.windows.net";

// initialize the ServiceHost
var serviceHost = new ServiceHost(typeof(AzureExample));

// define the behaviour
var transportClient = new TransportClientEndpointBehavior
(TokenProvider.CreateSharedAccessSignatureTokenProvider(sharedAcces
sKeyName, sharedAccessKey));

// add the service endpoint
serviceHost.AddServiceEndpoint(typeof(IServiceEndpointPlugin),
new WS2007HttpRelayBinding(),
serviceBusEndPoint).EndpointBehaviors.Add(transportClient);

serviceHost.Open();

Console.ReadLine();
}

void IServiceEndpointPlugin.Execute(RemoteExecutionContext context)
{
// cast to Entity object
Entity entity = (Entity)context.InputParameters["Target"];

// get the lead's topic attribute value
var leadTopic = entity.Attributes["subject"].ToString();

// output to console
Console.WriteLine(string.Format(" Entity Name = {0}, Message Name
= {1}, Lead's Topic = {2}",
```

```
context.PrimaryEntityName, context.MessageName, leadTopic));
    }
  }
```

10. Run the listener application so that it can actively listen for messages passed to it and create the lead record inside Dynamics 365. This will invoke the `Execute` method in our listener application and output the remote execution context details in the console window.

In this section, we learned how to write a one-way listener, in the next section we will cover how to write a two-way listener application.

Writing a two-way listener and an Azure-aware plugin

Let us walk through all the steps in detail for writing a two-way listener:

1. In the case of a two-way contract, we need to implement a custom Azure-aware plugin that can receive the response back from the two-way listener application, but before that let's register a new service endpoint for a two-way contract as shown here:

2. The two-way listener application needs to implement the `ITwoWayServiceEndPointPlugin` interface and use `WS2007HttpRelayBinding`. Also, the `Execute` method returns a string that enables the two-way communication. As mentioned earlier, with relay, it is real time, so the listener needs to be actively listening to the messages, unlike queue and topics.

3. In the following, we are self-hosting the service in a console application:

```
[ServiceBehavior]
class AzureExample : ITwoWayServiceEndpointPlugin
    {
        static void Main(string[] args)
        {
            // get the shared access key name
            // shared access key value
            // service bus endpoint from the Shared Access Policy
            Connection String.
            var sharedAccessKeyName = "RootManageSharedAccessKey";
            var sharedAccessKey = "[KeyValue]";
            var serviceBusEndPoint =
            "https://[ServiceBusNamespace].servicebus.windows.net";

            // initialize the ServiceHost
            var serviceHost = new
ServiceHost(typeof(AzureExample));

            // define the behaviour
            var transportClient = new
            TransportClientEndpointBehavior
        (TokenProvider.CreateSharedAccessSignatureTokenProvider
        (sharedAccessKeyName,
          sharedAccessKey));

            // add the service endpoint
            serviceHost.AddServiceEndpoint
            (typeof(ITwoWayServiceEndpointPlugin),
                new WS2007HttpRelayBinding(),
                serviceBusEndPoint).EndpointBehaviors.
                Add(transportClient);

            serviceHost.Open();

            Console.ReadLine();
        }

        string ITwoWayServiceEndpointPlugin.Execute
```

```
(RemoteExecutionContext context)
{
    // cast to Entity object
    Entity entity =
    (Entity)context.InputParameters["Target"];

    // get the lead's topic attribute value
    var leadTopic =
entity.Attributes["subject"].ToString();

    // output to console
    Console.WriteLine(string.Format
    ("  Entity Name = {0}, Message Name =
    {1},
    Lead's Topic = {2}",
        context.PrimaryEntityName,
        context.MessageName, leadTopic));

    // return the message back to the
    custom azure aware plugin
    return "Message Processed";
}
}
```

4. To read the message returned from the listener application in a two-way relay, let us write a custom Azure-aware plugin.

5. The first thing we need here is the GUID of the service endpoint we registered. We can get the GUID, **ServiceEndpointId** from the properties window of the service endpoint registered as shown here:

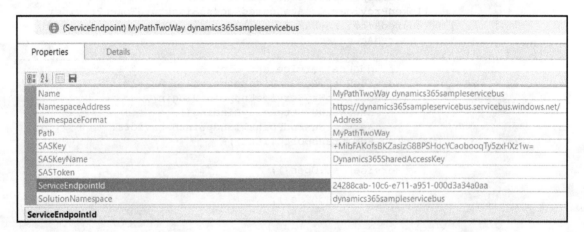

6. Here, `IServiceEndpointNotificationService` will provide us with the service endpoint, for which we will pass the service endpoint entity reference to it.

7. We need to call the `Execute` method of the notification service to post the execution context to the Azure Service Bus. The `Execute` method returns the response received from the listener application, which we are then tracing using the `ITracingService` inside our custom Azure-aware plugin:

```
public class AzureAwarePlugin : IPlugin
    {
        public void Execute(IServiceProvider serviceProvider)
        {
            // set the Service Endpoint Id
            var serviceEndpointId = "[serviceEndpointGUID]";

            // Obtain the execution context from
            the service provider.
            IPluginExecutionContext context =
            (IPluginExecutionContext)
                serviceProvider.GetService
                  (typeof(IPluginExecutionContext));

            //Extract the tracing service for use in debugging
            sandboxed plug-ins.
            ITracingService tracingService =
            (ITracingService)serviceProvider.GetService
            (typeof(ITracingService));

            // Extract the notification service for posting
            execution context
            IServiceEndpointNotificationService
            notificationService =
            (IServiceEndpointNotificationService)
            serviceProvider.GetService(typeof
            (IServiceEndpointNotificationService));

            var response = notificationService.Execute(new
            EntityReference("serviceendpoint", new
            Guid(serviceEndpointId)), context);

            if (!string.IsNullOrEmpty(response))
            {
                tracingService.Trace("Response = {0}", response);
            }
        }
    }
```

8. Register the plugin and add a new step for the **Lead on Create** message to it. The custom Azure-aware plugin can be registered as synchronous, unlike the OOB Azure-aware plugin.

9. Create a lead record to trigger the plugin. Make sure our two-way listener application is running and ready to receive the message.

10. The listener application, on successfully receiving the context passed from the Azure Service Bus, returns the string **Message Processed**.

11. Inside Dynamics 365, go to **Settings** | **Plug-In Trace Log** to verify the same:

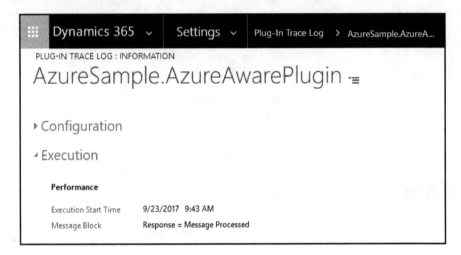

 To enable logging for the Plug-in Trace Log, go to **Settings** | **System Settings** | **Customization** tab. Select **All options** to enable logging to the Plug-in Trace Log field.

In the next section, we will cover how to write REST listener applications, which is similar to the two-way listener application, the main difference being that it uses a REST endpoint.

Writing a REST listener

Let us walk through all the steps in detail for writing a two-way REST listener. As it uses a REST endpoint, it allows us to create a relay service in Node.js which can be executed on multiple platforms such as macOS, Windows, Linux and so on:

1. Before writing a REST listener, let us first register a new service endpoint as shown here:

2. The REST Listener needs to implement the `IWebHttpServiceEndpointPlugin` interface and use `WebHttpRelayBinding`. Here again, we are self hosting the service in a console application:

```
[ServiceBehavior]
class AzureExample : IWebHttpServiceEndpointPlugin
    {
        static void Main(string[] args)
        {
            // get the shared access key name
            // shared access key value
            // service bus endpoint from the Shared
```

```
                                 Access Policy Connection String.
                                  var sharedAccessKeyName = "RootManageSharedAccessKey";
                                  var sharedAccessKey = "[KeyValue]";
                                  var serviceBusEndPoint =
                                 "https://[ServiceBusNamespace].servicebus.windows.net";
                                  // Create the service host for
                                 Azure to post messages to.
                                  var serviceHost = new
                                 WebServiceHost(typeof(AzureExample));

                                  // define the behaviour
                                  var transportClient = new
                                  TransportClientEndpointBehavior
                             (TokenProvider.CreateSharedAccessSignatureTokenProvider
                             (sharedAccessKeyName,
                                  sharedAccessKey));


                                  // Using an HTTP binding instead of a
                                  SOAP binding for this RESTful
                                   endpoint.
                                  WebHttpRelayBinding binding = new
                             WebHttpRelayBinding();
                                  binding.Security.Mode =
                                  EndToEndWebHttpSecurityMode.Transport;

                                  // add the service endpoint
                                  serviceHost.AddServiceEndpoint
                                   (typeof(IWebHttpServiceEndpointPlugin),
                                     binding, serviceBusEndPoint).
                                    EndpointBehaviors.Add(transportClient);

                                  // Begin listening for messages posted to Azure.
                                  serviceHost.Open();

                                  Console.ReadLine();
                          }

                         string IWebHttpServiceEndpointPlugin.
                          Execute(RemoteExecutionContext context)
                         {
                                  // cast to Entity object
                                  Entity entity =
                                  (Entity)context.InputParameters["Target"];

                                  // get the lead's topic attribute value
                                  var leadTopic =
                         entity.Attributes["subject"].ToString();
```

```
                  // output to console
                  Console.WriteLine(string.Format
                  ("  Entity Name = {0}, Message Name =
                  {1},
                   Lead's Topic = {2}",
                      context.PrimaryEntityName,
                      context.MessageName, leadTopic));

                  // return the message back to the
                  custom azure aware plugin
                  return "Message Processed by Rest Listener";
              }

          }
```

3. Back in Dynamics 365, create a lead record to trigger the plugin, which calls the `Execute` method of the listener application. The listener, on receiving the message, returns the string **Message Processed by Rest Listener**, which is traced by the plugin in the Plug-in Trace Logs as shown here:

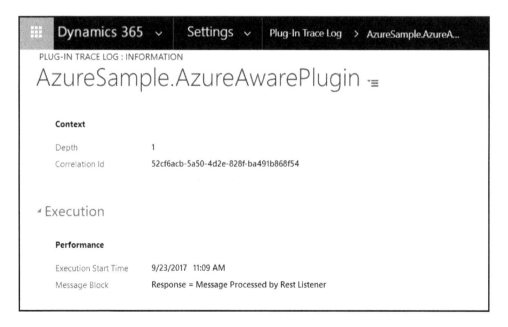

In this section, we learned how to write a REST listener, in the next section we will cover how to write an event hub listener application.

Writing an event hub listener

Let us walk through all the steps in detail for writing an event hub listener. To create an event hub listener:

1. Go to Azure Portal, search for event hubs, and create a new event hubs namespace.
2. Select **Event Hubs** inside **Event Hubs Namespace** and click on **Add Event Hub** to create a new event hub.
3. For the event hub created, add a new `SharedAccessKey` with appropriate rights and copy its connection string and use it while registering a new service endpoint in the plugin registration tool as shown here:

4. Add a step to trigger the plugin on **Create** of the Lead record.
5. For the event hub listener application, create a new console application, add the following NuGet Package in it—`WindowsAzure.ServiceBus`.

6. The following is the sample code for our event hub listener application. Here we are using the `EventHubClient` object to create the receiver:

```
var connectionString =
"Endpoint=sb://[namespace].servicebus.windows.net/;SharedAccessKeyN
ame=[KeyName];SharedAccessKey=[KeyValue];EntityPath=[QueueName]";

// create the Event Hub Client object
var client =
EventHubClient.CreateFromConnectionString(connectionString);

// create the event hub reciever
EventHubConsumerGroup consumerGroup =
client.GetDefaultConsumerGroup();
var eventHubReciever =
consumerGroup.CreateReceiver(client.GetRuntimeInformation().Partiti
onIds[0]);

while (true)
{
Console.Write("Press [Enter] to retrieve a message from the Event
Hub.");
string line = Console.ReadLine();
Console.WriteLine("Waiting for a message from the eventhub... ");

// call the Recieve method
var message = eventHubReciever.Receive();

// get the JSON result
string jsonResult = Encoding.UTF8.GetString(message.GetBytes());
// output to window
Console.WriteLine("JSON Output" + jsonResult);
}
```

7. Create a new lead inside Dynamics 365.

8. Running our event hub listener, we see the expected JSON output inside the console:

```
Press [Enter] to retrieve a message from the Event Hub.
Waiting for a message from the eventhub...
JSON Output{"BusinessUnitId":"3533cccb-0cb4-e711-a82c-000d3a33a7cb","CorrelationId":"e7980cb5-2c9b
-4683-be09-5f2489f4e444","Depth":1,"InitiatingUserId":"4457e7b8-7196-4e33-83a8-0590869db0fa","Inpu
tParameters":[{"key":"Target","value":{"__type":"Entity:http:\/\/schemas.microsoft.com\/xrm\/2011\
/Contracts","Attributes":[{"key":"confirminterest","value":false},{"key":"statecode","value":{"__t
ype":"OptionSetValue:http:\/\/schemas.microsoft.com\/xrm\/2011\/Contracts","Value":0}},{"key":"add
ress2_shippingmethodcode","value":{"__type":"OptionSetValue:http:\/\/schemas.microsoft.com\/xrm\/2
011\/Contracts","Value":1}},{"key":"isprivate","value":false},{"key":"followemail","value":true},{
"key":"msdyn_ordertype","value":{"__type":"OptionSetValue:http:\/\/schemas.microsoft.com\/xrm\/201
```

The recommended way to receive events from event hubs is by using the event processor host—`https://docs.microsoft.com/en-us/azure/event-hubs/event-hubs-dotnet-standard-api-overview#event-processor-host-apis`. (The source code for the chapter includes the example of receiving events using the event processor.)

Summary

In this chapter, we covered Azure Extensions provided within Dynamics 365 and how to configure and write listener applications for different supported contract types.

In the next chapter, we will look at the new Editable Grid introduced with CRM 2016 and different properties that are supported.

9
Using Editable Grids in Apps

The Editable Grid feature in Dynamics 365 allows end users to update records from a view or grid directly, which makes updating records more convenient and easy. It is also possible to do the same task using an Excel sheet, but to update data with an Excel sheet takes more time than editing records from the grid.

In this chapter, we will be covering the following points related to Editable Grid:

- Overview of Editable Grid
- Prerequisite privileges required for Editable Grid
- Supported entity, views, and fields to Editable Grid
- Steps required to configure Editable Grid
- Using JavaScript for Editable Grid
- Using business rules for Editable Grid
- Editable Grid on mobile devices

Overview of Editable Grid in Dynamics 365

Editable grids support a wide variety of features. The following list outlines the main CRM components supported by Editable Grid:

- Entity or sub-grid level record editing
- Personal views as well as system views
- Mobile clients
- Keyboard or mouse navigation support
- Record grouping and sorting

- Record filtering
- Grid columns moving and resizing
- Pagination (supports sub-grid with multiple records to fit on grid view)
- Saving changes from one session to another for grouping, sorting, filtering, pagination, and moving and resizing columns
- Lookup fields
- Rollup fields and calculated fields
- Security role
- JavaScript events
- Business rules
- End users using charts and search can also access the action bar with the help of read-only grids

Prerequisite and security privileges required for configuring Editable Grid

Before we discuss how to configure Editable Grid in Dynamics 365, it is important to understand the prerequisite security privileges, which are required for a particular user before being able to configure editable grids. The following table summarizes the minimum privileges required to configure Editable Grid in Dynamics 365:

S. no.	Entity name	Read	Write	Create
1.	Solution	Yes	-	-
2.	Customization	Yes	Yes	-

A detailed look at the security roles areas via CRM screens is as follows:

1. Navigate to **Settings** | **Security Roles** and update **Read** and **Write** privileges for **Customizations**, as shown in the following screenshot:

2. Navigate to **Settings** | **Security Roles** and update **Read** and **Write** privileges for **Solution**, as shown in the following screenshot:

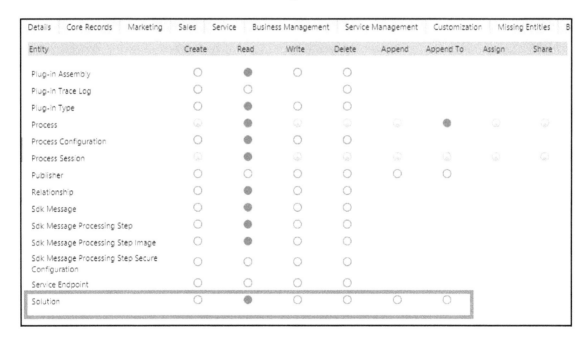

 Note: System Administrator and System Customizer roles already have available required prerequisite privileges to configure Dynamics 365 editable grids. The preceding security privileges need to be configured in case certain security roles other than the previously mentioned ones need access to create or edit a Dynamics 365 Editable Grid.

Entities and views supported by Editable Grid

Most of the out-of-the-box entities, views, and so on, support editable grids; however, certain entities and views do not support Editable Grid in Dynamics 365.

Few conditions are required if you want to configure Editable Grid for an entity. The following mentioned are the conditions need to be fulfilled when configuring an Editable Grid:

- Entity is customizable
- Entity should be a reference or custom entity
- Entity should not be a child entity

Editable subgrid supports all the view types in Dynamics 365, except RollUp and associated views.

The following sections outline the list of entities supported for editable grids based on the platform (web/tablet/phone).

Supported out-of-the-box entities

Web/tablet/phone

The following table outlines entities that are supported by web, tablet, and phone user interface of Dynamics 365:

Account	Case	Knowledge Article Views	Rating Model
Appointment	Category	Knowledge Base Record	Rating Value
Bookable Resource	Characteristic	Lead	SLA KPI Instance
Bookable Resource Booking	Competitor	Opportunity	Social Activity

Bookable Resource Booking Header	Contact	Order	Social Profile
Bookable Resource Category	Email	Phone Call	Sync Error
Bookable Resource Category Assn.	Entitlement	Price List	Task
Bookable Resource Characteristic	Feedback	Product	Team
Bookable Resource Group	Invoice	Queue	User
Booking Status	Knowledge Article	Quote	-

Tablet/phone only

The following table outlines entities that are supported by tablet and phone user interface of Dynamics 365:

Activity	Email Template	Note	Process
Attachment	Expired Process	Opportunity Product	Queue Item
Channel Access Profile Rule Item	Invoice Product	Opportunity Sales Process	Quote Product
Competitor Address	Knowledge Article Incident	Order Product	Sharepoint Document
Connection	Lead to Opportunity Sales	Organization	Translation Process
Connection Role	Mailbox	Phone to Case Process	-
Email Signature	New Process	Price List Item	-

Web only

The following table outlines entities that are supported by the web user interface of Dynamics 365:

Campaign	Channel Access Profile Rule	Fax	Quick Campaign
Campaign Activity	Contract	Letter	Recurring Appointment
Campaign Response	Entitlement Template	Marketing List	Sales Literature
Channel Access Profile	External Party	Position	SLA

Supported and unsupported data types by Editable Grid

Editable Grid supports most of the field types available in Dynamics 365. The following field types are supported Editable Grid:

- Single line of text
- Multiple lines of text
- Option set
- Multi-select option set
- Two options
- Status reason
- Whole number
- Floating point number
- Decimal number
- Currency
- Date and time
- Image

The following field types are not supported in an Editable Grid:

- State
- Customer type field
- Composite field
- Party list
- Related entity fields based on a lookup field

Configuring editable grids for main entity views

Now that we have a basic understanding of the supported entities, views, and field types available with Editable Grid, we will have a look at configuring editable grids for an entity.

Let's look at an example of this feature on the view of an **Accounts** entity. When editable grids are configured for any entity, all the views available for the selected entity are editable.

Following are the steps to follow to configure the editable grids in Dynamics 365 for an Account entity:

1. Go to **Settings** | **Customizations**, as shown in the following screenshot:

2. Select **Customize the System**, as shown in the following screenshot:

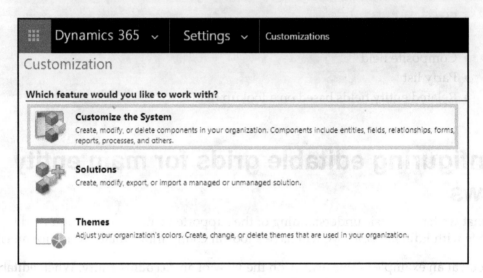

3. Select **Account** entity, as shown in the following screenshot:

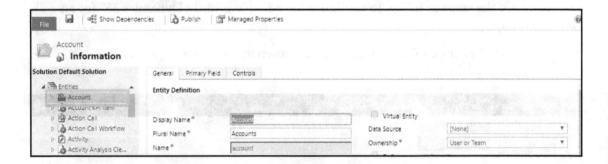

4. Select **Control**, then click on **Add Control...**, as shown in the following screenshot:

5. On the **Add Control** dialog box, select **Editable Grid**, and then click on the **Add** button, as shown in the following screenshot:

6. In the **Editable Grid** row that is added, select the form factor you want to apply the grid to. This makes the editable grid control the default control for the selected form factor. We are selecting the **Web** option in this particular example:

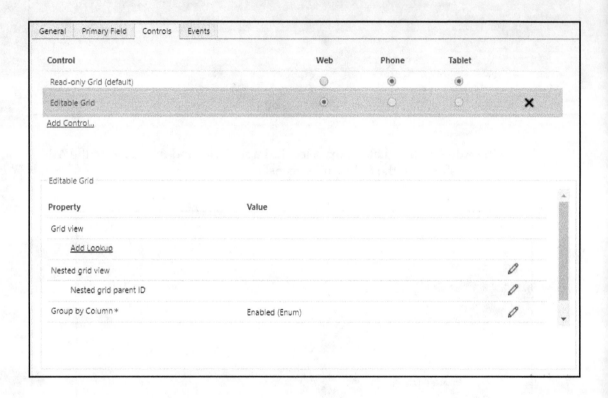

7. Now, save the changes and **Publish** it, as shown in the following screenshot:

8. To see the changes, navigate to **Accounts** entity. Click on any of the entity rows in the current view and try to edit the **Address** field:

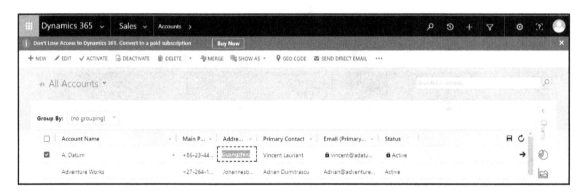

9. After you are done with editing the fields, click on the **Save** button to save your changes to Account entity records.

Configuring editable sub-grid for forms

The editable grid can also be configured for sub-grids on Dynamics 365 entity forms. Editable grids make it convenient to edit related records from a Parent entity form. For example, a user can be on an **Accounts** entity form and may wish to update related contacts available on it.

Here, we will be creating an editable subgrid for contacts on an Account entity form. The following steps will make a contacts sub-grid of the **Accounts** entity editable by users:

1. Go to **Settings | Customization**, as shown in the following screenshot:

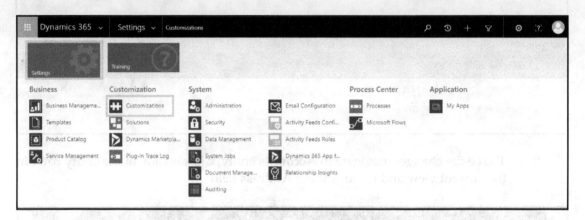

2. Click on **Customize the system**, as shown in the following screenshot:

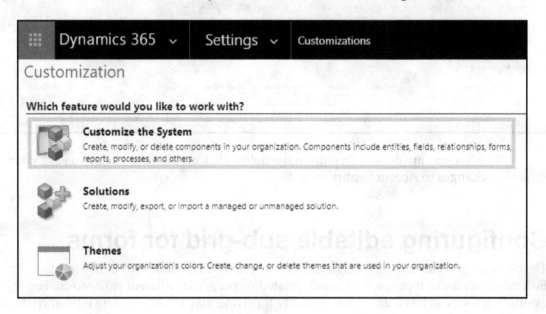

3. Click on the **Account** entity and select **Forms**, as shown in the following screenshot:

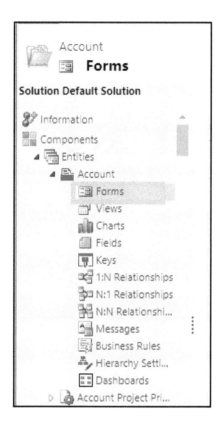

4. Select the **Main** form of **Account** and open it:

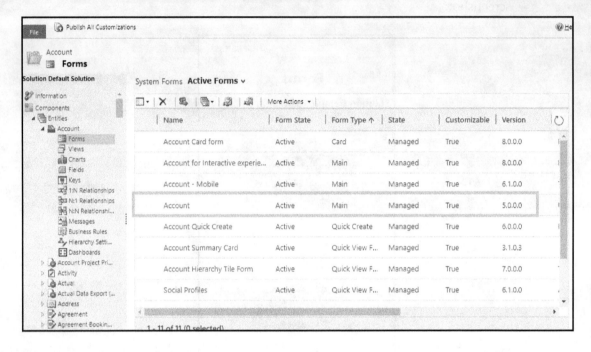

5. Select the appropriate **CONTACTS** subgrid, and then click **Change Properties** on the ribbon:

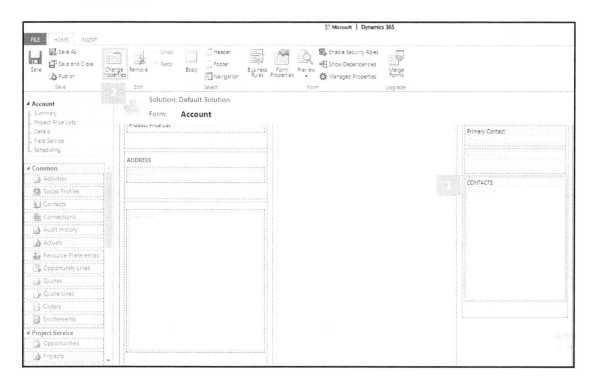

6. In the **Set Properties** dialog box, select **Controls**, click **Add Control**, and then
   follow the same steps listed earlier:

7. On the **Add Control** dialog box, select **Editable Grid**:

8. Select the web option to subgrid, then the OK button. **Save** the form as follows:

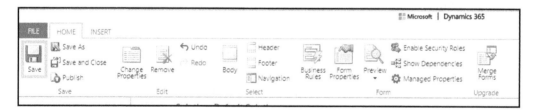

9. After saving, **Publish** it:

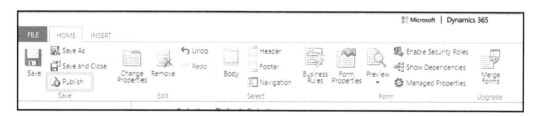

10. To see the changes, go to an account record and check contact sub-grid:

Using JavaScript in Editable Grid

JavaScript is used in Dynamics 365 to provide customer-side validation, and for other client-side requirements. Editable grids also support JavaScript. The editable grid supports three types of events, which are mentioned in the following points:

- **OnRecordSelect** – This event is triggered when the user selects a record in an editable grid
- **OnChange** – This event is triggered when any of the columns on the editable grid entity row is changed
- **OnSave** – This event is triggered by the **Save** button

The following gives a brief example of using JavaScript with Editable Grid:

Following is a scenario, which we will implement on an editable grid for opportunity:

- If the probability is greater than 70%, then set the rating of opportunity to **hot**
- If the probability is between 50% to 69%, then set the rating to **warm**
- If the probability is less than 50%, then set the rating to **cold**

Prerequisite: To start working on this example, first add out of box fields, namely `Rating` and `Probability`, to any of the views of the opportunity entity. Also, configure the opportunity entity main grid to Editable Grid, using the instructions explained earlier in this chapter.

1. Create a new JavaScript Web resource `OpportunitySetRating`, and use the following code in it:

```
function OpportunitySetRating(executionContext) {
  //Get opportunity entity
  var OpportunityObject =
   executionContext.getFormContext().data.entity;
  //Get Attributes from Opportunity record
  var probablityAttribute =
   OpportunityObject.attributes.getByName("closeprobability");
  var ratingAttribute =
   OpportunityObject.attributes.getByName("opportunityratingcode");
  //Rating options
  var hotRatingOption = 1;
  var warmRatingOption = 2;
  var coldRatingOption = 3;
  //Check Probability attribute contain data
  if (probablityAttribute != null) {
```

```
//Check probablityValue attribute contain data
var probablityValue = probablityAttribute.getValue();

// Check Probability Value
if (probablityValue < 50) {
    ratingAttribute.setValue(coldRatingOption);
}
else
    if (probablityValue > 50 && probablityValue < 70) {
        ratingAttribute.setValue(warmRatingOption);
    }
    else
        if (probablityValue > 70) {
            ratingAttribute.setValue(hotRatingOption);
        }
// End of if else
    }
}
```

2. After enabling the **Editable Grid** on an Opportunity entity (which is mentioned as a prerequisite), click on the **Events** tab under entity customization settings:

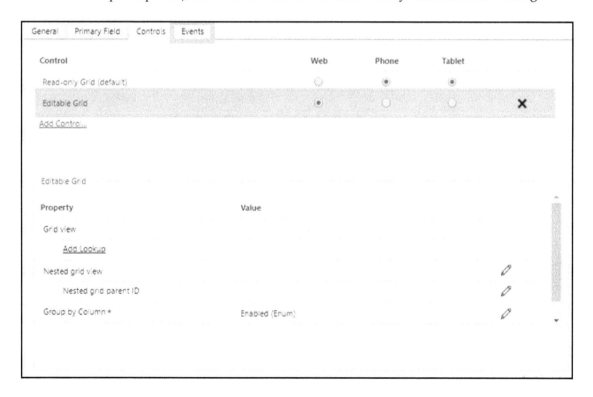

3. Add the newly-created JavaScript web resource to **Form Libraries**:

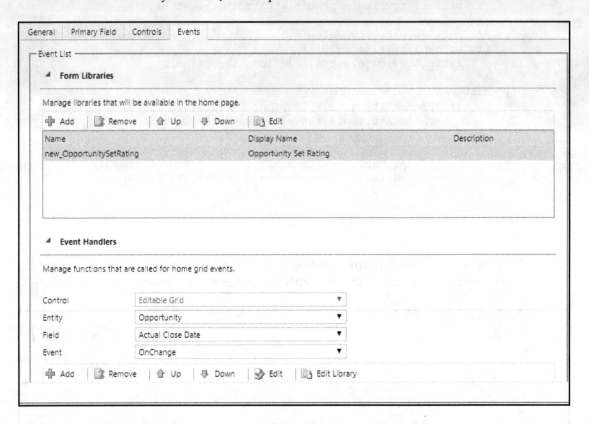

4. On **Event Handlers**, select the **Field** as **Probability** and select
   Event OnChange (similarly, you may choose handlers for **OnSave**, and
   OnRecordSelect in case they're needed. We are not using them in the current
   example):

General   Primary Field   Controls   Events

◢ **Event Handlers**

Manage functions that are called for home grid events.

Control	Editable Grid ▼
Entity	Opportunity ▼
Field	Probability ▼
Event	OnChange ▼

➕ Add   ☒ Remove   ⬆ Up   ⬇ Down   ✍ Edit   📖 Edit Library

5. Set the **Event Handlers** property for the event as **OpportunitySetRating** (mention the function name from the JavaScript Web Resource):

Handler Properties   ✕

Details   Dependencies

Library   new_OpportunitySetRating   ▼

*Function   OpportunitySetRating

☑ Enabled

Parameters

☑ Pass execution context as first parameter

Comma separated list of parameters that will be passed to the function

                                                        OK   Cancel

6. Finally, save the changes and **Publish** all customizations:

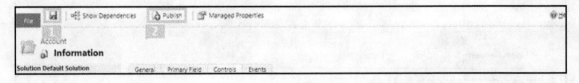

Save and publish

5. Now, navigate to the Opportunity entity and select the view to which you added the **Rating** and **Probability** fields. When you change the value of **Probability**, you will notice changes in the **Rating** field:

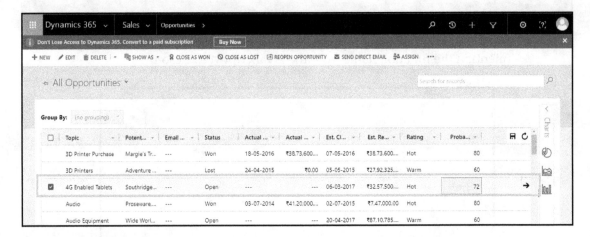

Editable Grid and business rules

In Dynamics 365, Business Rules provides a convenient way to apply validations to the fields of an entity. The Business Process Flow will trigger on changing the value of a field to perform specified operations. Editable Grid supports business rules in Dynamics 365. Editable Grid supports the following business rules operations:

- Show error message
- Set field value
- Set business required
- Set default value
- Lock or unlock field

To use Business Rules on Editable Grid, there is no need to do more configuration. You can achieve this by making a simple business rule on form level. This business rule will be in action when you change a record's data on the editable grid.

We will create a simple business rule to unlock the main phone field if the preferred method of contact is a phone, or otherwise lock that field. Following are the steps to follow to apply business rules to an editable grid:

1. Go to **Settings** | **Customization**, as shown in the following screenshot:

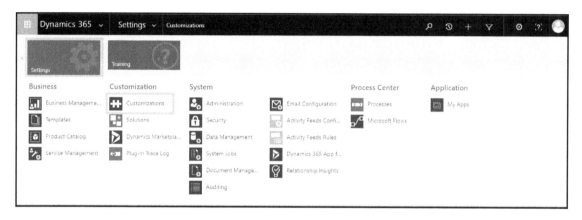

2. Click on **Customize the System**, as shown in the following screenshot:

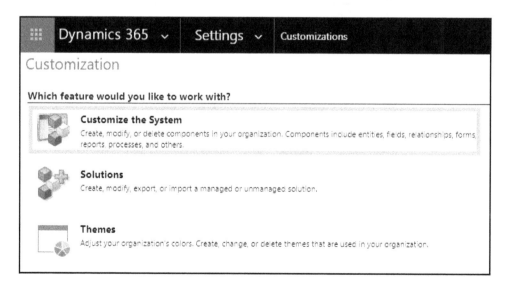

3. Now, expand the **Account** entity and click on **Views**, as shown in the following screenshot:

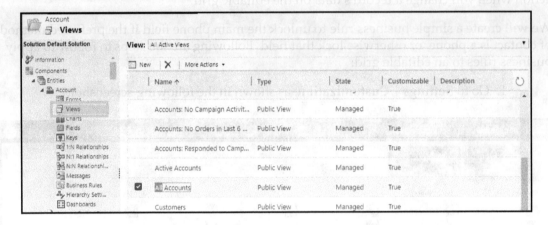

4. Select the **All Accounts** view and add two columns:

    1. **Preferred Method Of Contact**

    2. **Main Phone**

This is demonstrated in the following screenshot:

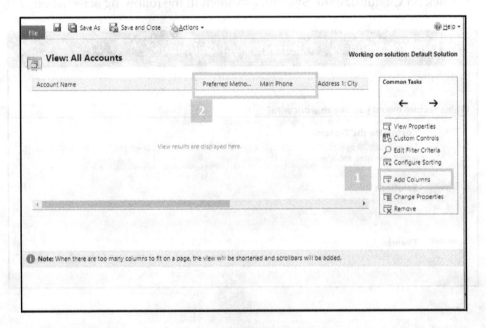

5. Now create a new Business Rule, as mentioned earlier. Add a **Condition** to check whether the Preferred Method of Contact value is a phone, then add a **Lock/Unlock** rule of the main phone to unlock, on else condition set add **Lock/Unlock** rule of the main phone to lock:

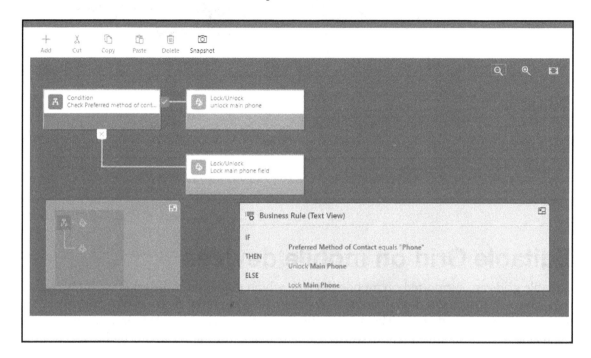

6. When you are done with the preceding steps, set the scope of the business rule to **Entity**:

7. Save and activate the business rule, and make sure you publish all the changes you made earlier.

8. Now, navigate to the Account entity and select the **All Accounts** view. You will notice the fields on View now change the value of the preferred method field, and check the result:

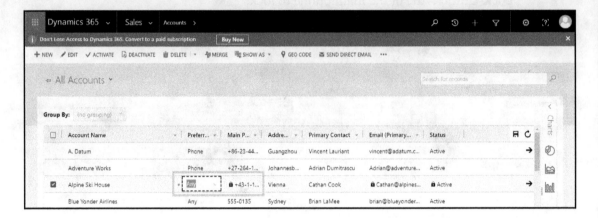

Editable Grid on mobile devices

Editable grids are supported on mobile devices, which makes editable grids useful because they save users time and data on mobile devices. There are other features that are only supported by mobile devices. The main distinct feature is that Editable Grid is available on the dashboards of mobile devices, which is not available for the web. This makes an editable grid a more powerful feature on mobile devices.

Let's make Active cases view as editable, which is available on mobile device dashboards.

Following are the steps for making an editable grid allow viewing on dashboards for mobile devices:

1. Go to **Settings** | **Customization**, as shown in the following screenshot:

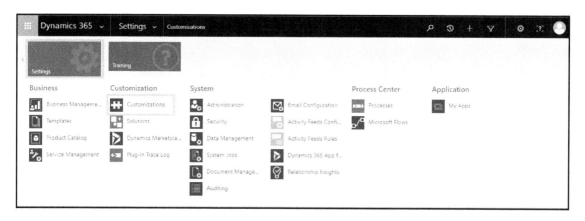

2. Click on **Customize the System**, as shown in the following screenshot:

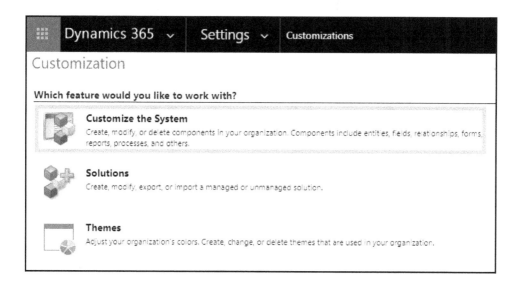

3. Expand **Entity**, and select the **Case** entity. Add an **Editable Grid** control on Case entity, and also make sure it is available for a phone:

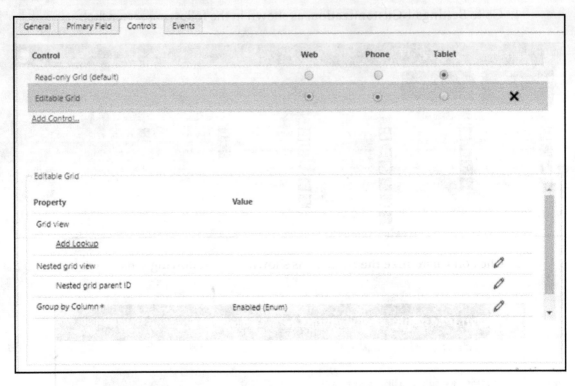

Editable Grids under Control tab

4. Save and publish the changes you have made:

Save and publish

5. To see results, open the Dynamics 365 mobile application and navigate to **Cases**:

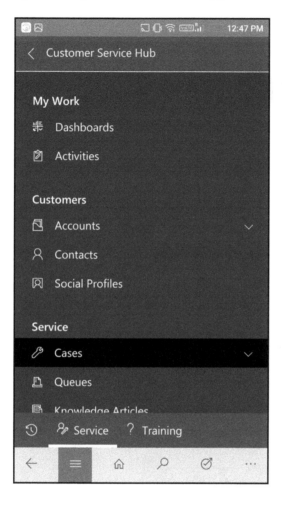

6. When the **Case** record appears onscreen, select record on case record and edit record topic, like so:

Summary

In this chapter, we have seen Editable Grid features they are supported on the web and mobile platforms. We also discussed different supported and unsupported entities, views, and fields that support Editable Grid.

In the next chapter, we will learn all about configuring Microsoft cognitive services.

10
Configure Microsoft Cognitive services

In Chapter 9, *Using Editable Grids in Apps*, we learned how to configure Editable Grid and how to make use of different methods and events supported by the Grid. In this chapter, we will look into Microsoft Cognitive Services and how to integrate them with Dynamics 365. Microsoft Cognitive Services is a collection of APIs, which can be used to add artificial intelligence capabilities into applications.

 The Cognitive Services Integration with Dynamics 365 is still in Public Preview and is only available for instances in the **United States** (**US**) region.

In this chapter, we will be covering the following points:

- Overview of Microsoft Cognitive Services
- Connect Dynamics 365 with Microsoft Cognitive Services
- Implement Text Analytics APIs for suggesting knowledge articles, similar cases, and document suggestions

Understanding Microsoft Cognitive Services

Microsoft Cognitive Services can be defined as a collection of APIs that can be easily configured and consumed to bring powerful artificial intelligence capabilities to applications, websites, and bots. Microsoft Cognitive Services are standard JSON-based REST APIs which can be consumed from a number of popular languages like Curl, C#, Java, JavaScript, PHP, Python, and so on. Early in 2015, Microsoft had released a set of technologies under Project Oxford that allowed developers to build more intelligent apps incorporating Machine Learning aspects, which was then later rebranded to Microsoft Cognitive Services. Currently, Microsoft Cognitive Services consists of different APIs such as Computer Vision API, Video API, Bing Speech API, Text Analytics API, Recommendations API, Bing Image Search API, and so on, categorized into Vision, Speech, Language, Knowledge and Speech.

 A list of different Microsoft Cognitive Services APIs is available at `https:/ /azure.microsoft.com/en-in/services/cognitive-services/ directory/`.

Let us have a quick look at these different APIs:

- **Vision APIs**: These allow an app to recognize faces, emotions, and understand images and videos. It includes Computer Vision API, Video API, Face API, Emotion API, and so on. To see Face API in action, we can browse to `https:// azure.microsoft.com/en-us/services/cognitive-services/face/` and can submit an image, and Face API will analyze the image and will return the result in JSON as shown in the following screenshot, in the Detection result:

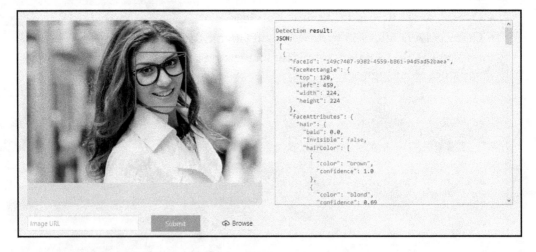

- **Speech APIs**: These allow an app to recognize speech, convert speech to text and text to speech. It includes Speech Recognition API and Text to Speech API. Too see Speech API in action, browse to `https://azure.microsoft.com/en-us/services/cognitive-services/speech/`and either play any of the samples or start recording. The Speech Recognition API will convert the spoken word to text as shown here:

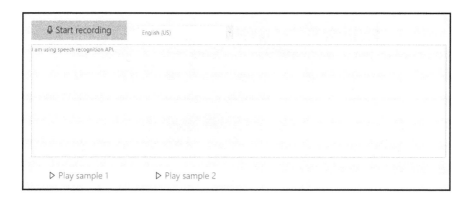

- **Language APIs**: This allows an app to evaluate sentiment and topics to understand what users want, detect and correct a misspelling and other capabilities. It includes Text Analytics API, Translator Text API, Bing Spell Check API and so on. To see spell check capabilities in action, browse to `https://azure.microsoft.com/en-us/services/cognitive-services/spell-check/`. On entering `Spell` incorrectly as `Spel` and clicking on **Submit**, it is autocorrected to **Spell** as shown in the following screenshot:

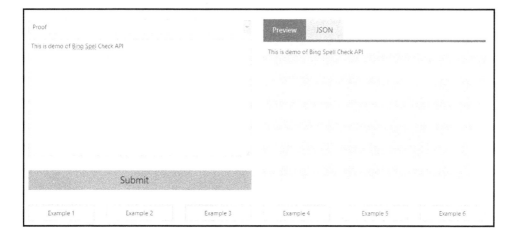

- **Knowledge APIs**: This allows an app to give recommendations based on customers, wants, decision-making capabilities and integration with a rich knowledge base collected from the web, academics, and so on. It includes Recommendation API, QnA Maker API, Academic Knowledge API, and so on. An organization can use Recommendation API to understand sales behavior and recommend related products to customers during purchase, which can result in increased sales. To see the QnA Maker API in action, browse to `https://azure.microsoft.com/en-us/services/cognitive-services/qna-maker/`and search for a particular keyword. Searching for `Login` matches with the question **how do I login to the qna maker portal?** and returns the appropriate answer as shown in the following screenshot:

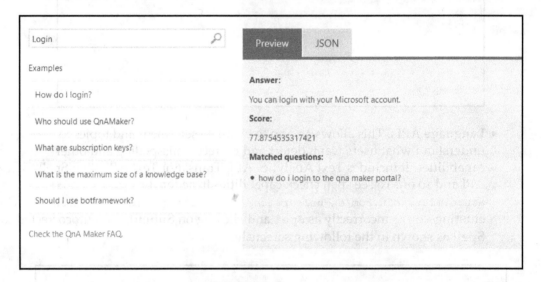

- **Search APIs**: Using this, an app can have access to web pages, images, videos, news and so on, along with autosuggestion capabilities using the power of Bing APIs. It includes Bing Autosuggest API, Bing Image Search API, Bing News Search API, Bing Web Search API and so on. To see the Bing News Search API in action, browse to `https://azure.microsoft.com/en-us/services/cognitive-services/bing-news-search-api/` and search for `Dynamics 365`. The Bing New Search API will respond with all the news pertaining to the Dynamics 365 as shown in the following screenshot:

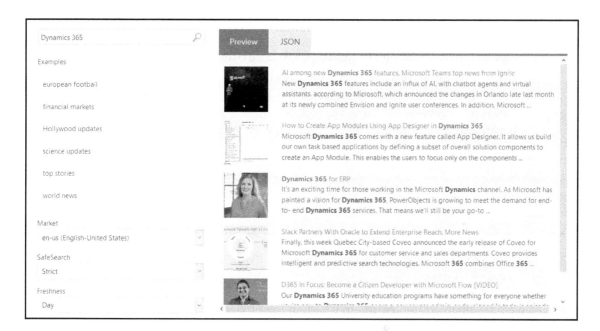

Documentation, quick starts, tutorials and samples for Cognitive Services are available at `https://docs.microsoft.com/en-us/azure/#pivot=productspanel=cognitive`.

Enabling Dynamics 365 Microsoft Cognitive Services Integration

The Cognitive Services Integration with Microsoft Dynamics 365 was introduced with the December 2016 Update for Dynamics 365 Online. The Cross-sell Product Recommendations Preview and Case Topic Analysis preview using Text Analytics Topic Detection API that was introduced with the December 2016 Update are no longer available in the Dynamics 365 July 2017 Update.

Microsoft recommends using Product Relationships for cross-sell product recommendations instead of Recommendation API, as this feature will be removed as of February 15, 2018. `https://www.microsoft.com/en-US/dynamics/crm-customer-center/define-related-products-to-increase-chances-of-sales.aspx`.

To enable Microsoft Cognitive Services Integration in Dynamics 365:

1. Open Dynamics 365, go to **Settings | Administration**
2. Click on **System Settings**, open the **Preview** tab
3. Select **Yes** for **Enable the Dynamics 365 Text Analytics Preview** under **Text Analytics Preview for Case Topic analysis, Suggest Similar Cases and Suggest Knowledge Articles** section

---

Text Analytics Preview for Case Topic analysis, Suggest Similar Cases and Suggest Knowledge Articles

Enable the Dynamics Dynamics 365 Text Analytics Preview   ● Yes ○ No

⚓ For more information, see the Dynamic 365 Customer Center

---

4. Select **OK** for the **Text Analytics Preview Confirmation** dialog box, to give your consent to share your data with the Azure Machine Learning Text Analytics API

Now, as we have enabled the feature in CRM, in the next section we will connect Text Analytics API with Dynamics 365.

Connecting Text Analytics API with Dynamics 365

To connect Dynamics 365 with Cognitive Services:

1. Go to **Settings|Administration** and select **Azure Machine Learning Text Analytics Service Configuration**
2. Give your consent to share the data by clicking on **Continue**
3. For configuring the Text Analytics Connection, we would need the Azure Service URL and the Azure Account Key
4. Log in to the Azure Portal `https://azure.microsoft.com/en-us/free/` using an existing account or set up a free trial `https://azure.microsoft.com/en-us/free/`

5. Click on **Create** to create a new Text Analytics API service under **AI + Cognitive Services**

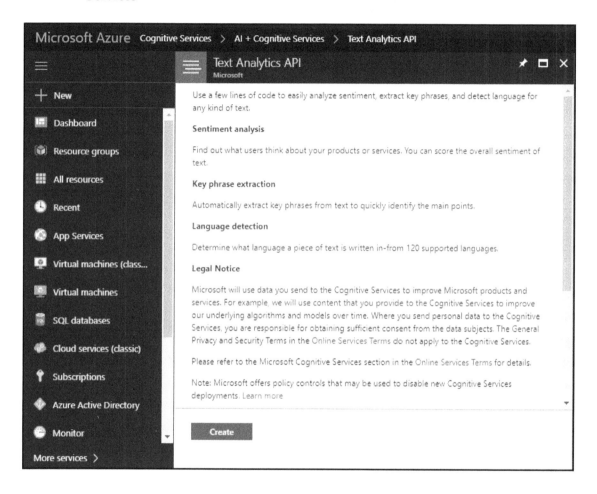

6. Provide required details such as Name, Subscription, Location, Pricing, and Resource Group. Check the confirmation box and click on **Create**:

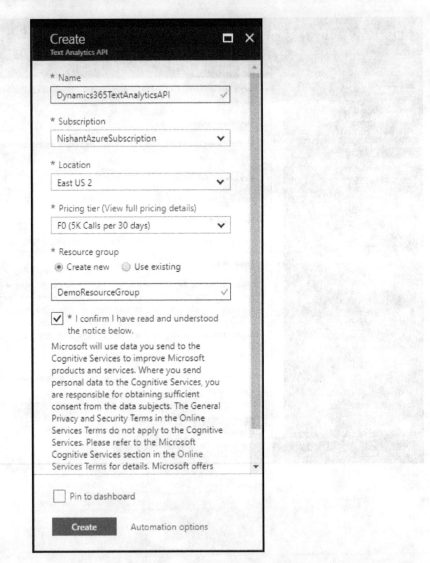

7. Open the **Text Analytics API** created, go to the **Overview** section and copy the Endpoint

8. Similarly, go to the Keys section, under Resource Management, and copy the Key's value

9. Paste the values in the **Azure Service URL** and **Azure Account Key** fields in **Text Analytics Connection inside Dynamics 365** and click on the **Test Connection** button to validate the connection. The **Last Connection Status** field will show the status as **Success** on successful verification. Click on **Activate** to enable the connection as shown in the following screenshot:

In this section, we successfully connected Text Analytics API with Dynamics 365. In the next section, we will see how we can make use of Text Analytics API to suggest similar KB Articles to users.

Configuring Knowledge Base Suggestions in Dynamics 365

Through Knowledge Base Suggestions, Dynamics 365 can suggest similar Knowledge Base articles to the user related to the case the user is working on. This can help the user to quickly resolve the case, which would result in higher customer satisfaction.

For enabling Knowledge Base Suggestions, first, we need to set up a knowledge search field in Dynamics 365:

1. Go to **Settings** | **Service Management** and select **Knowledge Search Field Settings.**
2. Click on **New** to create a **KNOWLEDGE SEARCH MODEL** as shown in the following screenshot:

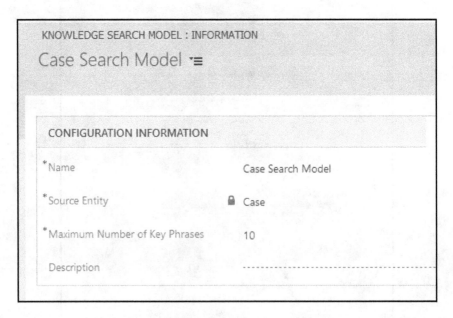

3. For a **KNOWLEDGE SEARCH MODEL** record:
   - **Name:** Name specifies the name of the model.
   - **Source entity:** Source entity specifies the entity to enable a text search rule for finding matching records. Out of the box, we can select **Case Entity**. To enable it for any other entity, we need to open that entity for customization and enable **Knowledge Management** under **Communication & Collaboration**. In the following screenshot, it is seen that we have enabled **Knowledge Management** for the Lead Entity:

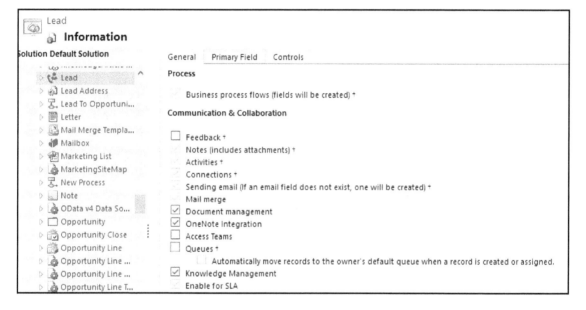

   - **Maximum number of key phrases:** This specifies a maximum number of key phrases to be taken into consideration. Allowed values are between 0 to 1,000.
   - **Description:** This specifies the optional description for the model.

4. After creating the model, next we need to define the fields which will be used for a keyword or key phrase determination. Here, we have defined a **Text Analytics Entity Mappings** record on the **Case Title** field of case entity, as shown in the following screenshot:

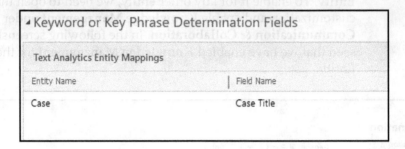

5. For a **Text Analytics Entity Mappings** record:
   - **Entity name:** Specifies the source entities which have Knowledge Management enabled. Here Activity Entities and Entities having $1 - N$ or $N - 1$ relationship to the source entity can be selected
   - **Field name:** Specifies Single Line of text, Multiple Line of text and Option Set fields of the selected entity for finding matching knowledge base records.

6. Click on **ACTIVATE** to enable the Model, as shown in the following screenshot:

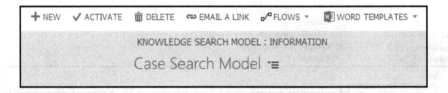

7. Update the Case form to add the Knowledge Base Suggestions. Enable **Turn on automatic suggestions** and select **Text Analytics** in the **Give knowledge base (KB) suggestions using** field, as shown in the following screenshot:

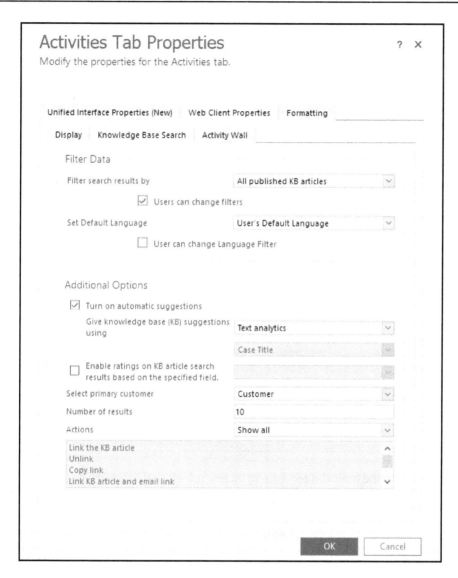

8. Click **OK** to close the properties dialog box and click **Save** and **Publish** the form.

9. To see it in action, open any of the case records, and go to KB records. Here, based on the Case title—that is, **Need help with 3D printer components**, clicking on the **KB RECORDS** tab shows the corresponding Knowledge Based article matching the title of the case, as shown in the following screenshot:

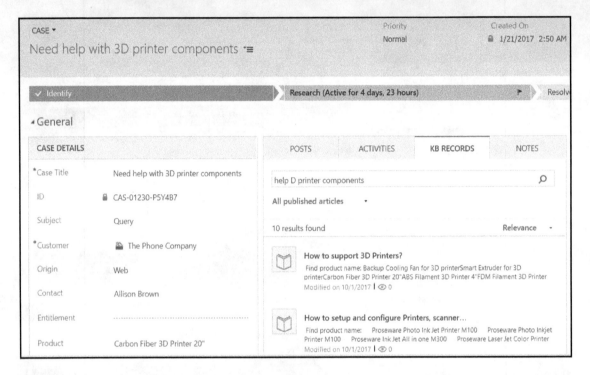

Similarly, we can define a model for a Lead entity (or any other entity having Knowledge Management enabled) based on the Topic field as a keyword or key phrase determination field, and can customize the lead to include KB Records suggestions. Based on the **Topic**, that is, **Audio**, the **KB RECORDS** suggests a KB article having **Audio** in its title, as shown in the following screenshot:

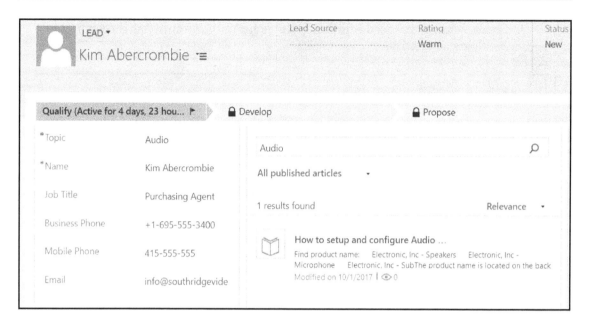

In this section, we covered configuring Knowledge Base Suggestions, in the next section, we will learn how to configure Dynamics 365 for similar records suggestions.

Configuring Similar Records Suggestions in Dynamics 365

Through Similar Record Suggestions, users while working on a particular record inside Dynamics 365, can quickly find similar records and can use this information to better serve their customers. For example, while working on a case, users can find similar cases and can use the information in those similar cases to resolve the current case.

To configure Similar Records Suggestions in Dynamics 365:

1. Connect Text Analysis Connection with Dynamics 365, which we have already done earlier
2. Inside Dynamics 365, go to **Settings** | **Data Management** and select **Similar Records Suggestions Settings.**

3. Create a new **Advanced Similarity Rules** for the Case entity as shown in the following screenshot:

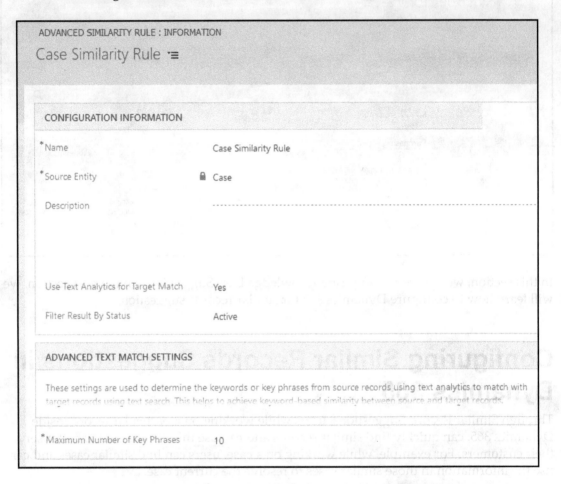

In the **ADVANCED SIMILARITY RULE** record:

- **Name**: Specifies the name of the rule.
- **Source Entity**: Specifies the entity on which the rule is being configured. It supports **Lead, Opportunity, Contact, Account, Case**, or a custom entity that has N - N relationship with them.
- **Description**: Specifies the optional description of the rule.
- **Use Text Analytics for Target Match**: Specifies whether to use the Text Analytics service or Dynamics 365 for keyword matching.

- **Filter Result by Status**: Specifies filter criteria for the result. For **Case**, it can be **Active**, **Resolved**, and **Cancelled**.
- **Maximum Number of Key Phrases**: Specifies Maximum number of keywords to be considered while performing text searches. Allows values between 0 to 1,000.

4. After we have created the similarity rule, we need to define the fields based on which matching will be done and suggestions will be made. Create a new **Match Fields** for Case records on the Case Title field as shown here:

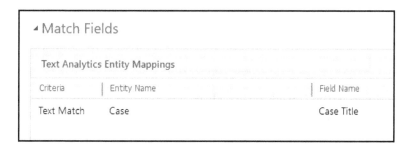

In the **Text Analytics Entity Mappings** record:

Following are the two types of Criteria that can be defined

- **Text Match**: Specifies that the text in the **Case Title** field will be used for finding key phrases or keywords for the match.
- **Exact Match**: Specifies that the text should be matched exactly. For **Exact Match**, only source entity fields can be specified.
- **Entity**: Specifies an entity on which a text search rule is to be created. A Source entity like **Lead**, **Opportunity**, **Contact**, **Account**, **Case**, or a custom entity that is related to the source entity and Activity entities like Email, Fax, letter and so on, can be specified.
- **Field**: Specifies the field on which similarity analysis needs to be run. The field can be of type Single Line of Text, Multiple Line of Text, or Option set.

5. Click on **Activate** to enable the rule.

6. To see it in action, open any of the case records. Here we have opened a case record with the title **Service Requested**:

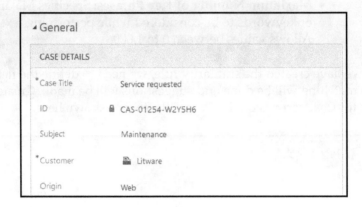

7. Scroll down to the **Case Relationships** tab, click on + (plus) on the **SIMILAR CASES** sub grid.

8. The **Find Similar Cases** dialog displays all the similar Case records as shown here:

9. We can then select the similar case record suggested and click on **Found a Solution** to associate the record as shown:

10. This connects the **Service required soon** record to the **Service requested** through the connection as shown here:

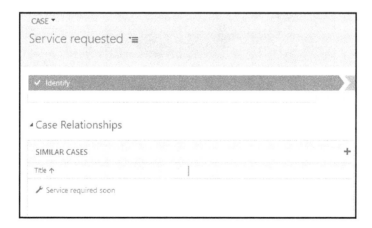

In this section, we covered configuring Similar Records Suggestions; in the next section, we will learn how to configure Dynamics 365 for Document suggestions.

Configuring Document Suggestions in Dynamics 365

Through Document Suggestions, users can be made aware of all the important relevant documents related to the record that they are working on, which can help them while working on a high priority case or a big opportunity. The suggested documents could be of type Word, Excel, PowerPoint, OneNote, Adobe PDF, and text files. Microsoft Azure Text Analytics uses the Similarity Rule defined to find the related records and then presents the list of suggested documents associated with them. The users can either open the document or can copy those documents to the current record. Document Suggestions searches only the locations and documents that the user has access to. The locations where it can search include SharePoint Sites, One Drive, Office 365 Groups, and external URLs:

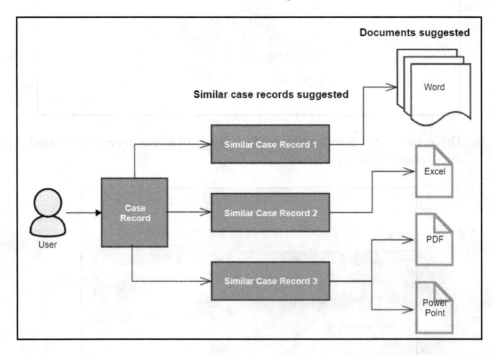

To set up SharePoint
Integration: `https://technet.microsoft.com/library/dn531154.aspx`

To enable OneDrive for Business: `https://technet.microsoft.com/en-us/library/mt622109.aspx`

Deploy office 365 Groups: `https://technet.microsoft.com/en-us/library/dn896591.aspx`

To configure Similar Document Suggestions in Dynamics 365:

1. Connect Text Analysis Connection with Dynamics 365, which we have already done.

2. Inside Dynamics 365, go to **Settings** | **Document Management** and select **Manage Document Suggestions**:

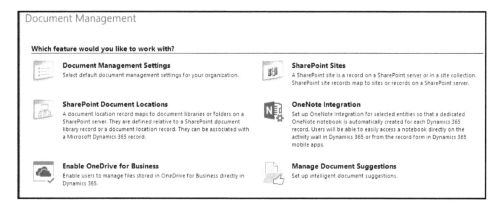

3. If entities are not configured for Document Suggestions we will get the following notification:

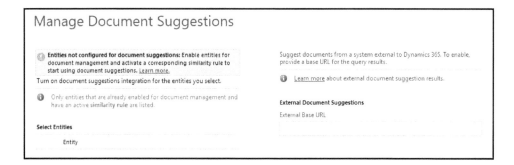

4. Let us enable it for **Case** entity. Open **Case Entity for Customization** and enable **Document Management** and publish the Entity:

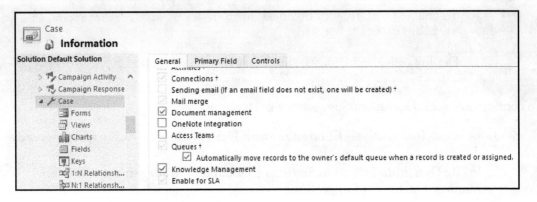

5. Select the **Case** entity in **Manage Document Suggestions** and click on **Apply**:

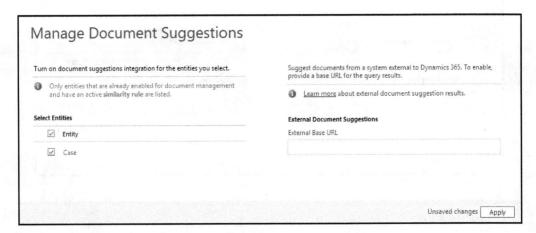

6. After enabling Document Suggestions, the next step is to create a Similar Record Suggestion rule for Case entity. Go to **Settings**| **Data Management** | **Similar Record Suggestions Settings**. Here, we will use our existing rule that we had created earlier based on **Case Title**, as shown in the following screenshot:

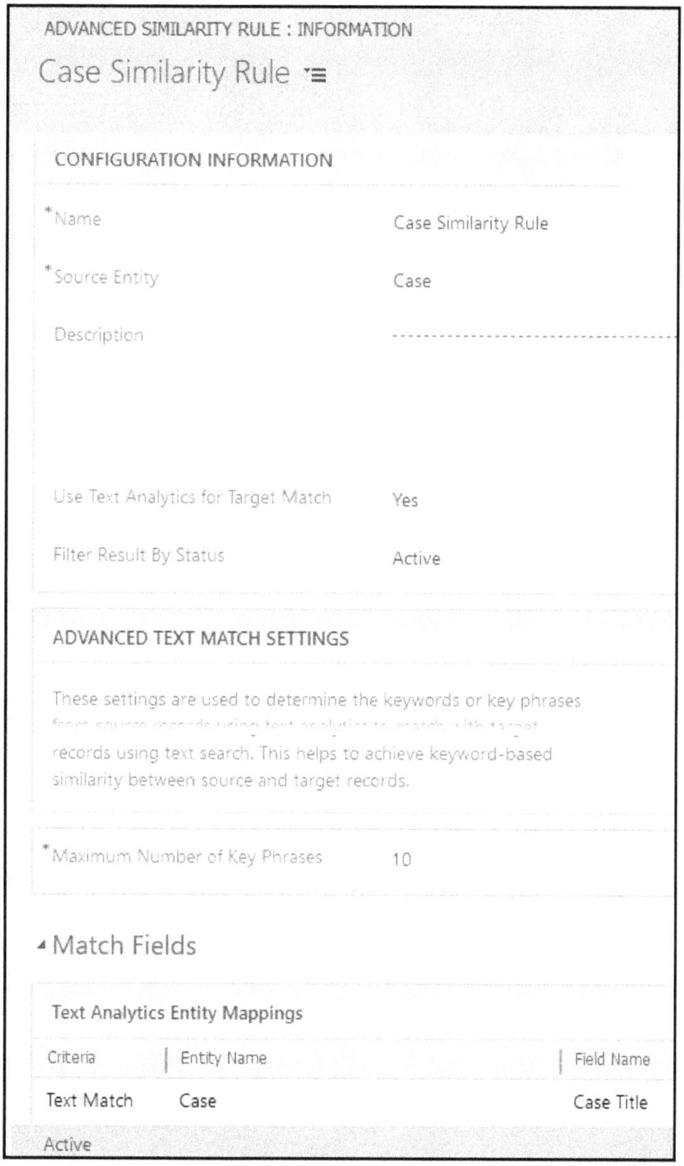

ADVANCED SIMILARITY RULE : INFORMATION

Case Similarity Rule ☰

CONFIGURATION INFORMATION

*Name   Case Similarity Rule

*Source Entity   Case

Description   -

Use Text Analytics for Target Match   Yes

Filter Result By Status   Active

ADVANCED TEXT MATCH SETTINGS

These settings are used to determine the keywords or key phrases from source records using text analytics to match with target records using text search. This helps to achieve keyword-based similarity between source and target records.

*Maximum Number of Key Phrases   10

◢ Match Fields

Text Analytics Entity Mappings

Criteria	Entity Name	Field Name
Text Match	Case	Case Title

Active

7. To see it in action, let us open the same case record that we opened in the case of Similar Record Suggestions that is, with the title **Service Requested** which resulted in 10 similar case records being suggested, as shown in the following screenshot:

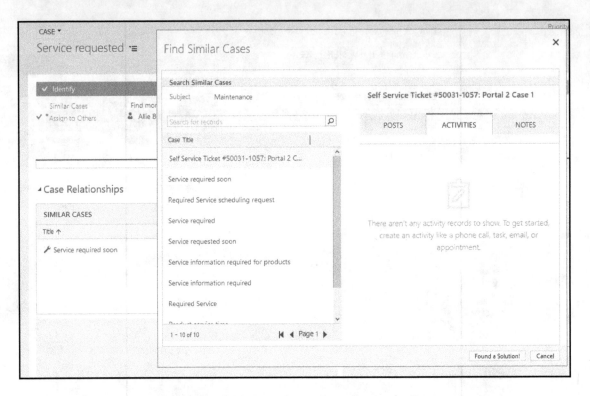

8. Open the associated Documents link for the case record.

9. Click on the **SHOW SUGGESTIONS** ribbon button on the **Document Associated Grid**:

10. **Document Suggestions** will list all the documents that are associated with the similar case records suggested earlier, as shown here:

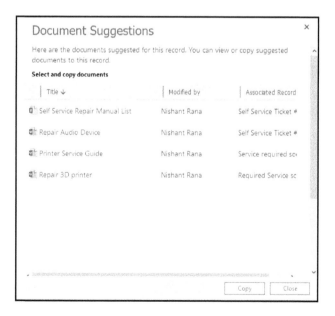

11. Select the documents to be copied to the existing case record and click on **Copy**:

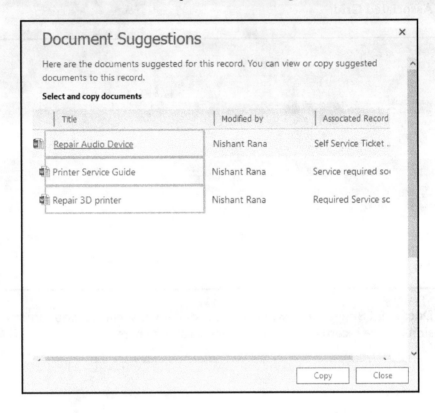

12. This copies the selected documents with the current case record:

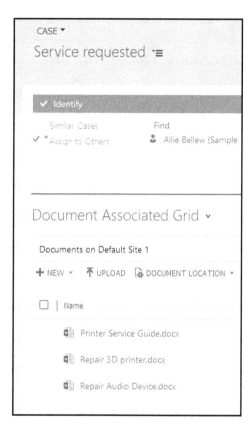

In this section, we covered configuring **Document Suggestions**, in the next section, we will learn how to monitor the Text Analytics Service inside the Azure Portal.

Monitoring the Text Analytics Service inside the Azure Portal

To monitor our configured Text Analytics Service:

1. Log in to the Azure Portal
2. Open the Text Analytics API created
3. Select **Metrics** in the **MONITORING** section, which allows us to select various metrics like **Data In**, **Data Out**, **Total Calls**, **Total Errors**, and so on, and displays the result in a line chart:

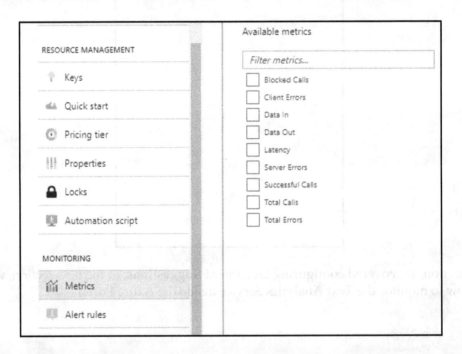

4. The following screenshot shows a line chart with the **Data In** and **Data Out** metrics selected for the past 24 hours. We can also specify the **Chart type** to be of type **Bar** and can also filter the **Time range** to be **Past Hour**, **Past Week** or define a **Custom** range:

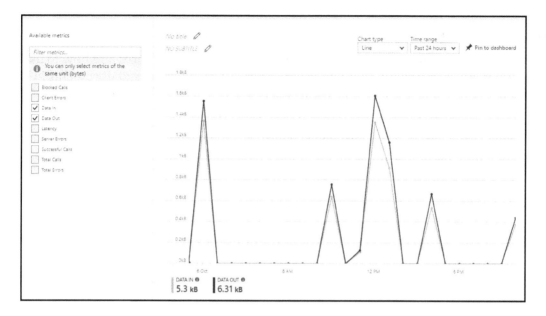

5. Similarly, here we can see the report with different metrics like **Blocked Calls**, **Client Errors**, **Server Errors**, **Successful Calls**, **Total Calls**, and **Total Errors** selected:

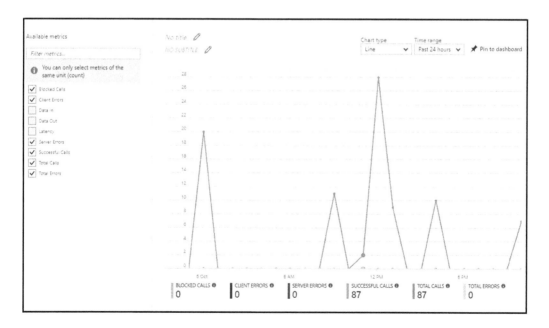

Summary

In this chapter, we covered an overview of Microsoft Cognitive Services and how to use Text Analytics API for suggesting knowledge articles, similar cases, and documents in Dynamics 365.

In Chapter 11, *Train the Users Through Learning Path*, we will look at the Learning Path authoring, which allows us to create our own custom Help experience for our Dynamics 365 users. Through this new feature, we can reduce training time and costs and make users more productive using Dynamics 365.

11

Train the Users through Learning Path

Dynamics 365 Learning Path was introduced in Dynamics 365 version 9.0. This feature allows you to add customizable Help in Dynamics 365 when the user opens pages. It also allows users to follow Help and work simultaneously, providing adaptability, and easy learning of Dynamics 365.

In this chapter, the following topics will be covered to increase your understanding of Learning Path:

- Learning Path overview
- Prerequisites for Learning Path
- Enable Learning Path in Dynamics 365
- Content Library of Dynamics 365 Learning Path
- Steps to create and configure Learning Path
- Understanding of Learning Path

Learning Path overview

Dynamics 365 Learning path is an effective and efficient feature that allows users to simultaneously learn and adapt Dynamics 365. This feature is only available for Dynamics 365 online.

Learning Path Help is available for the user on the loading of a page or on a click of the **Help** button. Learning Path provides training for text, videos, and URLs. It gives a complete walk-through to do work in Dynamics 365. Learning Path supports the export and import into different organizations, which means it is convenient to export Learning Path from one organization to another.

Learning Path supports the localization of content for Help, which means Help content is created for Dynamic 365 users using Learning Path. All Help content is available in selected languages for Dynamics 365; this distinctive attribute makes Dynamics 365 Learning Path attractive to users.

Learning Path is accessible from tablet and mobile devices. It is even more reliable for different regions; soon it will be accessible in all remaining regions.

Prerequisites for using the Learning Path

Learning Path gives a tremendous amount of benefits to Dynamics 365 users. First, it is needed to complete the following prerequisites to use Learning Path:

- Dynamics 365 Learning Path is supported only in Dynamics 365 version 9.0. In Dynamics 365 2016 version 1, the user can only see the default Help created by Microsoft; to author content for Learning Path, the new Dynamics 365 version 9.0 is required.
- The system customizer or system administration role needs to be assigned for authoring Learning Path content.
- Learning Path in Dynamics 365 for the organization has to be turned on. The next part is to unable Learning Path for the organization.
- It is important to add users to the Learning Path group. This task is also covered in the next section.

Enabling Learning Path in Dynamics 365

Learning Path needs to be turned on in Dynamics 365 because, by default, it is turned off. The following steps will specify how to turn on Learning Path, as well as how to add users to the Dynamics 365 Learning Path group:

1. Log in to the Dynamics 365 9.0 instance using Office 365 credentials.
2. In Dynamics 365, **Opt Out of Learning Path** should be enabled. Select settings and click on **Opt Out Of Learning Path**. After this stage, Dynamics 365 controls will be redirected to the Dynamics 365 home screen. Take a look at the following screenshot:

3. The next stage is to enable Learning Path Authoring. Go to **Settings | Administration**:

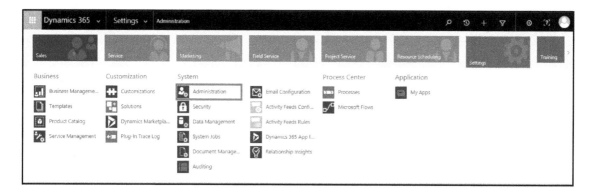

Select **System Settings**:

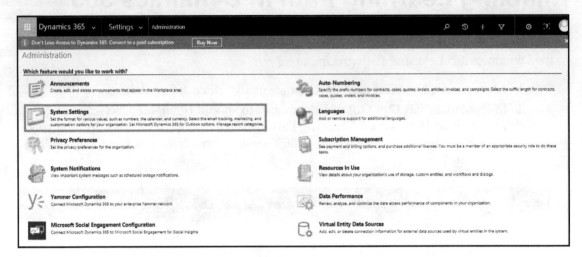

4. Select the **General** tab of **System Settings** | **Enable Learning Path** and **Enable Learning Path Authoring**. Click **OK** to save changes, as shown here:

5. Now, move forward to add users in the Learning Path group. Go to the Office 365 Admin Panel. Select **Groups**, click on **Learning Path Authors,** and add users to the group, as shown in following image:

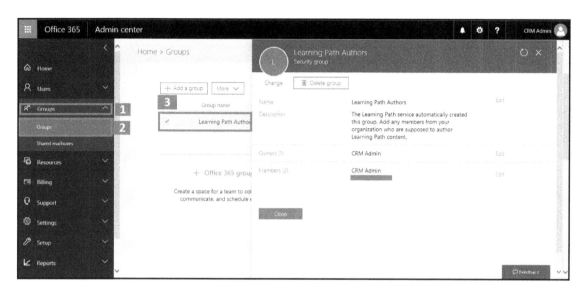

Content Library of Dynamics 365 Learning Path

The Learning Path Content Library is used to show the contents created and available for an organization. Additionally, it is used to manage, create, and interact with controls. The Content Library is accessible from the **Training** tab of the Dynamics 365 site map, or click on the **Content Library** option on the side bar.

The following image will explain the **Content Library** UI:

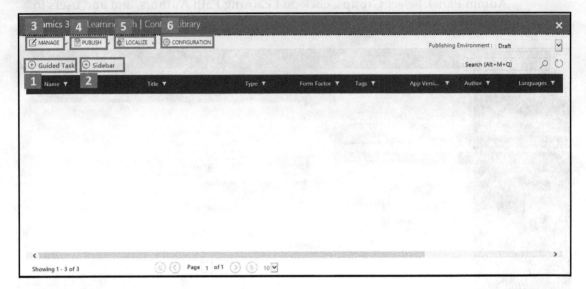

Consider the following points:

1. **Guided Task**:

   Guided Task contains a single or sequence of steps. Launching **Guided Task** is simple. It guides the user through a step-by-step process and helps the user to understand the new task. It ensures you add data as well as perform tasks simultaneously. It provides a **next** button to the user, which makes it efficient to use if the user is performing any task.

   It supports many things such as adding videos, links, and more information to help the user be more familiar with the Dynamics 365 UI.

2. **Sidebar**:

Sidebars appear when the user clicks on the **help** button, selects the link or the button on the page, and navigate page to that customizer design content. Dynamics 365 supports the creation of a Home Sidebar, which appears on screen when the user selects the **help** button or opens the Home Screen.

A system customizer can also create error sidebars, which are displayed for the user when there is a problem. Sidebars support the adding of links, information, and videos to help the end users.

3. **MANAGE**: This option allows the managing of content in the following way:
    - **Check in**: This option saves changes and makes the content available to other users
    - **Delete**: Use it to delete the content
    - **Export**: Export content to other organizations
    - **Import**: Import content from other organizations
4. **PUBLISH**: Publishes all changes to the content and makes them available for end users.
5. **LOCALIZE**: To add localization of content, use this option.
6. **CONFIGURATION**: This option is used to configure security roles, as well as the publishing environment.

Steps to create and configure Learning Path

Dynamics 365 covers the sales process from lead-to-opportunity. In this scenario, the lead to opportunity process flow is used for the **Learning Path** example. The following steps are to provide guidance to create the **Learning Path** for lead-to-opportunity:

1. In Dynamics 365, go to **Training** | **Content Library**:

2. The Content Library will open:

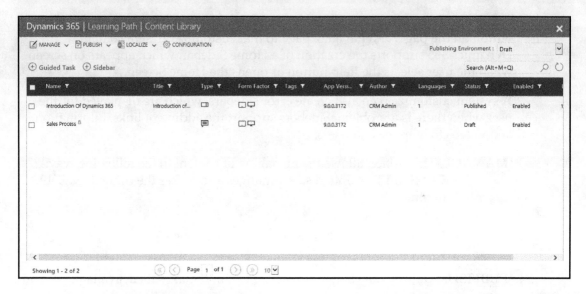

3. Select the **Sidebar** option:

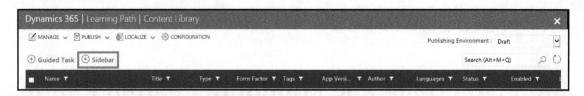

4. The Learning Sidebar form will open, fill in all the necessary fields. Enter a **Name**, choose a **Template**, and save the **Sidebar** form:

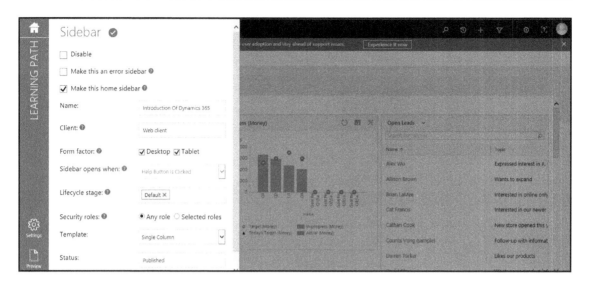

5. After this step, edit the sidebar template, enter the sidebar name, edit sections if necessary, and add URLs and images to the sections:

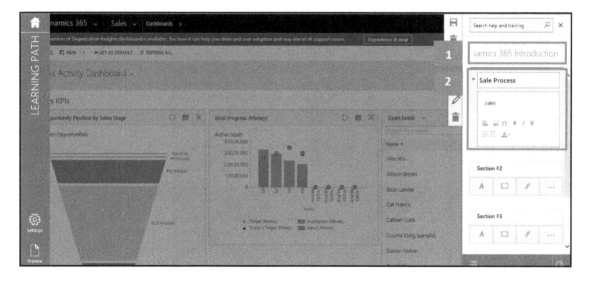

6. If there is a need to update the section property , click on the edit button of the section. This option will add **Content Types**, **Text**, **Button**, **List of Links**, and so on:

7. Select the save option of the Sidebar form:

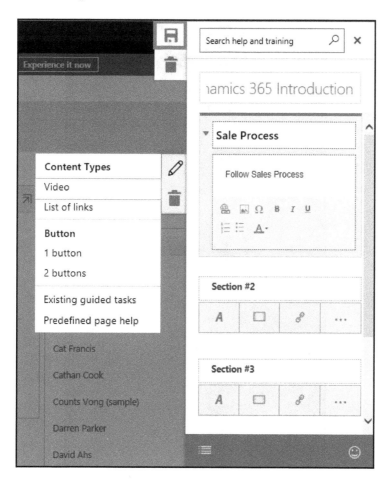

8. Select the **Preview** button on the left-hand side to see a preview:

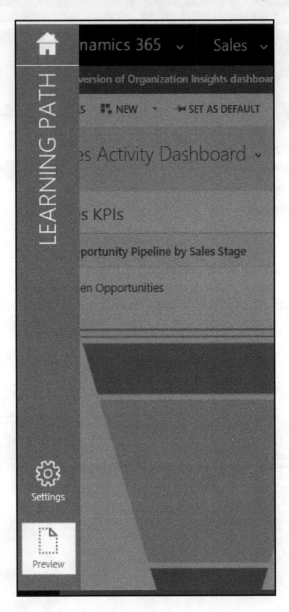

9. **Publish** or **Check in** the changes, after you have seen the preview:

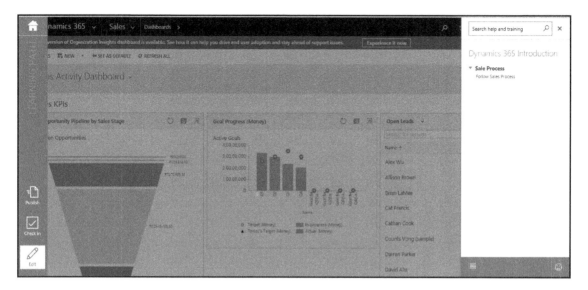

10. Select the Learning Path home button. This action will redirect you to the Learning Path Library:

11. Select the **Guided Task** option to create a guided task:

12. Fill all the required fields of the guided task and **Save** it, as shown in the following image:

13. In the **Flow Editor**, add the guide option for **Lead to Opportunity**. First, collapse the **Flow Editor** then select the **Leads** entity:

and then select the **Leads** tab, as shown in the following screenshot:

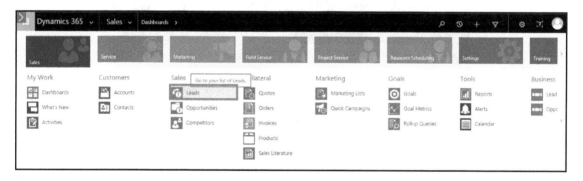

14. Expand the **Flow Editor**, when the lead records load:

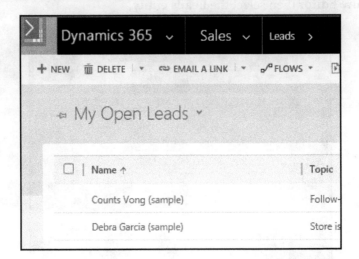

15. Select **Add New Step** and click on **Learning Step**:

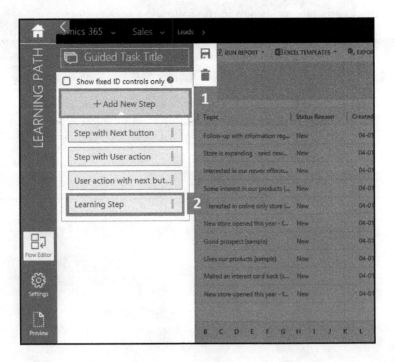

16. Drag and drop the newly created learning step to the new lead button. Add a title and description in the learning step:

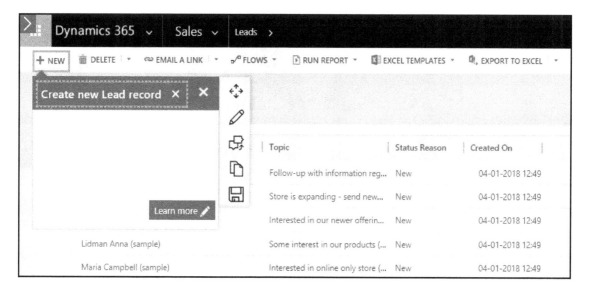

17. Click the **Save** button to save changes in the learning step:

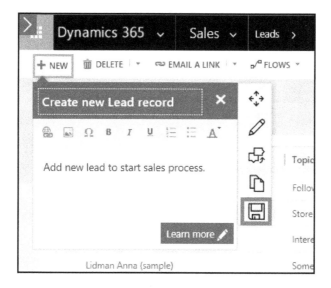

18. Click on the new button of **Create new Lead record** and open the new Lead form. To **Add New Step** to add on **CONTACT** section, select **User action with next button**. Use the following image:

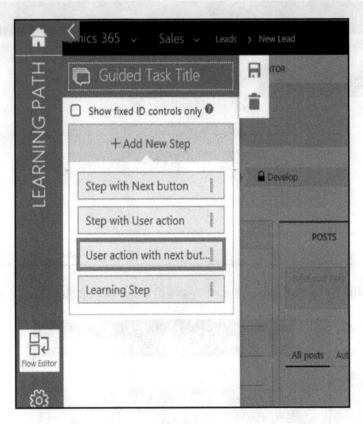

19. Drag and drop this learning step contact section of the **Lead** record. Add the step description and name. Select the **Save** button to save changes:

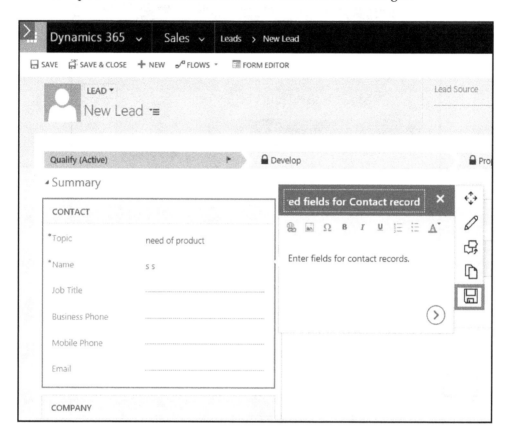

20. Repeat the same process for the **Company** section:

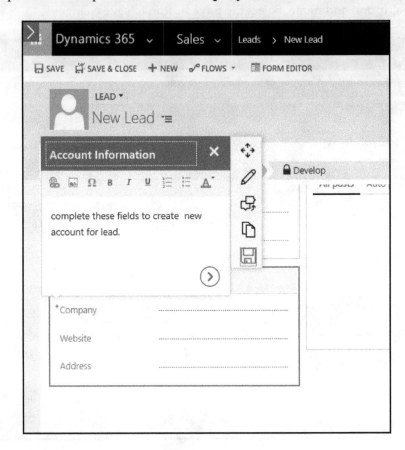

21. Create the same learning step for the **SAVE** button:

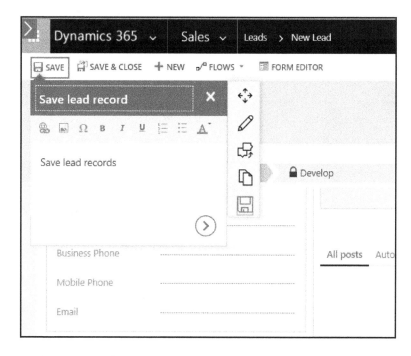

22. Repeat the process for the **QUALIFY** button:

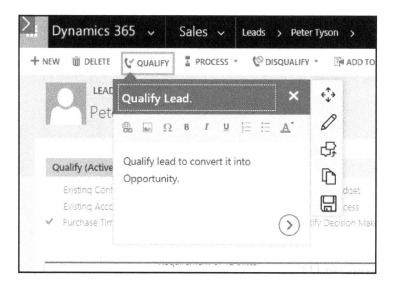

23. Add another step for the **Next** button of the business process flow:

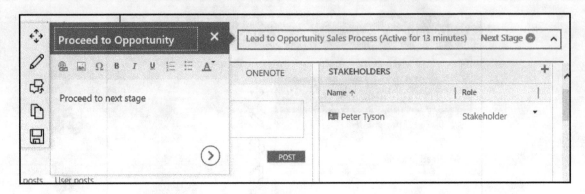

24. In the opportunity record, choose the **Step with Next button** Learning Step:

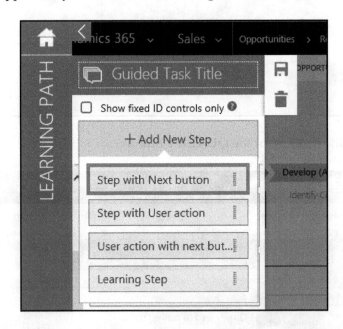

25. Drag and drop this step on the opportunity name. Repeat it with **Business Process Flow**, activity, and so on:

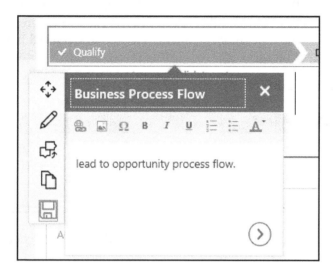

25. Now, save the guided task:

26. See the preview and **Publish** changes.

Publishing content and publishing group

Dynamics 365 Learning Path content is not available unless it is published. Publishing the content is possible from the Content Library. To publish the content in Learning Path, it first needs to be checked in. The following steps will help you understand how to publish content from the Content Library.

1. Go to **Content Library**:

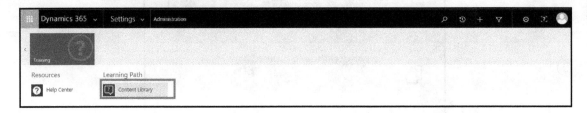

2. Select the contents of the content list to publish. If it is not checked in, then make sure you check in the content:

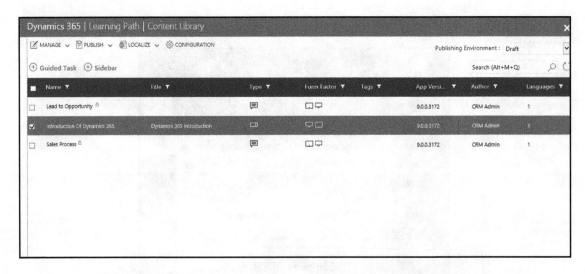

3. Click on the **Publish** button to publish changes:

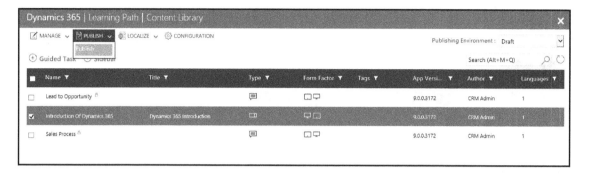

These are very simple steps to publish the contents.

Publishing the group is used to publish the content of Learning Path. A default publish group is created when Learning Path is enabled in an organization. This default publishing group uses the same name as the organization name. It is possible to create another publishing group and it is also possible to add more than one organization to the publishing group. Multiple organizations can be members of different groups, which makes content publishing into different organizations.

The following steps specify how to create a publishing group:

1. Go to **Content Library**:

2. Click on **CONFIGURATION**:

3. Select the new Publishing Group on **PUBLISHING CONFIGURATION**:

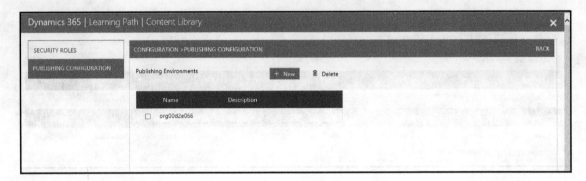

4. Complete the name and the optional description:

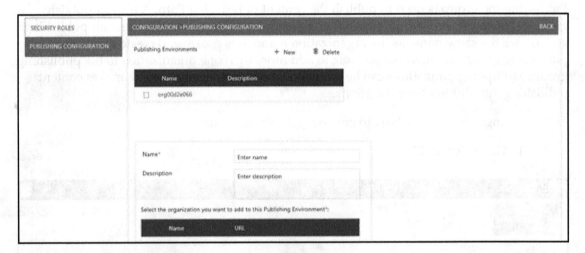

5. Include organizations in the publishing group.
6. Click **Save** and click **OK**.

Summary

In this chapter, we saw how to work on Learning Path in Dynamics 365, Content Library of Dynamics 365 Learning Path, the steps to create and configure Learning Path, and more. In the next chapter, we will cover web client refresh and unified interface, along with features such as Relevance Search and Relationship Insights.

12
Other New Features in Dynamics 365

In the previous chapter, we learned about the new authoring capabilities added to the *Learning Path* feature in Dynamics 365 that delivers contextually rich content for the end users using the application. In this chapter, we will look at some of the new features that were introduced in Dynamics 365 with the July 2017 and December 2016 update that we haven't covered in the previous chapters.

These are the some of the main topics we will cover in the chapter:

- Web client refresh
- Unified interface
- Activity timeline
- Multiselect option set
- Virtual entity
- Auto numbering
- Relevance Search
- Data Export Service
- Relationship Insights
- Live Assist
- LinkedIn Lead Gen Forms

Top new features introduced in Dynamics 365

With each update, a lot of new functionality, features, and enhancements are added in Dynamics 365. Some of these new features are targeted towards the end users who use the system on a daily basis, and others are for the administrators, customizers, or developers who are responsible for configuring, customizing, and developing solutions around it. In this chapter, we are going to look at some of these new features which we haven't covered in previous chapters.

Understanding visual changes introduced in the web client refresh

Web client refresh, which was introduced in the July 2017 update, is one of the biggest improvements made to the product, keeping in mind the feedback of the Dynamics 365 users related to the user interface. The user interface of the web client apps has been completely revamped, with the aim of making users working on the application more productive by increasing readability and accessibility.

Here are some of the major improvements in the web client:

- Containers, like sections, now have a defined border and any extra whitespace which is not part of any content has been gray shaded. Similarly, the main body is put inside the white container to separate it from the header and the rest of the content. Also, if the containers do not contain any data, it is clearly indicated using an icon and a message, as shown here in the activities list inside the social pane:

- Text wrapping can now be configured for labels and values in the form. We need to go to **System Settings** | **General** tab and Select **Yes** for the **Allow text wrapping in form fields labels and values** option to enable it:

- This is how the fields are displayed in the form with text wrapping enabled:

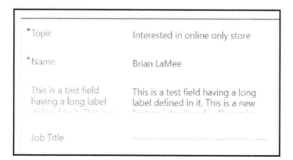

Styling changes include three new themes:

- CRM default theme
- CRM blue theme
- CRM orange theme

Themes also include the option to define colors for the page header and the section header through the **Page Header Fill Color** and the **Panel Header Fill Color** property.

Here, we have specified the following values for those properties:

- **Page Header Fill Color** – #ccffcc
- **Panel Header Fill Color** – #ccffff

This is how the changes show up in the Dynamics 365 interface:

We now have the option to define a color for sub grid headers inside the form. Open the form for customization, select the sub grid and in the **Edit properties** dialog box, we can specify **Panel header color** as shown here:

Selecting multiple options using multiselect option set

The multiselect option set is now available as a new attribute type in Dynamics 365. These are some of the key features about this new attribute type:

- The multiselect option set can be used in advanced find
- They are available for main forms, quick create and quick view forms
- The existing global option set can be used for creating the multiselect option set attribute
- The existing client side API's methods that are specific to the existing single valued option set applies to the new multiselect option set
- The multiselect option set is not supported in business rules and workflows

The following screenshot shows **Multiselect** option set the field with three items selected **Item 1**, **Item2**, and **Item 3**:

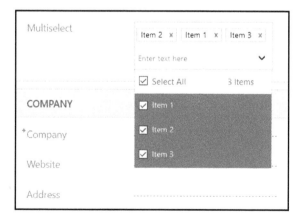

Doing advanced find with Does Not Contain Data filter

ADVANCED FIND view now supports a **Does Not Contain Data** filter for a related record. So basically, we can now write a query such as `Find all the lead records which do not contain any related tasks`. However, we cannot define any filter conditions for the related record in the current implementation as shown here:

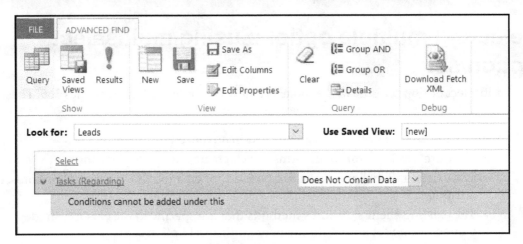

This is how the `fetch` XML looks for the preceding query:

```
<fetch version="1.0" output-format="xml-platform" mapping="logical"
  distinct="true">
  <entity name="lead">
    <attribute name="fullname" />
    <attribute name="companyname" />
    <attribute name="telephone1" />
    <attribute name="leadid" />
    <order attribute="fullname" descending="false" />
    <link-entity name="task" from="regardingobjectid" to="leadid"
      link-type="outer" alias="ac" />
    <filter type="and">
      <condition entityname="ac" attribute="regardingobjectid"
operator="null" />
    </filter>
  </entity>
</fetch>
```

Defining web resource dependencies

For JavaScript and HTML web resource, we can now specify dependencies. This makes sure that all the required dependent resources are available in the solution during export, or already existing in the target system to which the solution is being imported, otherwise it will result in failure. It also ensures that we do not delete any of the components accidentally without removing its dependencies first. For HTML and JavaScript, we can define dependencies on other web resource types such as CSS, HTML, JavaScript libraries, RESX and XML. In case of JavaScript, we can additionally define dependencies on attributes of a specific entity as shown here:

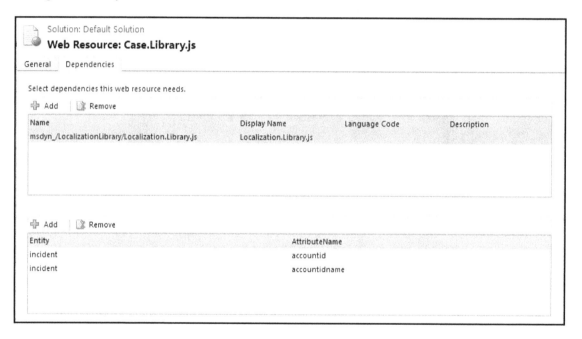

Understanding the new unified interface

Unified interface is a new framework introduced in the Dynamics 365 July 2017 update. With unified interface, we now have the same architecture under the hood across all the platforms. Currently, we have the following apps such as **Customer Service Hub** (which is a new version of **Interactive Service Hub**), **Field Resource Hub**, **Project Resource Hub**, and **Sales Hub** developed on unified interface as shown here:

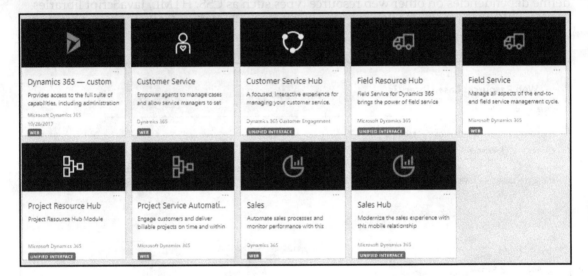

The unified interface has been built from the ground up keeping accessibility, consistency and performance in mind. It also brings faster development and deployment time, with a single set of customizations working seamlessly across different devices. For the end users, it will provide a uniform experience across tablet/phone client, mobile web client or App for Outlook which makes it more consistent, user-friendly and saves training costs.

Benefits of the new unified interface include:

- Easy access to favorite and recent records, dashboards and entities within the application at a single place from the left navigation panel:

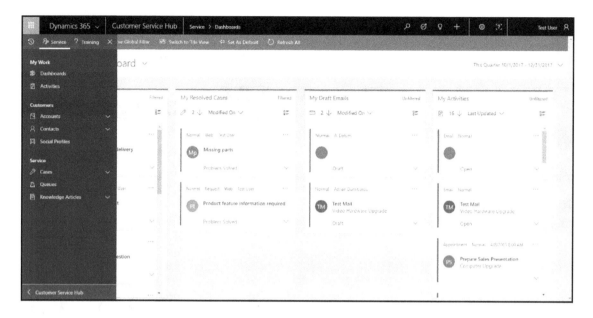

- Recently used records inside the unified interface can be pinned, as shown here:

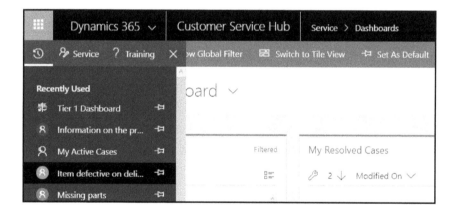

- The new responsive user interface of the unified client, autofits based on the screen size. On resizing the browser window, the unified interface displays an interface that fits the small screen, as shown here on the image on the right:

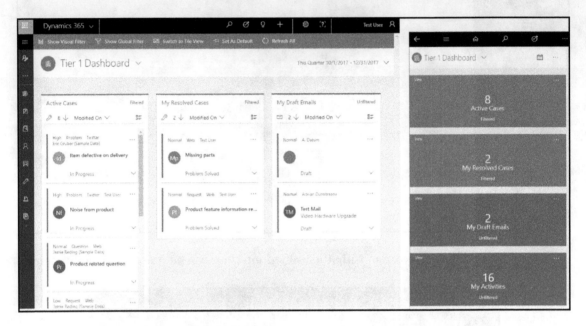

- Business process flows can now be displayed in floating mode along with docked mode:

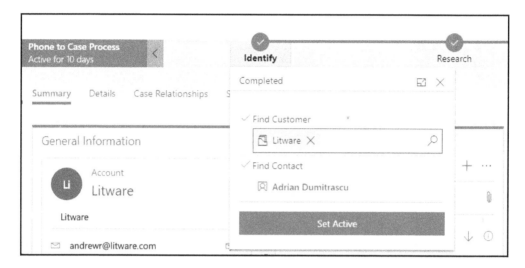

- The business process flow can be aligned vertically as shown here:

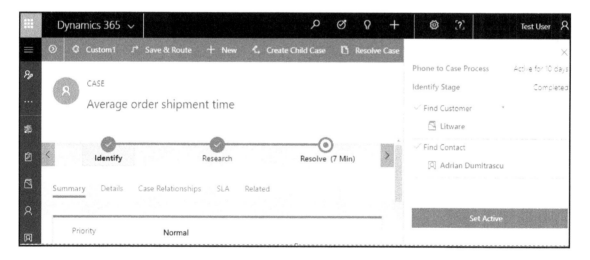

- New timeline control in the unified interface combines and gives a single view of all the activities, notes and posts, which can be filtered by record type, date and so on. It also allows the user to perform various actions based on the type of record as shown here:

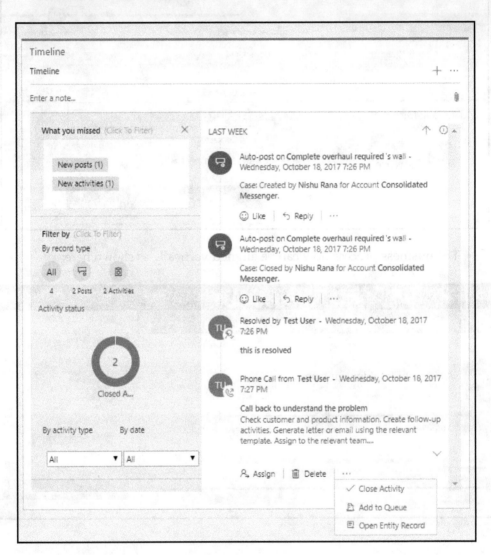

- Editor for knowledge base has been enhanced, which includes support for editing the HTML source as shown here:

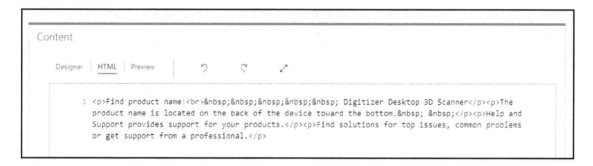

- It also includes the option to preview the content to check its compatibility with various devices:

Integrating external data using virtual entity

With the July 2017 update in Dynamics 365, we can now create a virtual type of custom entity. The name virtual applies because the data for the entity is not saved inside Dynamics 365. The virtual entity on runtime, that is when accessed, gets its data from the data source provider configured for it. Currently, it only supports the OData V4 data provider. With an earlier version of Dynamics 365, before virtual entity, if we had to fetch or retrieve data from external data sources, we had to write custom code for that. Now, once we have the OData service ready and exposed, it becomes more of a configuration thing inside Dynamics 365, that the system administrator or customizer can take care of, without depending on the developer.

To configure a virtual entity:

1. Go to **Settings** | **Administration** and select **Virtual Entity Data Sources**:

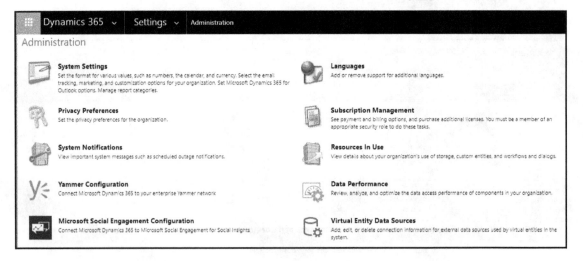

2. Click on **New** to create a new data source. Currently, it supports only **OData V4 Data Provider**:

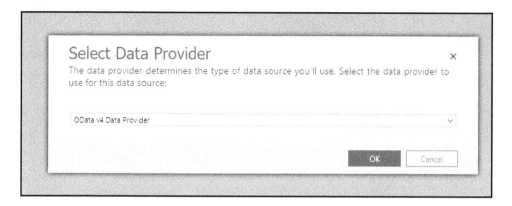

3. Specify the URL of the OData service, along with the required values to create the OData source record:

4. Now with the data source setup, the next step is to create the virtual entity. Go to **Settings** | **Customizations** | **Customize the System** | Select **Entities** and click on **New** to create a new entity. To create a virtual entity, we need to select the **Virtual Entity** checkbox.

5. For a virtual entity, the **External Name** property and the **External Collection Name** property should correspond to the entity name and the entity set name within the OData entity to which we want to configure inside Dynamics 365:

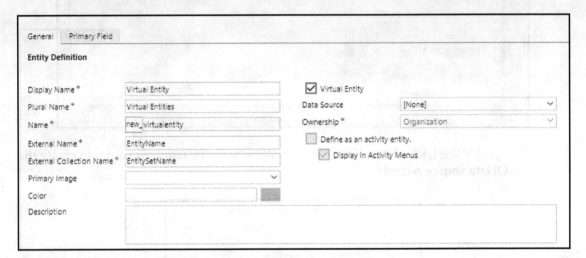

To learn more about OData go to the following link:
http://www.odata.org/documentation/

6. On creation of a virtual entity, two fields will be created by the system, which need to be mapped to the corresponding fields of the OData entity as part of the virtual entity configuration. Apart from the autocreated fields, we can also create new custom fields and can then map them to the corresponding fields of the OData entity for them to show up inside Dynamics 365.

7. Here, we are mapping the ID field created for the virtual entity with the primary key field (for example, EntityID) of our OData Entity. The primary key field must be of type GUID, otherwise we will get an exception:

8. Once we are done with creating and mapping all the fields of the virtual entity, we can publish the changes.

9. This virtual entity will be available just like any other entity. We can open the **ADVANCED FIND** view, select the virtual entity and run the query against it or open any of the records created for that entity to view it.

10. Here are certain points we need to consider while planning to use a virtual entity:
    - A virtual entity is read-only
    - A virtual entity is organization owned, however, the Dynamics 365 security features are not supported for a virtual entity
    - A virtual entity cannot be of type Activity
    - We cannot configure SLAs, business process flows against the virtual entity
    - A virtual entity doesn't support the creation of a quick create form
    - We cannot enable auditing and duplicate detection on them
    - Virtual entity fields cannot be used for rollups and calculated fields
    - Although we can use it inside an advanced find, Microsoft doesn't recommend using a query that joins the Dynamics 365 native data with virtual entity data
    - We cannot write workflow or plugins against a virtual entity

Implementing auto numbering

Auto numbering as a feature, has always been there in the Dynamics 365 starting version 3.0, but it has always been restricted to a few entities such as contracts, cases, articles, quotes, and so on.

Go to **Settings** | **Administration** and click on **Auto-Numbering** to see all the entities on which we can configure auto numbering:

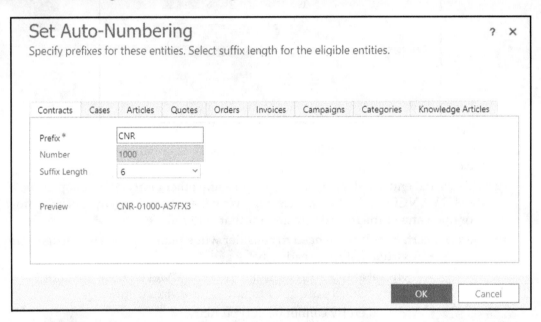

However, now with the Dynamics 365 July 2017 update, we finally have the ability to define autonumbering for other entities as well. Currently, we can only define it programatically using SDK's CreateAttribute request. We do not have the user interface to define it.

Here is the sample code that will create a new auto number field name, My Auto Number in the contact entity:

```
    CreateAttributeRequest createAttributeRequest = new
CreateAttributeRequest();
    createAttributeRequest.EntityName = "contact";

    var autoNumberAttributeMetadata = new StringAttributeMetadata()
    {
      AutoNumberFormat = "Auto Number - {SEQNUM:4} - {RANDSTRING:4} -
      {DATETIMEUTC:yyyyMMddhhmmss}",
```

```
        SchemaName = "new_autonumber1",
        MaxLength = 100,
        RequiredLevel = new AttributeRequiredLevelManagedProperty(
         AttributeRequiredLevel.ApplicationRequired),
        DisplayName = new Microsoft.Xrm.Sdk.Label("My Auto Number", 1033),
        Description = new Microsoft.Xrm.Sdk.Label("This is my first auto
number
        field through SDK", 1033)
    };

    createAttributeRequest.Attribute = autoNumberAttributeMetadata;
    var response = organizationService.Execute(createAttributeRequest);
```

The following image shows the auto number field generated with the format specified for a contact record:

Here are the properties specific to this new auto number attribute:

AutoNumberFormat	Specifies the format of the auto number field Static String along with: {SEQNUM:size} - Size of the sequential number {RANDSTRING:size} - Size of the random string to be generated {DATETIMEUTC:format}- Format for the date time
Schema Name	Specifies the schema name of the auto number field
Max Length	Specifies the maximum length of the auto number field
Required Level	Specifies the required level of the auto number field: • None • Recommended • Application Required • System Required
Display Name	Specifies the display name of the auto number field
Description	Specifies the description of the auto number field

We can use the Auto Number Manager plugin of XrmToolBox developed by Jonas Rapp to create, update and delete the auto number field through an intuitive user interface `http://anm.xrmtoolbox.com/`.

Using the `UpdateAttribute` request, we can update the format of the existing auto number field. This will only be applicable to new records created and will not apply to the existing records. We can also create multiple auto number fields for an entity.

An auto number field with an attribute required level as system required is not supported.

Using Relevance Search for improved search experience

Relevance Search brings the power of Microsoft's Azure Search to improve search performance in Dynamics 365. Data from the Dynamics 365 entities and the fields enabled for Relevance Search are synced with Azure Search DB, which performs an intuitive semantic search on it, and displays the results by relevance. Relevance Search searches across the fields in the entities and displays the results in the order of the most relevant to the least, unlike a categorized search, which displays results based on entity grouping. Also, compared to a categorized search which is limited to filtering the result by entity, the Relevance Search lets the Dynamics 365 user filter the result based on multiple conditions such as record type, owner, modified on, created on and any other filtering option defined for each of the entities, based on facets. As Relevance Search uses a semantic search, we do not need to specify a wild card in our search text. Relevance Search also highlights the matching words in the search results. Basically, once we have identified and configured the entities and their corresponding fields for Relevance Search, the full sync can take more than an hour, depending on the amount of data to be synced, when it runs the first time and then any subsequent changes made in Dynamics 365 can take up to 15 minutes to appear in the search.

Azure Search documentation can be found here: `https://docs.microsoft.com/en-us/azure/search/`.

Enabling Relevance Search

To enable Relevance Search:

1. Go to **Settings** | **Administration** | **System Settings**. In the **General** tab, check the **Enable Relevance Search** in the **Set up Search** section and give the consent to share the data with the external system:

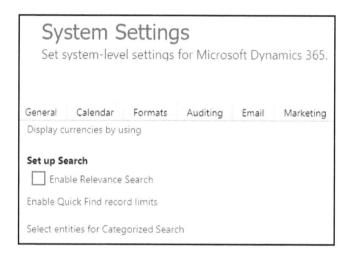

2. Next, we need to define entities and fields on which we want the Relevance Search to be performed. Go to **Customizations** | **Entities** and click on **Configure Relevance Search** to select the entities on which we need to enable the Relevance Search:

3. There is no limit on the number of entities that can be selected for the Relevance Search. The limitation is on the number of fields per organization, the maximum is 1,000 fields. Here, the lookup field is considered equivalent of adding 3 fields, option set as 2 and remaining fields as 1 field.

4. We can add the entities from the **Available Entities** list box to the **Selected Entities** list box, followed by publish. The **Total fields indexed** field in the progress bar shows the total number of fields used:

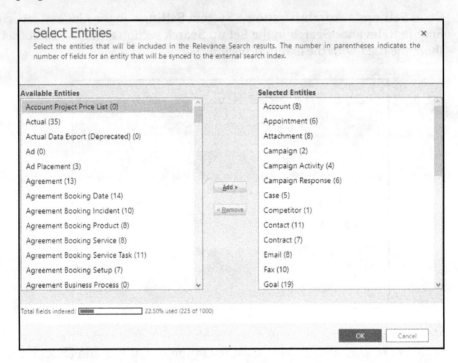

5. To enable a particular attribute of an entity for the Relevance Search, we need to add the field as **Find columns** in the **Quick Find** view of that entity. Only a single line of text and multiple lines of text will be searchable.

6. The first four fields defined in the **Quick Find** view will be displayed in the search results in the user interface.

7. Similarly, the first four facetable fields, that is fields of data types other than a single line of text or multiple lines of text, in the **Quick Find** view will be displayed as facets in the Relevance Search user interface.

8. The filter defined on the **Quick Find** view is also applied to the Relevance Search results. However, not all the operators are supported for filtering. The following is the list of the operators that aren't supported by Relevance Search:

Like	NotLike	BeginsWith	DoesNotBeginsWith
EndWith	DoesNotEndWith	ChildOf	EqualUserLanguage

Mask	NotMask	MaskSelect	Above
Under	NotUnder	UnderOrEqual	AboveOrEqual

The related entity fields in **Quick Find** view are not considered by Relevance Search as Find Column, View Column or in Filter.

9. To perform the Relevance Search, click on the search icon in the navigation bar and enter the text to start the search. Here, we have entered Eva as the search text:

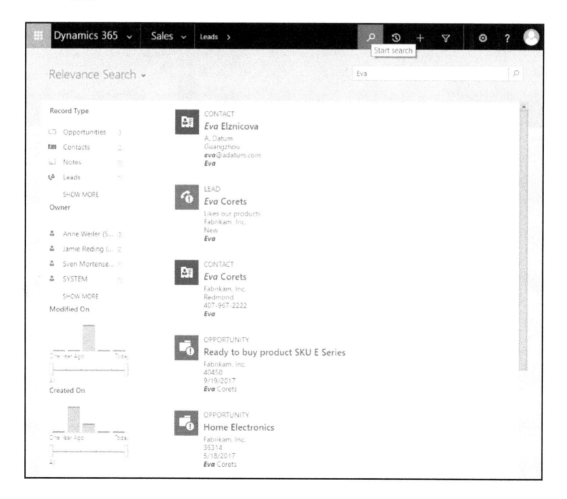

10. The search results are displayed in a list based on relevance and it includes results from all the searchable entities, which can be further filtered based on record type, owner, modified on, created on or any other facets defined. The matches are also highlighted in the result.

11. The user can also define the default search experience and configure facets fields for each of the entity configured for the Relevance Search:

   - To define a default search experience, navigate to the gear icon on the navigation bar, select **Options** to open the **Set Personal Options** dialog box. In the **General** tab, we can define either **Relevance Search**, **Categorized Search** or can let the last used search be the default search experience as shown here:

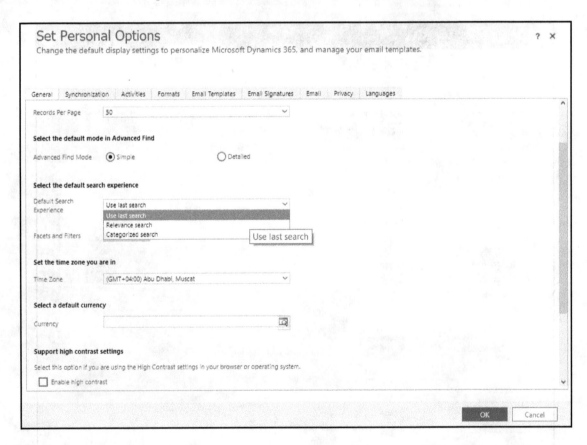

- Similarly, we can click on the **Configure** button for **Facets and Filters** to define facets for the Relevance Search. We can define up to four fields for each searchable entity as shown here:

Exporting Dynamics 365 data using Data Export Service

The Data Export Service can be defined as a scalable and secure cloud service that enables the replication of the Dynamics 365 online database into a Microsoft Azure SQL database or a SQL database on Microsoft Azure virtual machines. This Dynamics 365 data that can then be queried and used for various analytics and reporting scenarios such as Power BI or SQL-based SSRS reports, or to build any custom solutions on top of it. The Data Export Service synchronizes the entire Dynamics 365 data based on the export profile defined, for the first time and then on the subsequent run, it only synchronizes the delta changes to it.

Configuring Data Export Service

To configure Data Export Service:

1. We need to first link Office 365 Tenant with the Azure Subscription (in case they are separate), see `https://docs.microsoft.com/en-us/azure/billing/billing-add-office-365-tenant-to-azure-subscription`.

2. Next, we create an Azure SQL database. For this, sign in to the Azure portal and click on **Add** to create a new SQL database: `https://docs.microsoft.com/en-us/azure/sql-database/sql-database-get-started-portal`.

3. After successful creation of the Azure SQL database, open the SQL Server Management Studio to connect to the Azure SQL database. We can get the server name from the Azure portal and set the firewall rule that will allow us to connect to the Azure SQL database from SQL Server Management Studio:

✕ Tools	⧉ Copy	↺ Restore	↥ Export	🛡 Set server firewall	🗑 Delete
Resource group (change)				Server name	
RGDynamics365DB				dynamics365db.database.windows.net	
Status				Elastic database pool	
Online				No elastic pool	

4. Next, we need to create an SQL user that will be used by Data Export Service to write data inside the Azure database. For this first one, create a login, with master database selected:

```
Create login [dataexportserviceuser] with PASSWORD = '**********';
```

5. Assign a db owner role to the user on the Azure SQL database that you created to be used for exporting Dynamics 365 data:

```
Create user [dataexportserviceuser] from login
[dataexportserviceuser];

Exec sp_addrolemember 'db_owner', 'dataexportserviceuser';
```

 The database permission required for the database user for the data export connection string is given here: `https://technet.microsoft.com/en-us/library/mt744592.aspx#Anchor_1`.

6. Now, after having set up the database, we need to configure Data Export Service in Dynamics 365. Navigate to **Settings | Dynamics Marketplace**, locate Data Export Service and click on **Get it now**. Agree to the terms and conditions. This installs the Data Export Service solution in the Dynamics 365 instance:

7. This adds the data export link in **Settings** inside Dynamic 365. On clicking on it, we are presented with a disclaimer page, where we need to give consent on exporting data to an external system:

Enable popups for the domain `https://discovery.crmreplication.`
`azure.net/` in the browser for autosign in on navigating to **Settings** | **Data**
Export.

8. Once we are autosigned in, we can click on the **New** button to create a data
export profile:

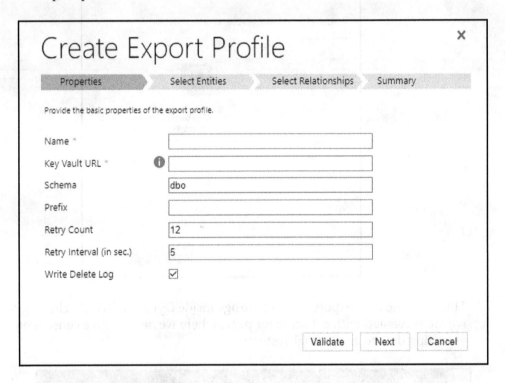

For the data export profile:

Name	Specifies the unique name for the export profile.
Key vault URL	Specifies URL of the key vault, which basically contains credentials and connection information for the Azure SQL database securely stored in it.
Schema	Specifies the schema for the database. The default is dbo.
Prefix	Specifies the prefix we want to give to the tables that will be created in the database.

Retry count	Specifies the number of times insertion or update of records are retried in case of any failure. Acceptable values are from 0 to 20. The default value is 12.
Retry interval	Specifies the interval between each retry attempt in case of failure. Acceptable values are from 0 to 3,600 seconds. The default value is 5 seconds.
Write delete log	Specifies optional setting for logging deleted records.

9. For the key vault URL, Microsoft has provided the PowerShell script which we need to generate it. To get the script, click on the blue information icon next to the key vault URL text box and copy it. Basically, here we need to specify values for the following placeholders inside the PowerShell script as shown here:

```
# ----PLACEHOLDER--------------------------------------------------- #
$subscriptionId = '[Specifies the Azure subscription to which the Key Vault belongs.]'
$keyvaultName = '[Specifies the name of the Key Vault. If the Key Vault does not exist,
the script will create one]'
$secretName = '[Specifies the name of the secret that is put into the Key Vault.
The secret holds the destination database connection string.]'
$resourceGroupName = '[Specifies the Resource Group for the Key Vault.]'
$location = '[Specifies the Azure region where the Resource Group and Key Vault is placed.]'
$connectionString = '[Specifies the destination database connection
string that would be placed as a secret in the Key Vault.]'
$organizationIdList = '[Specifies a comma separated list of all the CRM Organization Id
which will be allowed to export data to the destination database.]'
$tenantId = '[Specifies the Azure Active Directory Tenant Id
to which all the specified CRM Organizations belong to.]'
# ----------------------------------------------------------------- #
```

10. Go to the Overview section of the Azure SQL database to get the values for subscription ID, resource group name, location, and connection string.

11. For the connection string, we need to copy the ADO.NET connection string and replace the username and password with the SQL DB user's credential created earlier.

12. For the organization ID, go to **Settings** | **Customizations** inside Dynamics 365 and copy the ID from the *Instance Reference Information* section.

13. For the tenant ID, navigate to **Azure Portal** | **Azure Active Directory** | **App Registrations** | **Endpoints** and copy the tenant ID from the Federation Metadata Document URL.

14. Replace the placeholders in the PowerShell script and run the script. This will create a key vault record in the Azure Portal. To copy the key vault URL, navigate to **Azure Portal** | **Key Vaults**. Select the key vault created and click on **Secrets**. Copy the secret identifier value and paste it in the key value URL in **Create Export Profile** inside Dynamics 365 and click on **Validate**.

 Install and configure the Azure PowerShell Extension: `https://docs.` `microsoft.com/en-us/powershell/azure/install-azurerm-ps?view=` `azurermps-3.8.0`.

15. On successful validation, we would get the success message. Click on **Next** to select the entities that we want to be exported:

16. Here we have selected the Contact entity in the **Select Entities** step. As we have selected only one entity here, we will not get any relationships to select in the next **Select Relationships** step. In the last summary step, review the details and click on **Create** and **Activate** to create and enable the profile as shown here:

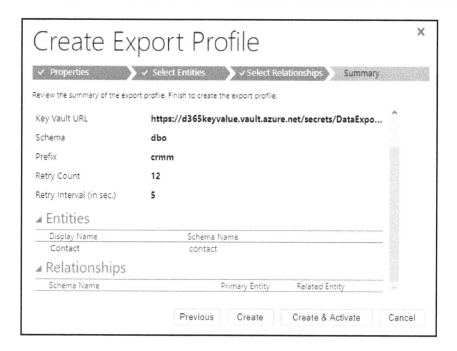

 The entities must have change tracking enabled for them to be added to the export profile.

17. Activating it will start the sync process. We can **Refresh** and check the export profile record for the sync status:

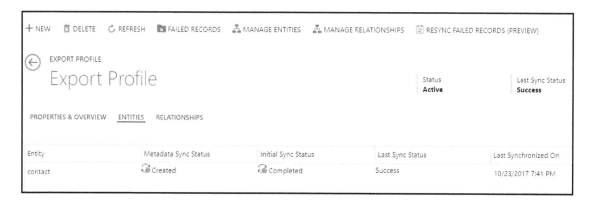

17. After a successful sync, we can see the exported data for the **Contact** entity in our SQL Azure database:

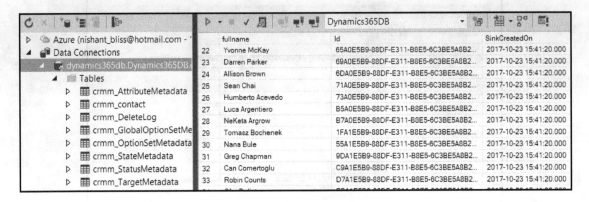

Configuring Relationship Insights

Relationship Insights leverages Microsoft Azure's machine learning capabilities to analyze information in Dynamics 365, Exchange and Office 365 and guide users to help them build more personalized and productive relationships with their customers. All the insights captured from these sources are displayed inside Dynamics 365, so the users will never have to leave Dynamics 365 and shuffle between different applications to figure out the next business activities they need to take.

The three key features of Relationship Insights are:

- Relationship Assistant
- Email Engagement
- Auto Capture

 Relationship Insights is still in preview, the feature is only available in the **North America (NA)** region.

Enabling Relationship Insights

To enable Relationship Insights:

1. Go to **Settings** | **Administration**. Open **System Settings**, inside the **Preview** Tab, select **Yes** to enable them under the **Relationship Insights** section:

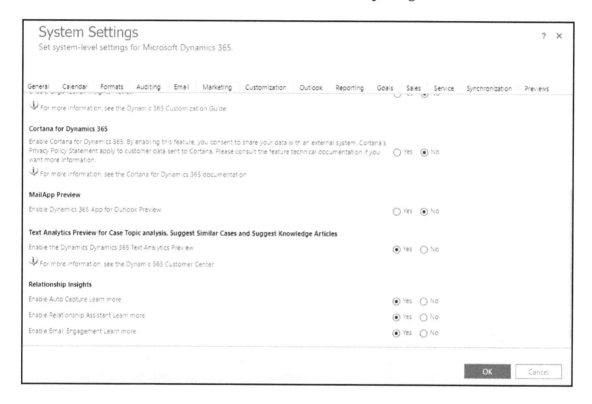

2. Go to **Settings** | **Relationship Insights** and click on **Install**. Select the **Dynamics 365 Relationship Insights** solution in the Dynamics 365 admin page, click on **Manage** and select **Accept** to give consent to Relationship Insights for accessing Dynamics 365 Online. This will configure Relationship Insights for the Dynamics 365 instance selected:

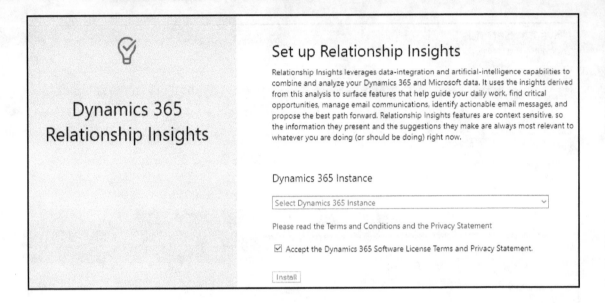

Configuring Relationship Assistant

There are two ways we can enable and configure Relationship Assistant: from **Settings** | **Relationship Insights** or from **Personal Options** settings. Relationship Assistant analyzes all the communications regarding the customer records the user is working on and generates the action cards. These action cards remind users of the actions to be performed such as emails to be sent today, reminding users about the opportunity of having close data approaching, or show analytics related to when an email or attachment is opened, or notifications about the account, case, contact and so on, record having no associated activity. The action cards are divided into the different categories as shown here:

Email Cards from Exchange requires **Exchange Online** to be configured.

Action cards can be viewed within the **ASSISTANT** tab in the social pane inside the form. The **Relationship Assistant** can also be added as one of the components inside the dashboard. The sample action card shown here, reminds the user of an opportunity closing within 14 days inside an opportunity form. The user can open the opportunity record from with in the action card and can work on it:

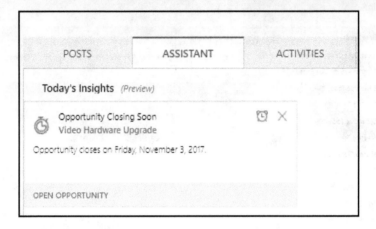

Configuring Auto Capture

Following are the steps to configure the Auto Capture:

1. Go to **Settings** | **Relationship Insights**, click on the **Auto Capture** tab to turn it on.
2. Auto Capture requires server-side synchronization and **Exchange Online** to be configured.

 Set up server-side synchronization: `https://technet.microsoft.com/en-us/library/dn531109.aspx`.

3. Auto Capture analyzes the email communication done through **Exchange Online** and displays relevant emails inside Dynamics 365 for tracking. Currently, these emails are private, which means they are only visible to the current user.

4. Here is how the mail sent to a contact from Exchange shows up in the **ACTIVITIES** tab of the social pane inside Dynamics 365:

5. The user can click on **TRACK** to track the activity inside Dynamics 365. The status changes from **Not Tracked** to **Tracking Pending**. After server side synchronizing finishes, (within 15 minutes), the mail starts getting tracked inside Dynamics 365:

6. Auto Capture, once turned on, will be enabled for all the users in that particular Dynamics 365 instance. The user can turn if off by going to the gear icon, open **Personal Options**, select the **Email** tab and select **No** for **Show email not tracked in Dynamics 365** in the **Activities** list option.

Configuring Email Engagement

Following are the steps to configure Email Engagement:

- Go to **Settings | Relationship Insights**, select the **>Email Engagement** tab and click on **Begin Setup**. This will start provisioning Email Engagement Services.
- Once provisioning is done, select the checkbox to turn on the **Email Engagement**.

To provide insights around attachments we need to enable server-side sync for SharePoint, Exchange and One Drive for Business in Dynamics 365: `https://technet.microsoft.com/en-us/library/dn531154.aspx` and `https://technet.microsoft.com/en-us/library/mt622109.aspx`.

3. Email Engagement provides insights around email communication such as whether an email or the attachments have been opened or not, whether a link has been clicked or not, suggesting the best time to send email based upon the open rates and so on.

4. After SharePoint integration is configured we need to enable document management for the Email entity; go to **Settings | Document Management | Document Management Settings** and check the **Email** checkbox. This is required if we want to follow attachments along with the email activity.

5. Email Engagement works only on email sent from inside Dynamics 365. To see it in action, create an email activity. You will notice a new section named Email Engagement in the email activity's form. By default, the emails created are followed. To unfollow it, we need to click on the **DON'T FOLLOW** link:

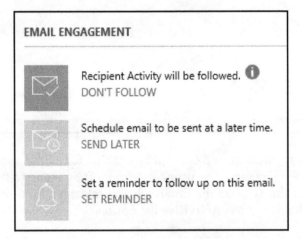

6. The email can also be scheduled to be sent later:

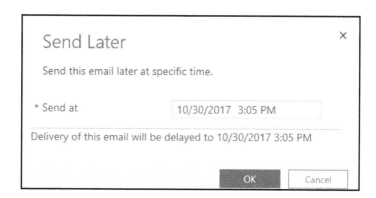

7. **Set Reminder** allows us to set conditions when we want to be notified:

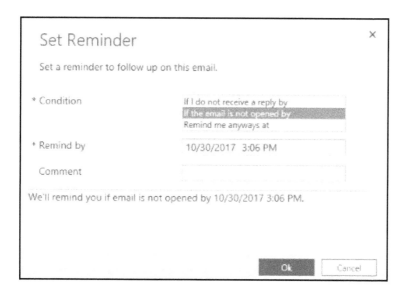

8. We can see the scheduling information added to the activity record as shown here:

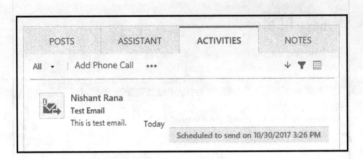

9. Action cards specific to **Email Engagement** show up in **Relationship Assistant**:

10. Similar to email, attachments can also be followed. To do so click on the + button in the attachment sub grid which opens up in the **Manage Attachment** dialog box. On successful upload of the document, we will see the option to **Follow** the attachment:

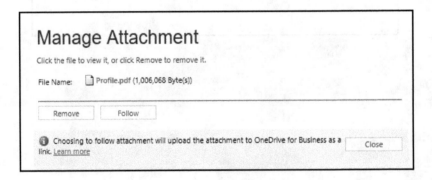

11. We can also see a section named **RECIPIENT ACTIVITY** added in the Email entity form for the emails that are being followed. It gives us the summary view of how many times an email was opened, the number of times attachment was viewed, links clicked and the total number of replies.

12. Along with the summary view, we also get the details of when and in which device the email was opened, when was the link clicked on, when was the attachment viewed, and so on, as shown here:

13. Email Engagement functionality also works for the email templates. If we are using email templates for our email, it will track details such as how many times an email that has used a particular template was opened, what is the rate of opening of that email, reply count, reply rate and total number of times templates were used for sending email, and based on those details captured will mark that email template as recommended, as shown here:

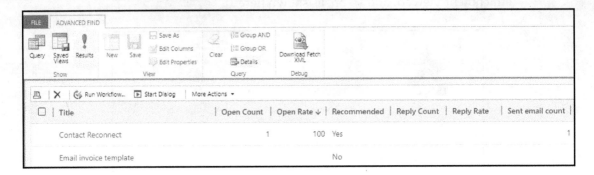

Configuring Dynamics 365 Live Assist

Live Assist for Dynamics 365 is an add-on for Dynamics 365 that adds chat, co-browse and video capabilities to Dynamics 365. It allows Dynamics 365 users to have a more personalized experience with the customer, which could lead to increased online sales, faster resolution of issues and so on.

To install it:

1. Navigate to **Settings** | **Dynamics Marketplace**, search for Live Assist and click on **Free Trial** to get started.
2. Verify the Dynamics 365 instance, and click on **Agree** to add the application to Dynamics 365:

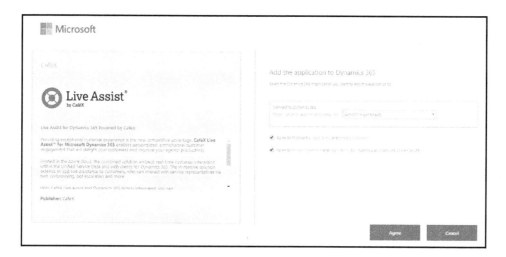

3. This opens up the Live Assist provisioning page, select the **Dynamics 365 instance**, provide a contact email address and click on **Submit** to start the configuration:

4. Once the provisioning is completed, a confirmation email is sent to the contact email address that was provided. The email will have the link to the Live Assist admin portal to which we can log in using our Dynamics 365 credentials and follow the instructions to complete the setup of Live Assist.

5. Through the admin portal (`https://admin.na1.liveassistfor365.com/portal/`), admin can manage the subscription and users, as in enabling or disabling a user or assigning the supervisor (admin) role to the users:

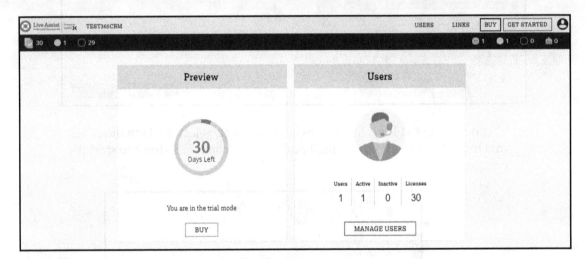

6. Inside Dynamics 365, we can see the Live Assist link added to the Business area inside **Settings**:

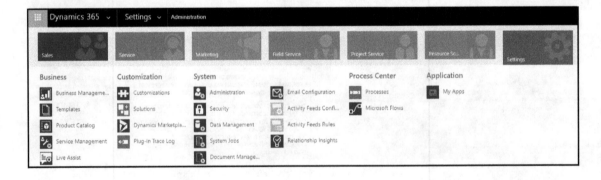

7. Along with the Live Assist panel in the right of Dynamics 365 as shown here:

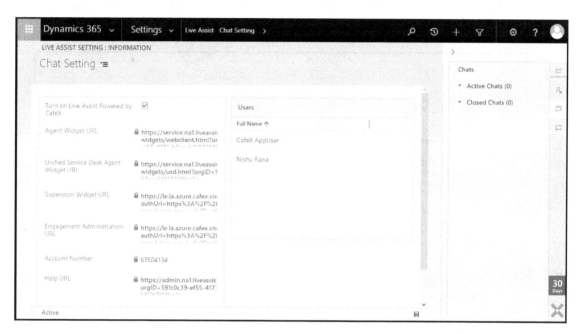

 Knowledge Base for Live Assist for Microsoft Dynamics 365: `https://www.liveassistfor365.com/en/support/knowledge-base/`.

8. To see it in action, we can use the Live Assist Demo Site. To access it we need to click the **Get Started** button in the admin portal and go to Step 3 inside it and launch Dynamics 365 and Demo Site:

9. We can click on the **Launch Dynamics 365** button to open Dynamics 365 and the **Demo Site** button to open a demo site provided by Live Assist for testing purposes:

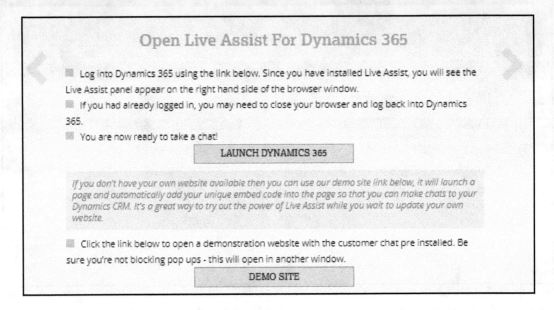

10. The demo site is a CafeX site designed for testing. The Dynamics's organizations Live Assist tag will be automatically embedded in the demo site.

11. The agent using Live Assist inside Dynamics 365 can chat and assist the visitor inside the demo site as shown here:

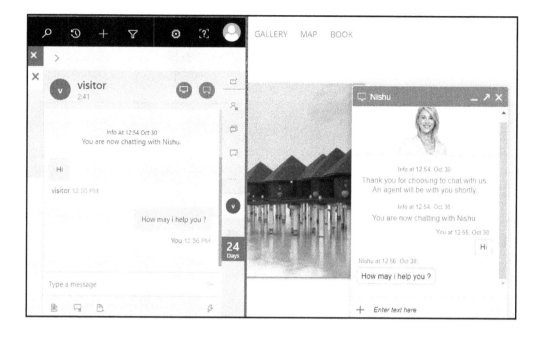

12. The agent can search for Knowledge Base, Open Chat Activity and Create Case record from within the Live Assist Widget inside Dynamics 365:

13. To start a co-browsing session, the user can click on the blue screen share icon inside the Live Assist Widget. The co-browsing allows customers or visitors to share the screen with the agents:

13. We can also open the chat window in full-screen mode, which includes functionality such as searching the contacts or cases and creating new contacts or case records, and also providing additional details about visitors, chats, devices, and so on, as shown here:

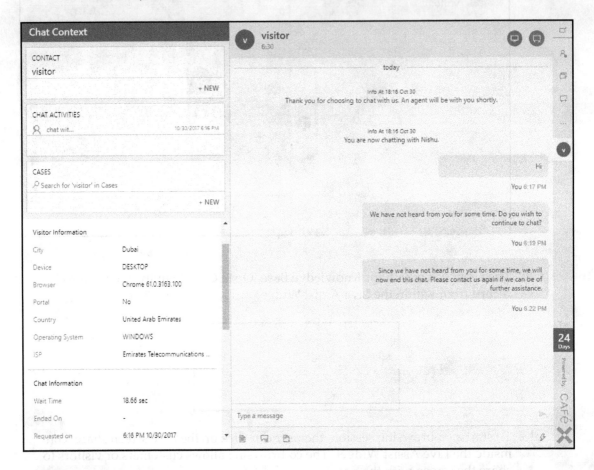

Configuring Dynamics 365 Connector for LinkedIn Lead Gen Forms

Using Dynamics 365 Connector for LinkedIn Lead Gen Forms, we can seamlessly synchronize LinkedIn leads from LinkedIn's Lead Gen Forms inside Dynamics 365. These leads can then be nurtured inside Dynamics 365.

Setting up LinkedIn Lead Gen Forms: `https://business.linkedin.com/ marketing-solutions/native-advertising/lead-gen-ads`.

To configure it:

1. Go to **Settings | Dynamics Marketplace**, search for `Dynamics 365 Connector for LinkedIn Lead Gen Forms` to install it. Click on **Free Trial** and follow the instructions to start the installations process.

2. Inside the LinkedIn **Organization Selector** page that shows up, select the **Organization** and click on **Continue** to start the setup:

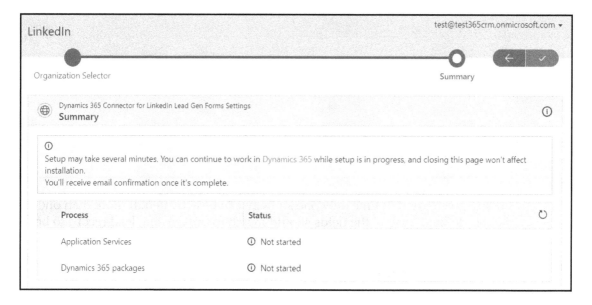

3. We will receive a confirmation email when the setup completes successfully. This installs the `LinkedInLeadGenIntegration` solution inside Dynamics 365.

4. Whenever a new lead is synced from LinkedIn, Dynamics 365 looks for the **Matching Lead Fields** defined in the active **LINKEDIN LEAD MATCHING STRATEGY** record to determine whether to create a new lead or update an existing lead record inside Dynamics 365.

5. LinkedIn Leads are created as LinkedIn Form Submissions records inside Dynamics 365. They contain the answers provided by the LinkedIn Member during the submission of the form. The existing lead records are matched with these answers based on the field defined as matching fields.

6. A user with a LinkedIn Lead Gen Forms Connector Administrator security role can define the **Email Lead Matching Strategy**. Here is the default record created inside Dynamics 365, having matching fields defined on email address:

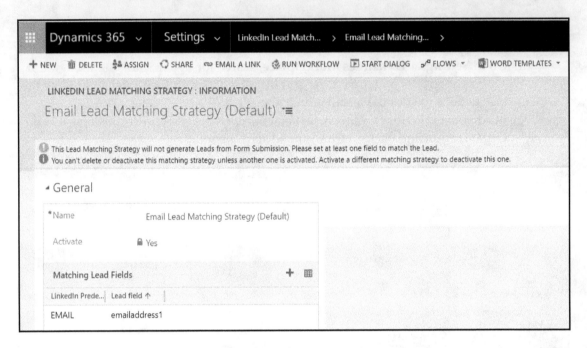

7. At any given point of time only one strategy can be activated. If more than one field is defined then all the fields should match for an existing lead record to be updated. If only subsets of fields match, then we can configure whether a new lead record should be created or no action is to be taken, in the **On Matching Fail** property of the **LinkedIn LeadGen Integration Configuration** record:

8. Next, we need to authorize Dynamics 365 to sync data from LinkedIn's Campaign Manager. Go to **Settings | LinkedIn User Profile** and click on **New** to create a new user profile record. To add a linkedIn account to this new user profile, click on the **Authorize** button. Enter the LinkedIn account credentials and select **Allow**:

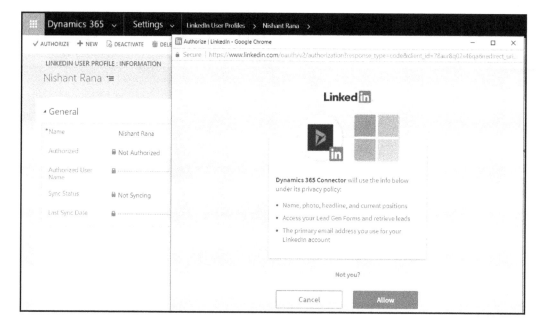

9. Select **Yes** to allow Dynamics 365 to access LinkedIn data in the next screen that shows up.

10. This adds the LinkedIn account to the profile and starts the sync. We can also click on the **Sync Submissions** button to start the sync manually. This will start synching LinkedIn Form Submissions records with Dynamics 365:

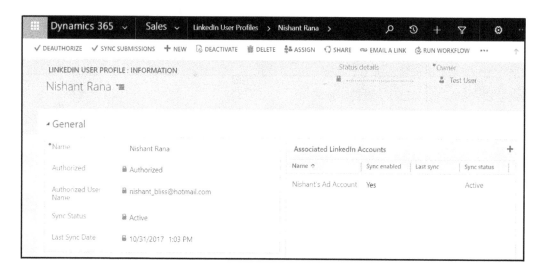

11. Inside Dynamics 365, we can open the lead record inside Dynamics 365 and see the details captured in the **LinkedIn Lead Info** section as shown here:

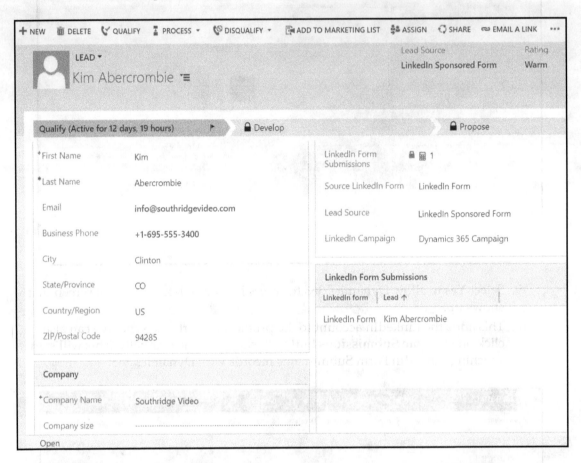

Summary

In this chapter, we covered some of the biggest changes in Dynamics 365 such as web client refresh and unified interface, along with features like Relevance Search and Relationship Insights that bring artificial intelligence into Dynamics 365. We also looked at how we can export Dynamics 365 data with simple configuration steps, which can then be used for various analytics purpose.

Other Books You May Enjoy

If you enjoyed this book, you may be interested in these other books by Packt:

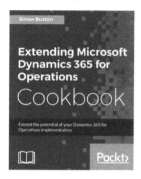

Extending Microsoft Dynamics 365 for Operations Cookbook
Simon Buxton

ISBN: 978-1-78646-713-3

- Create enumerated and extended data types
- Understand the importance of using patterns and frameworks while creating a unique concept for your solution
- Service and deploy your code and packages to improve performance
- Write and perform unit tests to automate the testing process
- Design your security model and policies to provide code access privileges
- Construct the UI and business logic to add Power BI to dashboards

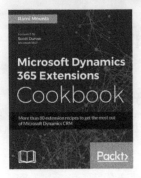

Microsoft Dynamics 365 Extensions Cookbook
Rami Mounla

ISBN: 978-1-78646-417-0

- Customize, configure, and extend Microsoft Dynamics 365
- Create business process automation
- Develop client-side extensions to add features to the Dynamics 365 user interface
- Set up a security model to securely manage data with Dynamics 365
- Develop and deploy clean code plugins to implement a wide range of custom behaviors
- Use third-party applications, tools, and patterns to integrate Dynamics 365 with other platforms
- Integrate with Azure, Java, SSIS, PowerBI, and Octopus Deploy
- Build an end-to-end DevOps pipeline for Dynamics 365

Leave a review - let other readers know what you think

Please share your thoughts on this book with others by leaving a review on the site that you bought it from. If you purchased the book from Amazon, please leave us an honest review on this book's Amazon page. This is vital so that other potential readers can see and use your unbiased opinion to make purchasing decisions, we can understand what our customers think about our products, and our authors can see your feedback on the title that they have worked with Packt to create. It will only take a few minutes of your time, but is valuable to other potential customers, our authors, and Packt. Thank you!

Index